Kelda.

C000257549

The Witchcraze of the 16th and 17th Centuries

ALAN FARMER

HODDER
EDUCATION
AN HACHETTE UK COMPANY

The Publishers would like to thank the following for permission to reproduce copyright material: Polity Press for tables on pages 10 and 62 from W. Behringer, *Witches and Witch Hunts*, Polity Press, 2004. Routledge for *The Witch-Hunt in Early Modern Europe*, B.P. Levack, Copyright 2006 Routledge, reproduced by permission of Taylor & Francis Books UK.

Acknowledgements are listed on page 220.

Although every effort has been made to ensure that website addresses are correct at time of going to press, Hodder Education cannot be held responsible for the content of any website mentioned in this book. It is sometimes possible to find a relocated web page by typing in the address of the home page for a website in the URL window of your browser.

Hachette UK's policy is to use papers that are natural, renewable and recyclable products and made from wood grown in sustainable forests. The logging and manufacturing processes are expected to conform to the environmental regulations of the country of origin.

Orders: please contact Bookpoint Ltd, 130 Milton Park, Abingdon, Oxon OX14 4SB. Telephone: +44 (0)1235 827720. Fax: +44 (0)1235 400454. Lines are open 9.00a.m.–5.00p.m., Monday to Saturday, with a 24-hour message answering service. Visit our website at www.hoddereducation.co.uk

© Alan Farmer

First published in 2016 by
Hodder Education
An Hachette UK Company
Carmelite House, 50 Victoria Embankment
London EC4Y 0DZ

Impression number   10 9 8 7 6 5 4 3 2
Year   2019   2018   2017   2016

Cover photo © The Granger Collection, NYC/TopFoto
Produced, illustrated and typeset in Palatino LT Std by Gray Publishing, Tunbridge Wells
Printed and bound by CPI Group (UK) Ltd, Croydon CR0 4YY

A catalogue record for this title is available from the British Library

ISBN 978 1471838385

Contents

Dedication

Keith Randell (1943–2002)

The *Access to History* series was conceived and developed by Keith, who created a series to 'cater for students as they are, not as we might wish them to be'. He leaves a living legacy of a series that for over 20 years has provided a trusted, stimulating and well-loved accompaniment to post-16 study. Our aim with these new editions is to continue to offer students the best possible support for their studies.

CHAPTER 1

Witch-hunting in early modern Europe

From the mid-fifteenth to the mid-eighteenth centuries, but mainly in the period 1560–1660, thousands of Europeans were tried and executed for witchcraft. This chapter will examine the factors that led to the rise of witch-hunting by focusing on the following themes:

★ The rise of witch-hunting

★ The legal foundations of witch-hunting

★ Explanations of witch-hunting

Key dates

1420s	Large-scale witch-hunts in the Alpine region	**1517**	Martin Luther's *Ninety-Five Theses*: the start of the Reformation
1484	Pope Innocent VIII's papal bull *Summis desiderantes affectibus*	**1560–1660**	Large-scale witch persecutions across Europe
1486	Kramer published *Malleus Maleficarum*		

1 The rise of witch-hunting

▶ *Why was there a growth of witch-hunting in the early modern period?*

Most people in **early modern Europe** believed in the reality of witches and witchcraft. When Europeans talked about witchcraft in the sixteenth and seventeenth centuries, they were invariably referring to two types of activity:

- Black or maleficent magic: the performance of harmful deeds by means of some sort of occult or supernatural power, for example, by killing a person by piercing a doll made in his or her image, inflicting sickness by reciting a spell or blighting crops by bringing down hail.
- White magic: the performance of good deeds which could help the growth of crops, cure disease, foretell the future and help to counter evil sorcery.

'White' witches (often known as 'cunning folk' in England) were usually considered a 'good thing' at a local level. By contrast, most Europeans thought that evil witches should be hunted down and persecuted.

 KEY TERM

Early modern Europe
The period from c.1450 to c.1700; the years that are regarded as bridging the medieval and modern worlds.

Developments in Christian doctrine

Until the thirteenth century, mainstream Christian teaching denied the existence of witchcraft, condemning it as a pagan superstition. However, two developments in Christian doctrine in the late medieval period contributed significantly to the early modern witch-hunts:

- the identification of witchcraft as **heresy**
- the notion of the Devil's pact.

The threat of heresy

In the two centuries after 1200, a number of groups, notably **Cathars**, **Waldenians** and **Lollards**, were perceived to be a threat to the Catholic Church. The **Inquisition** was given the task of protecting Christian orthodoxy from the 'internal' threat of heresy. Historian Robert Thurston (2001) speaks of a shift in Christian society from a 'relatively open and tolerant' attitude to that of a 'persecuting society', which took an aggressive stance towards minorities such as heretics, Jews and (eventually) witches. In the minds of some Church leaders, these groups were all part of a vast diabolical conspiracy to weaken and destroy Christianity. The catalogue of typical charges that would later be levelled at witches, of spreading diseases and engaging in orgies, emerged during the fourteenth century as crimes attributed to heretics. In 1326, Pope John XXII authorised the Inquisition to persecute witchcraft as a type of heresy.

The Devil's pact

Prior to the fifteenth century, most European witchcraft trials were prosecutions for *maleficium*. Witches were rarely executed. However, in the 1420s and 1430s, a number of trials took place in the Alpine regions of France, Switzerland and Italy in which suspected witches were accused of holding large meetings at which they worshipped the Devil (or Satan). This idea developed, so much so that by 1500 many educated Europeans believed that witches, in addition to practising harmful magic, had made a pact with – and paid homage to – the Devil in return for promises of material reward. As a sign of their allegiance, the Devil imprinted a distinctive mark on a witch's body, usually in a concealed spot. He also gave witches instructions for their maleficent work and equipped them with the necessary potions and images they would need to ply their trade.

By the sixteenth century, demonological experts insisted that witches gathered periodically with other witches to perform a series of blasphemous rites at a **sabbat** (see Source A, page 3). The witches would sacrifice children, feast on their bodies, dance naked and engage in sexual intercourse with the Devil, demons and other witches. There was also a belief that witches could fly, especially on broomsticks, an explanation for their seeming ability to attend midnight gatherings in areas many miles from home without their absence being noticed.

🔑 **KEY TERMS**

Heresy A belief contrary to the authorised teaching of the Catholic Church.

Cathars Twelfth-century French dissidents from Catholicism. The sect, sometimes known as the Albigensians, was wiped out in the fourteenth century by the Inquisition.

Waldensians Members of a dissident Christian group which began in the French Alps in the twelfth century. Religious persecution scattered them to other areas including Bohemia and Germany.

Lollards Followers of English reformer John Wycliffe (c.1329–84) who advocated the primacy of the scriptures over the teaching of the Church.

Inquisition A tribunal, established in the thirteenth century, to preserve the supremacy of Catholicism by suppressing heresy by means of formally organised persecution.

Maleficium A harm committed by magic (plural *maleficia*).

Sabbat A witches' midnight meeting.

SOURCE A

The Witches' Sabbat, a seventeenth-century engraving by Matthäus Merian the Elder (1593–1650).

Demons and demonic possession

Theologians believed the Devil was assisted by large numbers of demons. One book, written in 1569, estimated there were 26 billion demons. Others, more conservatively, reckoned 6–7 million. Male demons were known as incubi, female ones as succubi. It was believed they could take on the appearance of a human or an animal form, for example, a black cat. (Hence the association of witches and black cats.)

In early modern Europe, witchcraft and demonic possession were considered to be distinct but related phenomena. Possession was the process by which a demonic spirit supposedly invaded the body of a human being, assumed control of its physical movements, and altered its personality. This assault on the possessed person resulted in bodily contortions and convulsions, the vomiting of foreign objects, insensitivity to pain, speaking in strange voices and so on. Demonic possession sometimes seemed to afflict not just individuals but groups of people, particularly children. The victims of possession could be distinguished from witches on the grounds that, being involuntary victims of demonic power, they were not responsible for their actions. Instead, witches were often persecuted for causing the possession of other people. In England, the connection between witchcraft and possession was so common that the words 'possessed' and 'bewitched' became almost synonymous.

Look at Source A. What do you think was the purpose of the illustration?

Rather than isolated individuals dabbling in the occult, witches were therefore increasingly seen as members of a heretical sect, a menace to Christianity. They thus needed to be hunted down and destroyed – in the same way that Cathar and Waldensian heretics had been persecuted:

- Inquisitors, appointed by the pope, were dispatched to investigate witchcraft.
- Just as heretics were burned at the stake, so were witches.

In December 1484, Pope Innocent VIII issued *Summis desiderantes affectibus* ('Desiring with passionate ardour'), a **papal bull** in which he declared witchcraft to be a *crimen exceptum* (an exceptional crime), thereby removing all legal limits on the application of torture in cases where evidence was difficult to find.

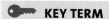 **KEY TERM**

Papal bull An edict issued by the pope.

? According to Source B, why were witches a menace to society?

SOURCE B

From a tract written by William West in 1594, quoted in Tracy Borman, *Witches: James I and the English Witch-hunts*, Vintage, 2014, p. xiii.

A witch or hag is she who – deluded by a pact made with the Devil through his persuasion, inspiration and juggling – thinks she can bring about all manner of evil things, either by thought or imprecation, such as to shake the air with lightnings and thunder, to cause hail and tempests, to remove green corn or trees to another place, to be carried on her familiar spirit (which has taken upon him the deceitful shape of a goat, swine or calf, etc.) into some mountain far distant, in a wonderfully short space of time, and sometimes to fly upon a staff or fork, or some other instrument, and to spend all the night after with her sweetheart, in playing, sporting, banqueting, dancing, dalliance, and divers [diverse] other devilish lusts and lewd disports [frolics].

The spread of the idea of demonic witchcraft

Literature became the main vehicle for transmitting knowledge about demonic witchcraft, especially with the introduction of the printing press in the late fifteenth century.

Malleus Maleficarum

The first witchcraft treatise that had a major impact was the *Malleus Maleficarum* (*Witches' Hammer*). First published in 1486 and reprinted thirteen times before 1520 (and a further sixteen times by 1660), it appeared under the name of two Dominican friars, Heinrich Kramer and Jacob Sprenger. Kramer, who had been appointed as an Inquisitor for southern Germany in 1478, was probably the sole author. The book was based on his own investigations. In 1484 he had prosecuted witches in Ravensburg. A witch-hunt in the Tyrol in 1485 followed. This was eventually halted by the bishop of Brixen, who opposed Kramer's brutal methods.

Malleus lent a new urgency to the eradication of witches, who, in Kramer's view, were invariably women. It was one thing to have a troublesome old woman in the community whose spells and potions might or might not be effective. It was quite another to imagine her as part of a conspiracy led by the Devil which aimed at Christianity's destruction. *Malleus* claimed that witchcraft was the worst of all crimes, combining heresy with terrible secular crimes such as murder and sodomy. Because it was difficult to trace, legal inhibitions and procedures had to be abandoned. About a third of the book was devoted to informing judges how to prosecute witches.

The immediate impact of *Malleus*

The upsurge of witch trials in the 1490s in central Europe was once seen as the result of the publication of *Malleus*. But while the book became influential, its significance should not be overstated. It did not on its own spark the witchcraze of the early modern period. In fact, its publication in Italy was followed by a noticeable reduction in witchcraft cases. Indeed, it may be that the rise of witch persecutions in the late fifteenth century had little to do with *Malleus*. Historian Wolfgang Behringer (2004) claims that the decades after 1470 were years of severe crises as plague rampaged through large parts of Germany, Switzerland and eastern France. People thus sought scapegoats. It may well be that Kramer exploited popular fears about witches that were already strong. It is also the case that witchcraft remained very much an intellectually contested area in the late fifteenth and early sixteenth centuries (see pages 5–7).

Witchcraft treatises 1560–1620

There was a European-wide decline in witch prosecutions from 1520 to 1560 and few witchcraft texts. However, after 1560 there was a marked increase in prosecutions and the printing of several new witchcraft treatises. These included:

- Jean Bodin's *On the Demon-mania of Witches* (1580). Bodin, a jurist, theologian and historian, was one of Europe's finest thinkers. He regarded witchcraft as a major threat and urged Christians to resist Satan's forces.
- Nicolas Remy's *Demonolatreiae* (1595). Remy, a judge from Lorraine, claimed to have executed more than 800 witches in sixteen years.
- Martin Del Rio's *Six Books of Discussions on Magic* (c.1600). Del Rio was a Spanish **Jesuit**. His work, printed 25 times between 1600 and 1755, became the most popular witchcraft treatise in the seventeenth century.

These and many similar works succeeded in making literate Europeans aware of the perceived threat of witchcraft.

The judicial process

As the number of witchcraft trials increased, so did the 'evidence' of diabolical practices. By extracting confessions, usually by torture (see pages 15–16), to the activities that they believed witches had engaged in, Inquisitors received confirmation of their suspicions. Knowledge of these trials spread to other

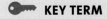 **KEY TERM**

Jesuit A member of the Catholic religious order the Society of Jesus, founded in 1534 by Ignatius Loyola. Jesuits were known for their aggressive religiosity as 'the soldiers of Christ'.

judges, both by word of mouth and by written manuals which used the testimony given at the trials to illustrate witches' activities. Accordingly, witchcraft trials validated the beliefs contained in literature and provided additional examples for new treatises. The treatises, in turn, seemed to confirm witchcraft's reality.

Universities

The process of transmission was assisted by European universities, which provided future judges with the growing body of demonological literature and also advised local jurisdictions, especially in Germany, how to conduct witchcraft prosecutions.

Different views of witchcraft

Accordingly, two different but related types of activity were denoted by the word witchcraft as it was used in early modern Europe: the practice of *maleficium* and **diabolism**. Both notions were contained in the prevailing stereotype of the witch, so much so that the presence of one usually implied that of the other. Nevertheless, some people were charged only with diabolism, others charged only with performing *maleficium*. Judges and prosecutors were more concerned with diabolical witchcraft. Charges of *maleficium* usually came from below – from the witches' neighbours – rather than from judicial officials.

The crime of *maleficium*, by itself, was probably not capable of sustaining the systematic prosecution of large numbers of witches. The **ruling elite** had to believe that witchcraft was a terrible – diabolical – crime and that it was being practised on a large scale by a conspiratorial sect of Devil worshippers. However, the idea of the witch as a Satanist was far less prevalent among the illiterate peasantry, who were far more concerned about the potential harm that they could receive from witches than from where they gained their power.

Nevertheless, the diabolical ideas of the elite trickled down:

- Charges against witches were read out at executions.
- Clergy preached against witchcraft.
- Cheap news-sheets, pamphlets and ballads about witches were printed and read to those who were illiterate.

The sceptics

Not all Europeans were convinced that witchcraft posed a serious threat. The notion that witches were in league with the Devil was contested from the late fifteenth century.

Renaissance humanism

In the early sixteenth century, some leading **humanists** took a stand against witch-beliefs in general and witch-hunts in particular:

KEY TERMS

Diabolism Devil worship.

Ruling elite The governing class, mainly comprising royalty, the aristocracy and the rich and powerful. The elite are the leading members of any social group.

Humanists Supporters of humanism – an intellectual movement that was strong in the late fifteenth and early sixteenth centuries. Humanists, while by no means rejecting Christianity, turned away from the theological bias of the medieval period and concentrated instead on human achievements.

- The great Dutch scholar, Erasmus, ridiculed zealous Inquisitors who sacrificed innocent victims in order to serve their foolish theories.
- The Italian Andrea Alciati branded the witch-hunts in the Alps as inhumane. He claimed that the Papal Inquisition was not so much fighting against witchcraft as creating it.
- The German philosopher Agrippa attacked the 'fantasies' of *Malleus*.

Johann Weyer

The most famous sixteenth-century critic of witch-hunting was Johann Weyer, a physician to the Duke of Cleves. 'The killing of witches is nothing but a massacre of the innocents', Weyer declared in *The Deceptive Tricks of Evil Spirits* (1563), a book that was something of a bestseller in France and Germany. Weyer used his medical knowledge to claim that the alleged *maleficia* of witches could be explained by natural causes and the confessions of witches were to a large extent the result of mental disorder. Weyer argued that the Devil was more powerful than was supposed, obviating the need for witches.

Reginald Scot

In England, Reginald Scot published *Discoverie of Witchcraft* (1584). Scot's scepticism was in part based on the absence of any biblical foundation for witch-hunting (see pages 86–7).

The course of witch-hunting 1480–1700

Despite the criticism of the sceptics, there was a spate of witch-hunts in the early modern period.

Witch-hunting 1480–1560

Between the 1480s and the 1520s, witches were tried in France, Italy, Spain, Germany, Switzerland and the Netherlands. Many of the persecutions occurred in northern Italy. One Dominican theologian suggested that the Inquisition of Como alone arrested an average of 1000 people a year for witchcraft and executed more than 100 of them annually in the first decade of the sixteenth century.

The years from 1520 to 1560 saw far fewer executions. This lull has been attributed to the development of scepticism among the learned elite and to the preoccupation of both ecclesiastical and secular authorities with the Reformation (see pages 21–2). Heretic-hunting was more common than witch-hunting.

There were exceptions to the decline in witch-hunting, however:

- There were witch burnings in various Swiss cantons.
- There were occasional witch-hunts in the Netherlands.
- Denmark saw a spate of witch-hunts with 52 executions in 1543.

The great witch-hunt c.1560–1660

The period of intense persecution took place between 1560 and 1660. In 1562, in the south-western German town of Wiesensteig, a place with barely 5000 people, 63 witches were executed. There were large hunts in the diocese of Trier in the late 1580s and early 1590s, in Scotland between 1590 and 1597, in Lorraine in the 1580s and 1590s, at Ellwangen in the 1610s, and in Würzburg and Bamberg in the 1620s. In Germany, witches were often burned in large batches. In the very small area of Quedlinburg, 133 witches were executed on one day in 1589.

The geographical distribution of witchcraft cases in this period was extremely uneven (as can be seen in Figure 1.1, below). In some areas there were very few

Figure 1.1 Witch-hunting hotspots 1400–1800. Places referred to in the text are labelled. Present-day borders are indicated on the map.

prosecutions. In others, thousands were tried. Within various jurisdictions, there were some decades when large numbers of witches were prosecuted and others when very few were tried. The trials emerged sporadically, flaring up in some areas while neighbouring territories remained unaffected. Small Catholic states within the **Holy Roman Empire** witnessed the largest number of trials and executions, relative to population. Nevertheless, there were regional variations. In Bamberg there were over 600 executions between 1622 and 1633. A few miles away, Rothenburg saw only a handful of witchcraft cases. Catholic Ireland and Protestant Netherlands had very low levels of persecution. Some countries (for example, Spain and the Netherlands) had ended their witch trials by 1610. In others, for example, Sweden, witch-hunts did not really take off until after 1660.

There was thus little consistency. If by a 'witchcraze' we mean a coherent, co-ordinated European campaign, it was not really a witchcraze at all.

The end of witch-hunting

After 1660, over most of western and central Europe, witchcraft trials and executions declined. A few areas in eastern Europe, as well as New England in North America, experienced serious witch-hunts in the late seventeenth and eighteenth centuries. But by the late eighteenth century witchcraft prosecutions came to an end. Traditionally, there have been two contenders for the final executions for witchcraft in Europe: the burning of Anna Goldi for bewitching a child in the Swiss canton of Galrus (1782) and the execution of two women for using magic to harm their neighbours' cattle in the Polish town of Poznań (1793).

The number of deaths

The number of witches killed was once believed to have been 9 million. But this number was a multiplication error made by an eighteenth-century writer. Because many judicial records have been lost, it is impossible to be fully accurate about the numbers of witches tried and executed. Present research, however, suggests that some 90,000–100,000 people were prosecuted for witchcraft in Europe and North America from 1400 to 1750. About half the trials took place within the Holy Roman Empire. Switzerland tried at least 10,000 people. Spain and Italy accounted for a similar number. Poland, France and Britain each saw some 3000 trials. Across Europe as a whole, some 40,000–50,000 witches were probably executed. This figure does not include unofficial lynchings of witches (which were probably rare) or the people who died in prison as a result of unsanitary conditions before being tried.

For many people at the time, the main concern was not so much how many witches had been executed but how many were still on the loose. For those who thought themselves to be bewitched, the experience was a terrifying one and the witch a figure who inspired fear.

 **KEY TERM**

Holy Roman Empire This territory comprised most of present-day Germany. From the thirteenth century, the emperors (in theory elected) were almost always members of the Habsburg family which ruled Austria. The Empire consisted of hundreds of small states.

Table 1.1 The severity of European witch-hunting

Country	Executions	Inhabitants	Ratio per capita
Turkey	0	Unknown	–
Ireland	4	1,000,000	250,000
Portugal	10	1,000,000	100,000
Iceland	22	50,000	2,273
Croatia	30	Unknown	–
Lithuania	50	Unknown	–
Estonia	65	Unknown	–
Finland	115	350,000	3,043
Latvia	150	Unknown	–
Netherlands	200	1,500,000	7,500
Russia	300	Unknown	–
Sweden	300	800,000	2,667
Spain	300	8,100,000	27,000
Liechtenstein	300	3,000	10
Norway	350	400,000	1,143
Slovenia	400	Unknown	–
Slovakia	400	1,000,000	2,500
Austria	500	2,000,000	4,000
Czech Republic	600	1,000,000	1,667
Hungary	800	3,000,000	3,750
Denmark	1,000	570,000	570
Britain	1,500	7,000,000	4,667
Italy	2,500	13,000,000	5,200
Belgium/Luxembourg	2,500	1,300,000	520
Switzerland	4,000	1,000,000	250
Poland	4,000	3,400,000	850
France	5,000	20,000,000	4,000
Germany	25,000	16,000,000	640

From W. Behringer, *Witches and Witch Hunts*, Polity Press, 2004, p. 150.

Who were the witches?

In early modern Europe, witches could be male or female. Men and women could make pacts with the Devil and/or practise *maleficium*. Nevertheless, across Europe as a whole witches were predominantly female – in excess of 75 per cent in most regions (see Table 1.2, page 12). Why was this?

The female stereotype

Most of the witchcraft treatises commented on the fact that most witches were women. A female witch-stereotype was therefore established by 1500. Women were generally seen as morally weaker than men and more likely to succumb to diabolical temptation (like Eve in the Garden of Eden story in the Bible). *Malleus Maleficarum* asserted that women were more gullible, carnal and prone to infidelity and carnality. 'When a woman thinks alone', declared Kramer, 'she thinks evil thoughts.' The notion that witchcraft stemmed from women's supposed carnal lust was strongly endorsed by most clerics. The view that women were driven by lust was especially pertinent for it was believed that the witches often became Devil-worshippers as a result of sexual temptation and then engaged in promiscuous sex at the sabbat.

This image of the lustful woman received strong visual reinforcement in engravings of the time. Albrecht Dürer's engraving *Witch Riding Backwards on a Goat* (see Source C) depicts a hag, calling up a hailstorm. Profoundly sexualised images of witches were developed by Dürer's apprentice Hans Baldung Grien, who depicted witches as the embodiment of female sexual power. This erotic art, which could be published only because it condemned the activities of the women it depicted, was, in many respects, the pornography of its day.

SOURCE C

Witch Riding Backwards on a Goat by Albrecht Dürer, *c.*1500.

How does the sixteenth-century illustration in Source C differ from a stereotypical twenty-first-century depiction of a witch? Why might the notion of what a witch looks like have changed?

Table 1.2 The gender of accused witches

Region	Years	Male	Female	Percentage of females
Holy Roman Empire (1648 boundaries)	1530–1730	4,575	19,050	76
South-western Germany	1562–1684	238	1,050	82
Rothenburg ob der Tauber	1549–1709	19	46	71
Bishopric of Basel	1571–1670	9	181	95
Franche-Comté	1559–1667	49	153	76
Geneva	1537–1662	74	240	76
Pays de Vaud	1581–1620	325	624	66
County of Namur	1509–1646	29	337	92
Luxembourg	1519–1623	130	417	76
City of Toul	1584–1623	14	53	79
Dept of the Nord, France	1542–1679	54	232	81
Normandy	1564–1660	278	103	27
Castile	1540–1685	132	324	71
Aragon	1600–1650	69	90	57
Venice	1550–1650	224	490	69
Finland	1520–1699	316	325	51
Estonia	1520–1729	116	77	40
Wielkopolska, Poland	1500–1776	21	490	96
Russia	1622–1700	93	43	32
Hungary	1520–1777	160	1,482	90
County of Essex, England	1560–1675	23	290	93
New England	1620–1725	75	267	78
Iceland	1625–1685	110	10	8

From B.P. Levack, *The Witch-Hunt in Early Modern Europe*, Routledge, 2006, p. 142.

Such images may have influenced the elite. But most witches were charged by their neighbours. The predominant stereotype of the witch in popular culture had invariably been female. Consequently, those who believed they were victims of witchcraft probably instinctively suspected women.

SOURCE D

? According to Source D, why were most witches women?

From William Perkins, *A Discourse of the Damned Art of Witchcraft* (1610). Perkins was a prominent Puritan clergyman in the late sixteenth and early seventeenth centuries. Quoted in J. Sharpe, *Witchcraft in Early Modern England*, Pearson, 2001, p. 43.

The woman being the weaker sex, is sooner intangled by the devil's illusions, with the damnable art, than the man. And in all ages it is found true by experience, that the devil hath more easily and oftner prevailed with women than with men … his first temptation in the beginning was with Eve a woman, and since he pursueth his practice accordingly as making for his advantage. For where he findeth easiest entrance, and best entertainment, thither will he oftenest resort.

Age

The available evidence suggests that most accused female witches were older than 50. Such women sometimes manifested signs of eccentric or antisocial behaviour. (Today such behaviour might be attributed to senility or dementia.) This could prompt witchcraft charges. However, it seems likely that many witches had been suspected of witchcraft for many years before they were prosecuted. When villagers first suspected someone, they generally did not immediately denounce her to the authorities. They sought some kind of reconciliation or sought help from cunning folk. Legal proceedings were often a last resort. Accordingly, most witches were fairly old when brought to trial.

Marital status

The percentage of unmarried witches (those widowed or who had never married) was higher than the percentage of such people in the female population. Arguably, in a **patriarchal society**, the existence of women who were subject to neither father nor husband was a source of concern. Possibly, single women were thought more likely to be seduced by the Devil.

The numbers of unmarried women was increasing: in some places they were almost a third of the population. This was probably the result of warfare or plagues. By 1600, nunneries, which had once accommodated a large proportion of the single female population, were in decline or had been dissolved as a result of the Reformation.

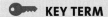 **KEY TERM**

Patriarchal society A social system which is dominated by men.

Social and economic status

Although not necessarily the very poorest members of society, most suspected witches struggled to survive, often resorting to begging. The dependence of the poor on a local community could arouse feelings of resentment, especially in times of economic crisis.

The personality of the witch

While not conforming to one single personality profile, witches frequently exhibited certain behavioural characteristics that explain why they were singled out for accusation:

- They were often described as sharp-tongued, bad-tempered and quarrelsome, traits that involved them in disputes with their neighbours.
- Many had been suspected of, and occasionally prosecuted for, other manifestations of immoral behaviour, for example non-attendance at church, cursing or fornication.

Healers

Many 'wise' or 'cunning folk' had reputations for curing disease. They served a useful function in most village communities. But if disease struck or people died unexpectedly, cunning folk could be accused of witchcraft.

Male witches

Not all witches were female. In Iceland 90 per cent of condemned witches were men, in Estonia 60 per cent and in Finland 50 per cent. Substantial numbers of male witches were prosecuted when hunts got out of control and confessing witches were forced to name accomplices.

Summary diagram: The rise of witch-hunting

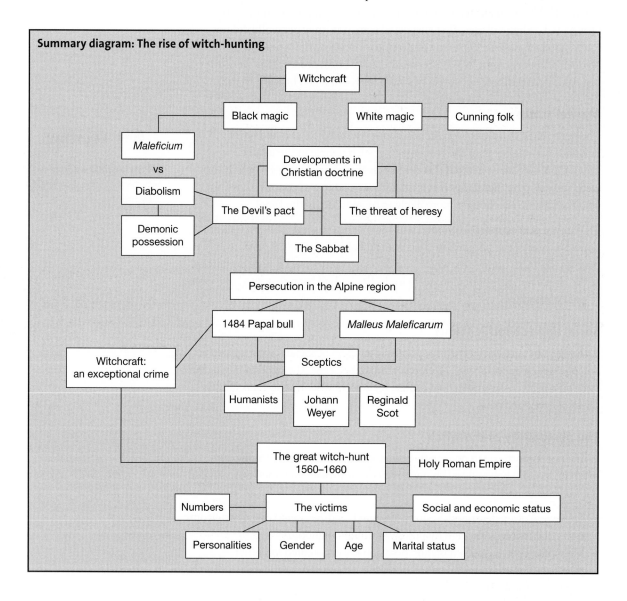

2 The legal foundations of witch-hunting

▶ *Why can the European witch-hunt be regarded as essentially a judicial operation?*

According to historian Brian Levack (2006), the great European witch-hunt was essentially a judicial operation. The vast majority of those executed for witchcraft were legally tried and sentenced. The prosecution of witches was facilitated by several legal developments that occurred across much of Europe between the thirteenth and sixteenth centuries. Continental courts, while varying from region to region, tended to concentrate power in the hands of individual judges. In England and Scotland, by contrast, ordinary jurymen – men not trained in the law – determined who was innocent and guilty.

The inquisitorial process

In the thirteenth and fourteenth centuries, the secular and ecclesiastical courts of continental Europe adopted an inquisitorial system of criminal procedure. Once an accusation was made, judges and their subordinates investigated the crime and decided whether the defendant was guilty. This they did mainly by interrogating both the accused and all available witnesses. Inquisitorial procedures had demanding standards of proof for establishing guilt in a **capital crime**: the testimony of at least two eyewitnesses or the confession of the accused was required. In witchcraft cases, however, it was difficult to produce two witnesses who could testify that a witch had performed *maleficia* before their very eyes, while the only persons who could give eyewitness accounts of sabbat attendance were alleged accomplices. Judges, therefore, were usually and heavily dependent on confessions.

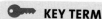

KEY TERM

Capital crime A crime punishable by a death sentence.

The use of torture

Torture was used on the Continent (but not in England) to obtain either a confession or information from an accused person. There was an awareness that confessions or allegations arising from torture could be unreliable. Innocent people were likely to say anything simply to escape the pain. Thus, rules were established with regard to the use of torture. While varying from place to place and over time, the rules generally agreed that:

- the victim should not die from torture
- certain people, for example children and pregnant women, were exempt
- judges should establish that a crime had been committed before allowing the use of torture
- testimony taken in the torture chamber was not admissible as evidence: the prisoner was required to repeat the confession 'freely'.

If the courts had adhered strictly to these rules then the European witch-hunt would have been more limited. But after 1484, witchcraft was seen as an exceptional crime (see page 4). Accordingly, the torture rules were relaxed and the system was abused. Judges, for example, were allowed to torture suspects for crimes that were believed to have been committed but for which there was no tangible evidence.

A common instrument of torture was the strappado, a pulley that raised victims off the floor by their arms, which were tied behind their backs. In the most severe forms, weights would be attached to the victims' feet and then the ropes would be jerked, a procedure that could dislodge the arms from their sockets. Thumb screws, leg screws, head clamps and the rack were commonly used. In Germany, many courts used the 'witches' chair', which was heated by fire from below.

Perhaps the most successful form of torture was forced sleeplessness. This had great appeal to humane judges. It was popular also because it was effective. One judge claimed that fewer than two per cent of all victims could endure it without confessing.

The use of torture had an enormous effect on the course of the European witch-hunts:

- Confessions under torture confirmed the evidence from witchcraft treatises.
- Torture meant that suspected witches were likely to confess and be convicted. When torture was used in witchcraft prosecutions, the rate of convictions could be as high as 95 per cent. When it was not used, as in England, the conviction rate was below 40 per cent.
- Torture ensured that more people were accused as alleged accomplices. Thus, chain-reaction hunts became possible.

Free confessions

Many suspects preferred to confess and be executed than to endure torture. However, not all 'free' witchcraft confessions represented conscious efforts to avoid suffering. A number of explanations have been put forward to explain free confessions:

- Some suspects may have actually invoked the Devil's aid and accordingly felt a sense of guilt.
- Some, particularly those who freely confessed to flying at night and copulating with demons, were probably mentally unstable.
- It has been claimed that those who confessed had experienced drug-induced hallucinations. This may have been the result of eating mouldy rye bread which could result in ergot poisoning, the symptoms of which include hallucinations and fantastic dreams.

SOURCE E

Torture by means of the strappado. A nineteenth-century French engraving.

What was the purpose of the weights in the foreground of the illustration in Source E?

Witch-testing

A number of other tests were used to identify witches. Most were legally dubious:

- Water in a pail was expected to shimmer when a witch walked past.
- Witches were made to recite the Lord's Prayer, which supposedly they could not do without faltering.
- If a death was attributed to witchcraft, suspects might be required to touch the corpse to see if fresh blood appeared – a sign of guilt.

- In England, midwives searched the bodies of the accused looking for teats where familiars or imps were supposed to suckle (see page 88).
- The Devil's mark was thought to be insensitive to pain and incapable of bleeding. The practice of pricking the witch with a needle to find the incriminating sign was thus developed.
- Witch 'swimmings' sometimes occurred (see Source F). The victim's left toe was fastened to the right thumb and the other way around. A line was passed under her armpits. She was then thrown into water. If she floated, she was assumed to be a witch: water was seen as a pure element and hence would reject anything impure. If she sank, she was presumed innocent.

SOURCE F

? Look at Source F. What exactly is taking place in the illustration?

Woodcut depicting the swimming test or water ordeal of Mary Sutton, who was accused of witchcraft and then executed, 1613.

Witchcraft and the secular courts

Ecclesiastical courts played an important role in regulating the moral and religious life of Europeans during the medieval and early modern period. To the extent that witchcraft involved the worship of the Devil, it was a spiritual crime. Many witches were in fact prosecuted in Church courts. But from the start of the great witch-hunt post-1560, European secular courts also took part in witch-hunting, either by cooperating with ecclesiastical courts or by trying witches by their own authority. Secular authorities had a legitimate interest in witchcraft because it was believed it could result in physical injury and might also be used for political purposes. Many states passed specific laws or included specific prohibitions against witchcraft in their criminal codes. These laws not only gave secular courts the right to hear witchcraft cases but also contributed to the growth of witch-hunting by publicising the crime and facilitating its prosecution.

By the late sixteenth century, Church courts were generally becoming weaker. Only in Spain, Portugal and Italy did the courts of the Inquisition remain strong. Elsewhere, especially in Protestant countries, Church courts became subordinate to secular courts. Without the mobilisation of this secular power, most witch-hunts would have been less intense. The retention of ecclesiastical jurisdiction helped to keep witch prosecutions to a minimum in Spain and Italy in the late sixteenth and seventeenth centuries because the Inquisition was sceptical about the crime of witchcraft. Papal Inquisitors, who initially had taken the lead in violating many of the procedural rules governing the use of torture, were among the first to recognise that these violations had resulted in many miscarriages of justice.

Elsewhere, clergy who were concerned about witchcraft sometimes put pressure on secular authorities to take stronger action. The most direct clerical influence on secular witchcraft prosecutions occurred in territories within the Holy Roman Empire where bishops or monks exercised civil power. In these quasi-ecclesiastical states, ruling clerics used secular officials and secular authority to prosecute witches.

Punishment

Across much of Europe, witches were burned at the stake, a punishment traditionally inflicted on heretics. In France, Germany, Switzerland and Scotland, the condemned were usually strangled before they were burned. In Sweden and some German states, witches were beheaded and then burned. In England, witches were hanged.

Non-capital punishment, especially for a first offence, was most common in England. This could result in a prison sentence. In Geneva, judges who could not determine guilt with certainty sometimes banished the accused.

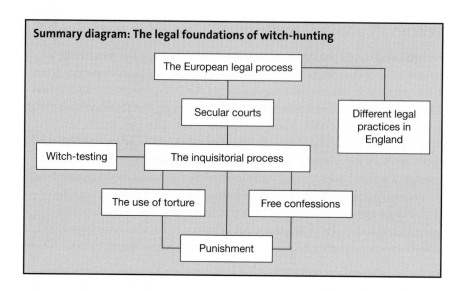

Summary diagram: The legal foundations of witch-hunting

3 Explanations of witch-hunting

▶ *What were the main causes of European witch-hunting?*

Legal changes and changes in Christian belief go some way towards explaining the European witch-hunts. However, scholars have put forward a variety of other theories to explain why the hunts occurred. Not all these scholars are historians. There has been interest in the history of witchcraft from a variety of disciplines: sociology, anthropology, criminology and feminist theory. All have brought their different insights to bear on the subject.

The contribution of anthropology

Some respected scholars, notably Alan Macfarlane (1970) and Keith Thomas (1971), attempted to compare present-day witch-hunts (for example in Africa) with those that occurred in early modern Europe. Historians today, however, are generally sceptical of **anthropological approaches**. Early modern Europe and modern Africa may have had similar witch beliefs but the cultures in which those beliefs were, and are, embedded, and from which they derived, mean that they are very different. Given the huge differences, it is dangerous to study witchcraft in modern Africa and assume it was the same in early modern Europe. The early modern European witch, for example, was regarded not as an isolated magical practitioner but rather, according to historian James Sharpe, 'as a member of an anti-Christian sect, a being eager to overturn the moral and physical universe of God, Christian believer, and Christian ruler alike'. The emphasis on the pact with the Devil is found in few other areas of the world.

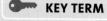 **KEY TERM**

Anthropological approaches Examinations of present-day societies (which are often seen as being 'pre-modern') which try to explain the actions of past societies.

Ignorance and delusion?

Today it seems inconceivable that people could actually believe in night-flying to the sabbat and sexual liaisons between witches and demons. Accordingly, it is easy to explain the witch-hunts as the result of mass superstition and general stupidity of people in the past. However, to regard early modern European beliefs as simply evidence of backwardness creates a barrier to the proper understanding of the witchcraft phenomenon and indeed to the period as a whole. It is important to realise that past societies invariably operated under a different cultural reality to our own. Most early modern Europeans, illiterate peasants and the educated elite alike, believed:

- that witchcraft existed
- in the existence of the Devil, who worked to turn mankind away from the path of righteousness.

There was some evidence for these beliefs. There were people who did practise harmful magic. There were others who freely confessed to making pacts with the Devil. Thus, when judicial authorities tried to eradicate witchcraft, they were not dealing with an entirely fabricated threat.

Early modern Europeans were perfectly able to explain misfortune without their minds leaping to witchcraft. But some misfortunes seemed bizarre, undeserved or both. Thus, for early modern Europeans the concept of *maleficium* was a rational reaction – an explanation for the inexplicable. To contemporaries, the victims were not the witches but the people who suffered at their hands. Witch-finding could be conducted by reasonable people, motivated chiefly by their compassion for the apparent victims of witchcraft.

Mass hysteria?

Historians of witchcraft are not keen on the rather crude concept of mass hysteria. Sometimes the term is apt. It is surely what occurred in a number of small German states when suspicion grew into accusations, accusations into trials, which in turn generated more accusations. But while mass hysteria could result in witchcrazes, it raises the question: why was there such hysteria?

The impact of the Reformation and Counter-Reformation

The profound religious developments that took place in the sixteenth century – the Reformation – are usually seen as encouraging the growth of witch-hunting. The early Protestant reformers, notably Martin Luther and John Calvin, shattered the unity of medieval Christendom. They aimed to restore the Church to its early Christian purity. They also proclaimed the autonomy of the individual conscience and favoured a direct relationship between a person and God, removing many of the clerical intermediaries that medieval Catholicism had established. Enthused by the new teaching, millions of Europeans left the

Catholic fold. Protestantism became the dominant religion in many parts of Germany, Switzerland, the Low Countries, England, Scotland, the Scandinavian countries, and in parts of France, Hungary and Poland.

The success of the Protestant Reformation encouraged the growth of a reform movement within Catholicism. This is known as the Counter-Reformation. Its main goals were to eliminate corruption within the Church, to educate the clergy, to inspire and strengthen the faith of the laity, and to reclaim the allegiance of those lost to Protestantism.

The battle for souls soon became a real war. Catholic armies fought against Protestants in a number of internal and international conflicts, the most significant of which were the civil wars in France in the late sixteenth-century and the **Thirty Years' War**.

Given that the Reformation and intense witch-hunting coincided in time, it is not surprising that some historians, like Hugh Trevor-Roper (1961), have claimed that the Reformation served as the mainspring of the European witch-hunt.

However:

- witch-hunting began almost a century before Luther nailed his *Ninety-Five Theses* to the church door at Wittenberg in 1517
- from 1520 to 1560, the early years of the Reformation, there were relatively few witchcraft prosecutions (see page 7)
- it is difficult to establish a direct causal connection between the Reformation and witch-hunting.

How did religious change contribute?

Witch-hunting occurred in both Catholic- and Protestant-controlled lands. Catholics took the lead in prosecution in some areas (especially south-west Germany), Protestants in others (for example, Scotland). It seems therefore that the Reformation and Counter-Reformation, to some extent different manifestations of the same European-wide religious revival, had similar effects on witch-hunting. Protestant and Catholic reformers alike exhibited a similar desire to extirpate witchcraft. Why?

Fear of the Devil

The Reformation increased Europeans' fear of the Devil. While not introducing a new conception of the Devil, Luther and Calvin stressed the Devil's presence. Luther saw his whole life as a struggle against Satan. 'The Devil', said Luther, 'liveth, yea and reigneth throughout the whole world'. Calvin thought much the same. Calvinist theologians, moreover, perceived the witches' pact with the Devil as being diametrically opposed to the Calvinists' covenant with God. While neither Luther nor Calvin was preoccupied with witchcraft as such, their concern at the threat posed by Satan encouraged many of their followers to take action against his agents – witches.

KEY TERM

Thirty Years' War This conflict from 1618 to 1648, mainly fought in Germany, involved most of the countries of western and central Europe and was one of the most destructive wars in European history. Initially a religious war between Protestants and Catholics, it eventually became a power struggle between France and Spain.

The Devil was just as frightening and omnipresent to Catholics. Indeed, for many Catholics Protestantism itself appeared to be the work of Satan. Thus, in both Catholic and Protestant circles there arose a zealous commitment to purify the world by declaring war against Satan and witches.

The attack on superstition and magic

Protestant reformers tried to purify the faith by eradicating Catholic superstitious beliefs and practices, eliminating vestiges of paganism and suppressing magic – the use of holy water, charms and amulets and so on. Campaigns against Catholic magic and superstition could easily lead to campaigns against witches.

The godly state

The Reformation bred a new moral mentality – the determination to create a godly state. In many places there was a considerable amount of legislation against moral offences. Sodomy, fornication, prostitution and adultery all came under attack – as did witchcraft. The goal of establishing a godly state was not restricted to Protestant states. Catholic rulers pursued the same ideal, their efforts often finding expression in witch-hunting. Some of the most intense witch-hunts took place in German principalities governed by Catholic prince-bishops who pursued witches in an effort to purify society as well as to promote their own image as the true defenders of Christian values.

The Bible and witchcraft

The Reformation established the Bible as the sole source of religious truth for most Protestants. There was also a new insistence on the literal interpretation of the Scriptures. Exodus 22:18 declared: 'Thou shalt not suffer a witch to live'. This text was used by preachers and judges to justify campaigns against witchcraft.

Religious conflict

The Reformation and Counter-Reformation led to bitter conflicts between Catholics and Protestants and between different Protestant denominations. This confessional strife, which often erupted into domestic and international warfare, played a role in witch-hunting. Some historians claim that a correlation can be established between the intensity of witchcraft prosecutions on the one hand and the extent of religious divisions on the other. Witch-hunting, it is claimed, was most severe in countries or regions where either large religious minorities lived within the boundaries of a state or the people of one state adhered to one religion and the people of a neighbouring state adhered to another. This was especially true in Germany, Switzerland, France, Poland and Scotland. In these areas, religious divisions and conflicts fostered political instability and violence. Religiously homogeneous areas, such as Catholic Spain and Lutheran Scandinavia, suffered less witch persecution.

However, while there may be a rough correlation between religious disunity/conflict and witch-hunting, this does not mean there was any direct causal connection between the two. Indeed, in many areas the most intense periods of witch-hunting were times of religious peace. Warfare could impede the operation of the regular judicial machinery that was used to prosecute witches. Interestingly, the dominant faith in a religiously divided area rarely used witchcraft prosecutions to dispose of their religious enemies. For the most part, witches belonged, at least formally, to the same faith as their prosecutors.

Consequently, the conflict between Protestants and Catholics did not necessarily inspire witch-hunting. Nevertheless, it may be that religious conflict made communities more fearful of moral subversion and more eager to rid their communities of corrupting influences like witchcraft. It may be that the belief that such corruption was taking place was stronger in areas where the heretical activities of either a Protestant or Catholic minority were close and threatening. Hunting witches allowed Protestant or Catholic communities to prove that God was on their side – and that they were on God's.

Conclusion

Some think Christianity in the early modern period was an oppressive ideology which fostered the persecution of alleged witches. Nevertheless, in reality, the connection between Christian belief and the persecution of witches is far from clear. Not all theologians agreed with the views put forward in *Malleus*. Many believed that God ultimately controlled the uncertainties of human existence, not the Devil or his agents. They thus opposed the persecution of witches.

Witchcraft and the early modern state

In the sixteenth and seventeenth centuries, several European states grew in size and power. Rulers brought the various territories over which they claimed jurisdiction under more effective political and legal control. 'It is no coincidence … that the great witch-hunt occurred during a period of extensive state-building throughout Europe', says Levack. Arguably:

- Rulers took a heightened interest in religious matters. In Scotland, for example, the government and Church sought moral conformity. Historian Christina Larner regards this as a vital factor in constructing an ideological base for large-scale witch-hunting. The good citizen was one who became closely identified with the good Christian as prescribed by the relevant secular ruler.
- It is unlikely that there could have been large-scale witch-hunts without the state's assistance and encouragement.

However, few governments of strong states actively promoted witch-hunting. The real initiative for witch-hunts came from the localities. Generally, the central or higher courts of most countries did more to restrict witch-hunting than to encourage it – unlike many local courts. Central judicial authorities were less likely to be affected by the hysterical mood that could engulf localities and usually more committed to the proper operation of the judicial system.

A country's government and legal system often made a major difference to the extent of witch-hunting. England, for example, had a long history of political and judicial centralisation and relatively few witch persecutions. The Holy Roman Empire, a patchwork of hundreds of autonomous territories, proved highly vulnerable to witch-hunts in the absence of central judicial regulations. Rather than being imposed by strong governments, in reality the worst witch-hunts occurred where central authority was weak.

The functionalist interpretation: pressure from below

Most historians now believe that witch persecution was driven more by attitudes from 'below' than pressure from the Church and state 'above'. This was the view of Alan Macfarlane and Keith Thomas in the early 1970s. Macfarlane's study of witchcraft in Essex, like Thomas's more general work, demonstrated that in England witchcraft accusations were the result of interpersonal tensions between villagers. Macfarlane and Thomas showed that accused witches were usually unpopular, antisocial people, known for begging from their neighbours and verbally cursing those who turned them away. If suspected witches were themselves angry, they made their neighbours even angrier. According to Thomas and Macfarlane, the witch trials had a functionalist purpose: they were used to eliminate antisocial members of the community and release pent-up local tensions. The Macfarlane–Thomas approach created a major shift in scholarly interpretation. Historians across Europe soon found similar evidence of popular pressures behind witch-hunting. Popular anxieties about the threat from witches forced – often reluctant – authorities to take action. Far more suspected witches died because of the fears of neighbours than on account of politically directed hunts.

The social and economic context

As well as stressing social functionalism as a crucial factor in witch-hunting, Thomas and Macfarlane emphasised the importance of socio-economic changes that they perceived taking place across Europe in the early modern period. These changes include:

- the population increase: for example, England's population doubled between 1540 and 1660
- an unprecedented rise in prices
- the decline in real wages
- the growth of towns
- increasing mercantile and agricultural capitalism
- the break-up of the traditional village community.

Such changes may have influenced witchcraft persecutions. The poorest members of society were particularly affected by the decline in living standards. As conditions deteriorated, the poor craved informal charity, charity which the richer elements of society were increasingly reluctant to give. Arguably, this engendered conflict within communities and may have contributed to a general mood of anxiety that encouraged witch-hunting.

The 'mini ice age'

German historian Wolfgang Behringer believes there was a correlation between intense witch-hunting and harsh climatic conditions. He claims that a 'little ice age', starting in the early 1560s, had a devastating effect on crops, particularly on vines. (Wine-producing areas of Germany saw intense persecution of witches.) Economic hardship, thinks Behringer, led to tension and a demand for scapegoats. Witches were the scapegoats. However, historians of climate are still divided over the chronology, impact and even the concept of a 'mini ice age'. There is thus no certainty that it had a major effect on witch-hunting.

The impact of disease

The early modern period was an age of epidemic disease of a severity not seen since the Black Death in the mid-fourteenth century. The most feared disease was the plague, which was particularly deadly in urban areas. In Geneva, Milan and other cities, witches were sometimes blamed for 'plague-spreading'. However, this was a relatively rare phenomenon. Most people at the time seem to have accepted that disease was simply a fact of life – and death. They did not usually blame witches for epidemics.

Class conflict?

It has been claimed that witch-hunting was a method used by the socio-economic elites as a form of control to consolidate their dominance over the poorer sections of the population. American anthropologist Marvin Harris (1973) claimed that witches were scapegoats victimised by the Church and secular authorities to divert public anger at a time of economic dislocation. 'The practical significance of the witch mania', says Harris, 'was that it shifted responsibility for the crisis of late medieval society from both Church and state to imaginary demons in human form.' Religious and secular authorities, claimed Harris, in leading witch-hunts not only exonerated themselves but made themselves indispensable, cementing their power. But, given that most of the witch charges came from 'below', not from the elite, this explanation is unconvincing.

It was once claimed by **Marxist historians** that witch-hunts were a product of the transition from feudalism to capitalism. This view is now seen as far too generalised to merit serious discussion. More interesting is the sub-Marxist view that the witch persecutions occurred at a critical period when a new way of economic life clashed with the old and that witch-hunting was to some extent a

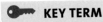 **KEY TERM**

Marxist historians
Historians who believe that history has been deeply shaped by economic circumstances. They are influenced by the ideology of the philosopher Karl Marx.

by-product of the anxiety engendered by rapid social change. Unfortunately for this interpretation, witch-hunts frequently occurred in areas where there was very little socio-economic change.

The counter-arguments

There are counter-arguments to the claims of Macfarlane, Thomas, Behringer and others that socio-economic pressures were responsible for witchcraft persecution:

- Arguably, socio-economic changes did not have as much impact on most people's lives as some historians claim.
- Even if the period 1560–1660 was an age of socio-economic tension and change, it does not follow that ordinary folk found in witch-hunting a release from the anxiety they were experiencing. Inter-personal tensions that led people to accuse others of witchcraft were probably no more intense in the early modern period than they had been in medieval times. Many of the personal conflicts that led to accusations were a constant feature of village life: they could just as easily develop in good times or bad, in times of rapid change or in times of relative stability.
- Although Behringer may have found a correlation between socio-economic hardship and the rise of witch-hunting in parts of Germany, elsewhere in Europe other historians have found no such connection. Indeed, recent research suggests that the witch-hunts declined during the 1630s when much of south-west Germany was facing serious hardship as a result of plague, famine and the Thirty Years' War.
- Witch-hunts often took place in areas which were free from war, famine or pestilence.
- It is dangerous to generalise about conditions which extended over two centuries and across Europe.

The geographical and social setting

Anthropological studies of pre-literate societies today suggest that magical beliefs are especially durable among an uneducated, superstitious peasantry living in close-knit, small communities where everyone knows everyone else and where undesirable people cannot be ignored – not dissimilar to conditions in early modern Europe.

However, witch-hunting was far from being just a rural phenomenon in early modern Europe. Some of the largest hunts in Germany took place within an urban environment.

Selfish motives

It has been suggested that some witch trials were engendered by selfish motives:

- Relatives of the accused might stand to inherit property.
- Governments might wish to acquire a witch's property.

- Some lawyers and officials may have encouraged witch-hunting in order to make money.
- Witch-finders sometimes profited by offering their services to local communities to help them identify witches.

But, in general, witchcraft cases were not very lucrative because the economic status of most witches was low. Only in those few cases (mainly in south-west Germany) in which wealthy people were accused may the possibility of profit have contributed to the zeal of the prosecutors.

Feminist interpretations

Given that the vast majority of accused witches were women, some feminist interpretations regard witch-hunting as a by-product of patriarchy and misogyny: evidence for men's oppression of women. There have been a number of feminist interpretations:

- The timing of the witch-hunts has been linked by some feminist historians to growing concern about female conduct. Economic change, especially growing commercialisation, it is claimed, elevated the public profile of women in a way that challenged male dominance, resulting in a 'gender crisis'.
- Barbara Ehrenreich and Deirdre English (1973) claimed that most of the women who were persecuted had been community healers and midwives. They argued that they were persecuted by the male medical establishment in order to eliminate female midwifery skills and extinguish knowledge about birth control in an effort to repopulate Europe. Unfortunately, this theory disregarded the fact that the majority of those accused were neither healers nor midwives. Indeed, in many parts of Europe, midwives were more likely to be found helping witch-hunters to examine suspects than being accused of witchcraft.

Unfortunately, many of those who were impressed by the feminist argument with regard to witchcraft had done little serious research. Claims, for example, that some 9 million women were killed in the witch-hunts were wrong. Misogyny may have been prevalent in the early modern period. But this did not mean that witch-hunts were male attacks, intentional or otherwise, on women. Few historians today see witch-hunting as deliberate male oppression of women. Ultimately, witches were pursued because they were thought to be witches, not because they were women. Interestingly, a high proportion of those accusing and giving evidence against witches were women. In Essex, for example, women were fifteen times more likely to give evidence in a witchcraft case than in other felony cases. Witchcraft accusations were often generated by disputes between women.

The reality of witchcraft

We tend to see witchcraft as a delusion, a non-existent crime. We thus assume that executed witches were innocent victims of a misguided judiciary and an oppressive legal system. Such assumptions are not necessarily valid. Some of those accused of witchcraft almost certainly did practise harmful magic: some may even have devoted themselves to Satan.

Over the last two centuries, several scholars have supported the view, first formulated by French radical Jules Michelet in 1862, that early modern witchcraft was a pre-Christian religion adhered to by the peasantry but attacked by the Church and the secular authorities. This notion was restated powerfully by Margaret Murray, an anthropologist, in *The Witch-cult in Western Europe* (1921) and by Gerald Gardner in *Witchcraft Today* (1954). The view that witchcraft is an ancient and coherent faith, however, has been largely discredited by historians:

- There is no evidence whatsoever that early modern witchcraft was an organised and structured religion or that witches gathered in large numbers for any purpose, diabolical or otherwise.
- Connections between early modern and modern witchcraft seem to be non-existent. Modern witchcraft is an invented religion, a synthesis of beliefs which owes little to the early modern period.

Children and witch-hunting

The role of children in witch-hunts was often important. Adults, conscious of the Devil's guile, took children's claims seriously:

- Claims made by the Throckmorton children in the Huntingdonshire village of Warboys led to the execution of Alice and John Samuel and their daughter Agnes in 1593. The Throckmorton girls suffered illness attributed to evil spirits infiltrating their bodies.
- In the Lancashire scare of 1634, a boy Edmund Robinson swore to magistrates he had been abducted to a sabbat and named at least fifteen witches. He later confessed to fraud (see page 105).
- A large witch-hunt began in Dalarna in Sweden in 1668, when a fifteen-year-old boy accused neighbours of witchcraft.
- Children, initially, were the key witnesses in the Salem witch trials (see pages 139–43).

Some children who accused people of witchcraft enjoyed the attention adults paid them and the opportunity to exercise power. Some may have been unable to tell fantasy from reality. Some were probably just evil.

Conclusion

Half a century ago, when historians began to take an interest in early modern witch-hunting, many believed that there must have been some kind of common causation underpinning what was taking place across Europe. But once historians began to study the witch-hunts in detail, it became apparent that witch-hunting was a more complex phenomenon than was once imagined. Witch-hunts varied from country to country and region to region. Given the differences, most historians now accept that no single 'big' explanation can account for Europe's witch craze. Robin Briggs (1996) warns that 'any attempt to suggest that there is a single cause, or even a dominant one, a hidden key to the mystery, should be treated with great suspicion'. Indeed, it is hardly possible to speak of a typical European witch-hunt. In many respects, the 'great' witch hunt was really nothing more than a series of separate hunts, each of which had its own causes and its own dynamics.

However, the witch-hunts do possess some common features. All involved the pursuit of a secret enemy of society. Most large hunts assumed that this enemy was not alone but part of a broader movement. Whatever the local circumstances of witch persecutions, they all depended on a general acceptance of the existence of *maleficium*. All large hunts involved a high degree of communal anxiety. This mood justified the exceptional legal procedures needed to uncover witches.

Historians today are most likely to stress the fundamental changes in the criminal law as the necessary precondition for the witch-hunts. Nevertheless, the witch-hunt was by no means only a judicial phenomenon. By the sixteenth century, in theology and the popular imagination as well as in law, the witch was regarded as a universal enemy. A range of emotions – fear, anger and hatred – lay behind the accusations. Most of the witch trials were motivated not by stupidity but by a belief that it was the morally appropriate course of action. Most of those involved in the judicial process seem to have acted 'from a spirit of duty and a concern for the public welfare', write Geoffrey Scarre and John Callow (2001). They describe the trials as 'a frightening example of how morally motivated action can lead to massive suffering'.

While some historians still assume that witchcraft charges were somehow not really about witchcraft, the reality is that most accusers believed witches to be witches. People might well cook up false accusations. But unless people, from kings to peasants, had believed in the reality of witchcraft, such charges would have made no sense.

Witch scares could devastate entire communities. But seen in context, they are the exceptions that prove the rule, the rule being that they were relatively rare. Rather than ask why so many people were killed as witches, it is equally valid to ask why only 40,000–50,000 Europeans were executed over a 300-year period. Given the pervasiveness of the factors which are normally regarded as having caused the craze, it may be that historians need to work out why there were so few – rather than so many – witch-burnings. This may have had something to do with early modern governments. Witch-hunts were often the response to pressures from below. Most governments were suspicious of such pressures. Surrender to popular passions ran counter to what most rulers were trying to achieve: the imposition of government on community. With regard to witchcraft, early modern governments may generally have been the heroes rather than the villains.

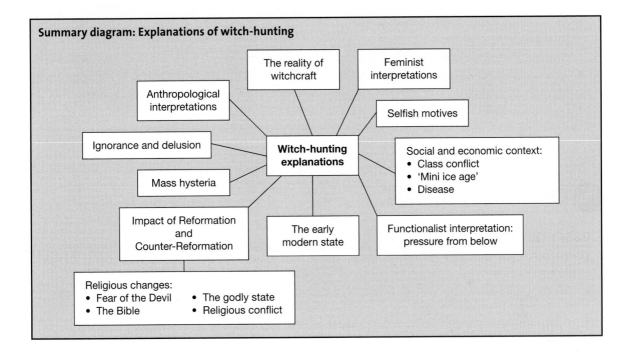

Summary diagram: Explanations of witch-hunting

- The reality of witchcraft
- Feminist interpretations
- Anthropological interpretations
- Selfish motives
- Ignorance and delusion
- **Witch-hunting explanations**
- Social and economic context:
  - Class conflict
  - 'Mini ice age'
  - Disease
- Mass hysteria
- Impact of Reformation and Counter-Reformation
- The early modern state
- Functionalist interpretation: pressure from below
- Religious changes:
  - Fear of the Devil
  - The Bible
  - The godly state
  - Religious conflict

Chapter summary

Large-scale witch-hunting began in the fifteenth century. There was a growth of belief among the elite that witches had made a pact with the Devil. Ordinary Europeans were more concerned about *maleficium*. Some 40,000–50,000 witches, the majority of whom were relatively poor women, were executed, mainly in the period 1560–1660. Changes in the legal process, especially the use of torture, encouraged witch-hunting. There are a host of explanations for witch-hunting: ignorance, mass hysteria, the impact of the Reformation, European state-building, pressure from 'below', social and economic factors, persecution of women. Most historians now accept that witch-hunting had many causes rather than one overriding cause.

Refresher questions

Use these questions to remind yourself of the key material covered in this chapter.

1 Why was there a growth in witch-hunting in the fifteenth century?

2 What was the impact of *Malleus Maleficarum*?

3 Why was there a major difference between elite and popular views of witchcraft?

4 When was the main period of witch-hunting?

5 What type of people were executed as witches?

6 Why can the witch-hunts be regarded as essentially a judicial operation?

7 To what extent did torture create witchcraft?

8 What was the impact of the Reformation on witch-hunting?

9 To what extent did state-building contribute to witch-hunting?

10 Was witch-hunting essentially driven from 'below'?

11 How important were socio-economic factors in the rise of witch-hunting?

12 Was witch-hunting essentially woman-hunting?

 Question practice

ESSAY QUESTIONS

1 'Witchcraft, a crime supposedly committed by women, was essentially a crime against women.' How far do you agree with this view in the period from 1560 to 1660?

2 'The great European witch-hunt was essentially a judicial operation.' How far do you agree with this view for the period from 1560 to 1660?

3 To what extent was witch-hunting in the period from 1560 to 1660 the result of social and economic change?

4 Assess the impact of the profound religious changes that took place in the period from 1560 to 1660 on the growth of witch-hunting.

CHAPTER 2

Popular culture in early modern Europe

Historians such as Keith Thomas and Alan Macfarlane have stressed that pressure for witch-hunting often began from 'below' rather than being initiated by governments or by the Church. It is thus reasonable to ask to what extent the witchcraze was affected by the popular culture of early modern Europe. This chapter will examine the issue of popular culture by examining the following themes:

★ The debate over popular culture(s)

★ Common cultures

★ Challenges to popular cultures

Key dates

1440s	Johannes Gutenberg began printing in Germany	**1488**	Publication of Lichtenberger's *Prognostications*
1476	William Caxton began printing in England	**1545–63**	Meeting of the Council of Trent

1 The debate over popular culture(s)

▶ *Was there such a thing as popular culture?*

Since the 1960s, the history of popular culture has been a field of research that has developed original and interdisciplinary approaches to historical sources and issues. In Britain, *Popular Culture in Early Modern Europe* by Peter Burke (published in 1978) was a pioneering and influential work. Popular culture, in Burke's view, denoted those beliefs, values, customs and practices belonging to the vast majority of ordinary Europeans who were non-noble and non-clerical commoners. The secular and religious elites had their own culture. Nevertheless, Burke thought that in the fifteenth and early sixteenth centuries most of the elite, with the exception of a small number of learned scholars and theologians, participated in popular culture.

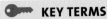

KEY TERMS

Renaissance An intellectual and cultural movement that began in Italy in the fourteenth century, spread to northern Europe and flourished until the mid-sixteenth century. Fundamental to the Renaissance (which means rebirth in French) were the revival of classical learning, art and architecture, and the concept of the dignity of man, which characterised humanism.

Enlightenment The name given to a school of European thought of the eighteenth century. Those influenced by the Enlightenment believed in reason and human progress.

Burke went on to claim that during the early modern period, the elites gradually withdrew from participating in much of this traditional world, a process encouraged in different ways by **Renaissance** humanism (see pages 6–7), the Reformation and Counter-Reformation (see pages 22–4), and later by the impact of the **Enlightenment** (see page 168). According to Burke, the Renaissance and Enlightenment promoted the values of reason and politeness, and by the eighteenth century the elite in both state and Church waged war on what they saw as the 'superstitious' values and the disorder, profanity and rowdiness resulting from many of the recreational pursuits of ordinary people.

In recent years, many scholars have questioned Burke's sweeping binary division between 'elite' and 'popular'. They have stressed instead cultural interaction and diversity. As well as the debate over 'popular', the notion of 'culture' has been a subject of controversy. In the nineteenth century, culture was used to refer to art, literature and music. But the word is now used to comprise almost all aspects of social life, from speaking, eating and drinking to the assumptions underlying everyday living.

Given the (often) heated debates over both of its components, the validity and usefulness of the term popular culture have been questioned.

Popular culture or cultures?

Today, most scholars emphasise the diversity of popular cultures and are sceptical of Burke's elite/popular divide. Given that the early modern period extended over some three centuries and the scale of Burke's study was the whole of Europe, it is hardly surprising that historians now distinguish a wide variety of different cultures with huge regional variations. Moreover, it is clear that by the late sixteenth century, partly as a result of increased literacy following the invention of the printed book (see pages 50–2), cultures evolved far more quickly than in the past.

Geographical cultures

In very broad terms it is possible to distinguish between the following cultures:

- A southern European culture, centred on the outdoor world of processions and parades, and with a tight restriction on women's freedom, and the more indoor and less exuberant culture of northern Europe.
- The more economically advanced western European states and the less advanced states of eastern Europe.
- Rural and urban cultures.
- Rural cultures of mountainous or pastoral regions and those of arable plains.

Elite cultures

The elites are generally seen to comprise the following:

- The nobles, generally great landowners, who played a major role in central and local government, possessed various traditional rights, and had more wealth than ordinary people.
- The learned elites, comprising university scholars and churchmen.

It should be self-evident that these two elites did not share one culture:

- Noble and learned elites had very different lifestyles and perspectives.
- The learned elites were by no means united. Scholars by 1500 were not necessarily churchmen. Scholarly activity had broken free from religious control in some – but not all – areas. By the seventeenth century, the ideas of some scholars, for example those of Galileo (see page 165) were at odds with those of Church leaders.
- As a result of the Reformation (see pages 21–2), churchmen – Catholics, Lutherans, Calvinists, Anglicans – were divided on a host of theological issues. There was thus no longer one common Church culture.
- Nobles were by no means one united class. At the top of European society were the royal families. Royal families and court nobility had very different cultural experiences from nobles who owned relatively little land.
- Nobles had different privileges in different parts of Europe.
- Some nobles, especially those in Italy and the Netherlands, had strong links to cities and were often involved in commercial activities. Elsewhere, for example in France and much of eastern Europe, nobles tended to shun both commercial activity and towns.
- Noble culture was constantly evolving, in different ways and at different times.

There were thus a host of different elite cultures. Nor was there a neat division between 'popular' and 'elite' culture. Certainly there were cultural manifestations that by dint of their sophistication or expense were exclusively the concern of the elite: court **masques**, for example. But across Europe in the sixteenth century all classes of people enjoyed festivals and bull- and bear-baiting.

Middling cultures

Historians have pointed to distinctive cultural traits found among the so-called 'middling sorts': merchants, professional men and substantial (but non-noble) farmers. Such groups cannot easily be labelled either 'elite' or 'popular'. Respectable middling-sort culture might stand equally distant from the cultures of both the disorderly poor and the rashly extravagant rich.

Urban cultures

Burke's bipolar cultural approach did not really fit the towns and cities which were growing in importance and in number across most of Europe throughout the early modern period. Many of Europe's largest and richest cities experienced

 KEY TERM

Masques A form of dramatic entertainment, consisting of a combination of verse, dance and music, usually with a plot based on a mythological theme. Masques were elaborately staged with expensive costumes and scenery.

spectacular growth. London, for example, had 60,000 people in 1500. By 1800 it had over a million. The rise in urban population was not the result of natural population growth. Cities tended to have above-average mortality and a particular proneness to epidemic disease. The population increase was the result of people from rural areas gravitating to towns hoping to improve their social and economic lot.

The largest cities, like Antwerp, Paris and London, characterised by a variety of economic functions, stood out as the centres of a sophisticated life. In the large cities there was considerable social interaction, high levels of literacy (see pages 51–2) and a diversity and multiplicity of cultures.

At the upper end of urban society were a few immensely rich merchants and bankers. There were also large numbers of prosperous and skilled professionals: smiths of all kinds, carpenters, bricklayers, builders, weavers and engineers. At the bottom of urban society were servants, labourers and young apprentices who were expected to complete a long and arduous training.

There was a varied and impressive cultural life in the early modern period. Much took place in public. But urban culture also took place in private, at home. In larger houses, families would gather to read and be read to, to share food and play music with friends. The growing sophistication of this culture was a consequence of the ever-widening reach of education.

Common cultures

Some nine-tenths of Europeans in the early modern period still lived and worked in the countryside in single homesteads, hamlets, villages and small towns, just as they had done throughout most of the Middle Ages. With some exceptions, the peasants were no longer **serfs** but legally free, able to dispose of their property and, if they chose, to leave their native villages. Most were occupied with growing crops, raising livestock and the countless other jobs connected with farming. Over most of Europe, the traditional village communities remained substantially intact for most of the early modern period.

There remains a lack of evidence of the cultures of ordinary people who lived in those communities. One major problem is that, while literacy was growing in the towns (see pages 51–2), the bulk of the population in the countryside could not read or write and have thus left few direct records. Much of what we know (or think we know) of what ordinary people did or how they felt comes from sources written or drawn by the elite.

Burke claimed that it was possible to reconstruct the entertainment culture of ordinary people by examining a much wider range of cultural media: songs, ballads, plays and paintings. Compelling glimpses into the lives of common people in the sixteenth century, for example, can be found in the paintings of

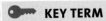

KEY TERM

Serf An agricultural labourer who was tied to working on his lord's estate.

Flemish artist Pieter Brueghel. His *Battle between Carnival and Lent* (1559) depicts a wide variety of popular pastimes (see Source A). It also provides a glimpse of ordinary people's clothes, dances, gestures and attitudes. Nevertheless, such cultural evidence can be variously interpreted. There are also other problems with regard to 'popular culture':

- There were quite large gradations of wealth and interest among ordinary people. In western Europe most ordinary people were peasants who paid rents to a landowner. In eastern Europe, by contrast, many were still serfs who were tied to the land and forced to provide labour and other services to the landowner.
- Religious differences between Catholic, Lutheran, Calvinist, Anglican and Orthodox Christians greatly affected lifestyles.
- Youth popular culture may have been different from 'middle-aged' and 'old' cultures.
- There were huge gender differences.

What does seem certain is that the recreational cultures of the countryside lacked the sophistication of urban cultures. There was little trace of the more refined domestic entertainments. Low levels of literacy limited access to books. Moreover, few country dwellings were sufficiently spacious to accommodate more than the smallest family gatherings. When country people sought recreation they did so at the inn or outdoors.

SOURCE A

Examine Source A. What does the source depict of popular culture in the Netherlands in the mid-sixteenth century?

Battle between Carnival and Lent by Pieter Brueghel, 1559.

Taverns were great centres of entertainment culture. It was here that people (mainly men) gathered to exchange news, make bargains, gamble and while away long winter hours. Sometimes they might be entertained by travelling musicians or divert themselves with songs or storytelling. The long narrative tale was a feature of many European cultures.

However, few country inns could hold large numbers of people. Large festive occasions thus generally took place in the open air. For country folk the winter celebrations of Carnival (see page 42) were often less important than the great festivals of May Day, midsummer and harvest time. These occasions were embellished by feasting, drinking and dancing. There were other opportunities for feasting, dancing and country sports of various kinds. Even the poorest serfs did not work incessantly and there were many holy days in the Church calendar (see page 41) prior to the Reformation. These gave most people at least one day off each week, with longer spells at the great festivals of Christmas, Easter and Whitsuntide.

More occasionally, diversions might be games connected with proving manhood. Football and stoolball (an early form of cricket) were both widely enjoyed in England by the sixteenth century. Tudor monarchs, like their medieval predecessors, regarded such ball games as a distraction from the more virtuous and military art of archery. Their efforts to stamp them out were in vain. In Scotland, people played a primitive form of golf. All European cultures enjoyed various sorts of animal fights, cockfighting or baiting bulls or bears. In Spain bull chases were popular.

Gender

Gender constituted one of the key foundations of the early modern European order, shaping almost every sphere of life – social, economic, religious, political and cultural. In the early modern period, women were considered – and probably saw themselves – as inferior to men. The dominance of men over women was anchored in theology and law. After all, Eve was held responsible for Adam's fall from Paradise. St Paul had also declared that women should be silent and submissive. The general intellectual opinion was that women were creatures of emotion, vulnerable to passions, deceit and infidelity, who needed a steady – male – hand. A husband's supremacy in marriage was considered sacrosanct. Gender-based assumptions led to exclusion of women from education, politics and many professions. Early modern society was patriarchal: male authority was undisputed within the family and in society at large by a web of laws, regulations and customs. There were some regional variations. Women probably had less freedom in southern Europe than in northern Europe. Foreign visitors, for example, sometimes described England as a paradise for women: in other parts of Europe, middle- and upper-class women were largely confined to the home. For women, chastity and fidelity were prerequisites for a good name, not education.

Husbands and wives had different but complementary roles within marriage. The husband's role was to provide for and govern the household. The wife's role was to manage the home, take primary charge of young children, and work with their husbands in agricultural or industrial production. Any couple straying too far from this pattern faced strong disapproval, ridicule or both (see pages 44–5).

Rather than meet in taverns to socialise, women gathered at the well or washing place and also in evening 'spinning-bees' devoted to work and gossip. At a local level, women played an important role in shaping public opinion through their 'gossip networks'. Public opinion was a weapon of some significance for retaining a good name: something that mattered to both men and women. By ostracising, mocking or rebuking troublesome neighbours or violent, unfaithful husbands, women might shame offenders into mending their ways.

Hardship

There were no fundamental changes in industrial methods, no new sources of power and energy, no major breakthroughs in farming and land transportation to transform the conditions of life in the early modern period. Consequently, the general lot of ordinary Europeans remained hard. Most people were dependent on the harvest – the heartbeat of the whole economy. This meant they were reliant on the vagaries of the weather. Plenty of families still went hungry in winter and lived on the breadline. Meat was a luxury for most peasants. Times of dearth were terrifying and for many potentially deadly.

While there is some evidence that there was a growing material prosperity, this could do little to mitigate the arbitrary quality of sudden misfortune. Epidemics struck with equal force in the seventeenth century as in the fourteenth. In fact, the growth of cities, unaccompanied by any breakthrough in public sanitation or hygiene, may have intensified their incidence. Many cities suffered 'plagues' of various types – deadly afflictions which modern medical science has struggled precisely to identify. Epidemics, which could kill a third of a city's population in a single year, led to panic that could lead to a search for scapegoats. Some people feared plague spreaders and some towns, like Geneva, tried to find those deemed responsible. In 1570, 115 people in Geneva were persecuted and 44 executed, invariably after torture.

The everyday hazards of work and an unbalanced diet took their toll on life and health. The birth of modern medicine was still centuries away. Such medical advances as there were in the period were more of a theoretical than practical nature. People continued to live in 1700, as they had in 1400, with pain and disability as the common lot, often to be endured over a long span of years.

Members of Europe's elites were shielded from some of life's brutalities. They had (more than) enough to eat, fuel to keep them warm and opulent clothing. They lived in large buildings and had servants to attend to their needs. But even the elite could be hit by epidemics and in an age before anaesthetics there were few conditions that justified the agony and risk of surgical operation. Childbirth was perilous for rich and poor, mother and child alike. In many areas, a third of children died before reaching the age of five. Death was literally all around and few lives were untouched by the sudden brutalities of its sheer unpredictability. In this at least, rich and poor, townsmen and country folk shared common concerns.

Conclusion

For most of the early modern period, it is impossible to talk of a common culture embracing all or even most ordinary Europeans. Instead, there were a host of popular cultures. Many historians today question whether it makes much sense to describe cultural media as 'elite' or 'popular'. Most tend to see popular culture as a variety of cultural practices and experiences which represent an intricate cultural mixture in which elements of both 'folklore' and 'learned' traditions found complex ways to intermingle. Thus, it is probably fair to say that many important features of early modern culture were shared by most people at every social level, certainly in 1500. If the substance of people's lives was markedly different, rich and poor shared the common culture of the Church. Popular superstitious religious practices had as deep a resonance with the aristocracy as in the community as a whole. All social orders were involved in the many festivals that took place across Europe. Rich and poor seem to have held broadly similar views on gender relations. In England, courtiers and artisans thronged the playhouses of Elizabethan London. Moreover, there was overlap and exchange, in both directions, between different cultural worlds. Some features, such as chivalric tales, descended from the elite to the popular, while others (dances and songs, for example) moved in the opposite direction. The elite did not just impose a higher culture on a popular one. Given the considerable interaction between the two, the borderline between popular and elite cultures was often a fuzzy one.

This is not to say that early modern culture was essentially democratic or that it was conducive to breaking down cultural barriers. The same cultural events could be experienced by citizens of different sorts or conditions in subtly different ways. A procession was in one sense a socially inclusive communal experience as it wound through the streets. But the position of all participants was carefully laid down to manifest and express publicly their place in the social hierarchy.

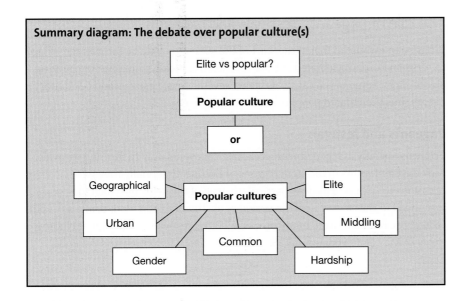

Summary diagram: The debate over popular culture(s)

- Elite vs popular?
- **Popular culture**
- or
- **Popular cultures**
  - Geographical
  - Urban
  - Gender
  - Common
  - Elite
  - Middling
  - Hardship

② Common cultures

▶ *To what extent were festivals of misrule and carnivals useful safety valves?*

Cultural historians have focused their attention on certain aspects of social life which they claim were held in common or shared by most Europeans. These include the significance of ritual, the importance of pageants, festivals and carnivals, public humiliation, moral regulation and the role of magic in society.

The significance of ritual

At the start of the sixteenth century, the strongest cultural bond was the religious framework of Christianity. Most Europeans, regardless of social origins, looked for moral direction, for hope and for consolation to the Church. Before the Reformation (see pages 21–2), most Europeans affirmed loyalty to the same Catholic Church. The Church's calendar and its sacraments provided an essential focus for piety and ritual:

- Baptism, first communion, weddings and funerals were not only religious ceremonies but also rites of passage marked with feasting, dancing and singing.
- Everyone was required to attend church on Sundays.
- A variety of saints' days provided opportunities for popular rituals and processions which reinforced communal ties and enhanced local pride. Indeed, any special occasion of the Christian year was used to celebrate festivals. Moreover, authorities saw nothing wrong in using the church or its ceremonies for purposes that were not exclusively religious.

The role of pageants, festivals and carnivals

It has been estimated that at the start of the sixteenth century the average village in western Europe celebrated at least seventeen festivals annually, not counting saints' days. Some of the carnivals lasted several days. Festivals and celebratory events thus punctuated people's hard-working lives.

Pageants and festivals

Festivals, usually associated with ecclesiastical events or with farming festivals, took different forms in different regions of Europe. Essentially they were occasions for excess. This was particularly true of the festivals which took place just ahead of the start of Lent – a period of abstinence from food, drink, sex and recreation. But there were many other exuberant festivals in the year, including those of May Day, Midsummer, St Valentine's Day, Halloween and All Fools' Day.

Festivals generally took place in the centre of a village or town. Usually there was some kind of procession or pageant with people dressed up to represent biblical, mythical or classical heroes. Often a play was performed or a mock battle fought. The cornerstone of most festivals in towns was provided by the **guilds**. They sponsored processions, feasts and special masses, often competing to put on the best and most lavish pageant, procession or play.

Rulers and great lords staged their own festivals, usually on a lavish scale. There would be enormous banquets, knightly jousts (long after the lance had disappeared from the battlefield), literary and musical competitions and elaborately staged theatrical presentations, often with a water festival. (The 'floats' of modern popular processions are a reminder of such festivals.)

Carnival

In southern and central Europe, in particular, carnival was an important part of popular culture. The carnival season usually began in January or February. People of all social classes celebrated the pleasures of the flesh – eating, drinking, dancing and sexual pleasure, before the abstinence of Lent. Carnival normally mocked the normal rules of order and morality. Many centred on the theme of the world turned upside down. The forms of topsy-turvy varied widely. In some places men adopted women's roles and dress and the other way around, or servants became masters and so forth.

Carnival festivities usually culminated in rowdy processions in which people often wore masks or ritual costumes, and special ceremonies (often the performance of a play of some kind or horse or foot races) on the main square. Figures suggest that carnival produced more conceptions than any other period, except the late spring period of May and June which saw May Day and Midsummer festivities. The last two festivals were regarded as more important than carnival in some northern European areas.

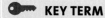

KEY TERM

Guilds Associations of workers, formed in medieval Europe, to further their members' common purposes and interests. Most guilds represented specific crafts or trades. They became very powerful, exercising a monopoly over both production and trade and controlling recruitment by the apprenticeship system.

The Feast of Fools

This seems to have been a popular festival across Europe in the early modern period. Held usually in December or early January, it went under different names in different places. It was called the Feast of Fools or Misrule in France and Germany. In England it was called the Day of the Boy Bishop. In Scotland it was known as the Abbot of Unreason. It may be that it had links to the Roman festival of Saturnalia but this is difficult to prove.

The festival was often organised by young clergy. Essentially, someone called variously a Lord of Misrule or a Bishop of the Fools was elected or chosen by lot. This person, for the period of the festival, had the power to command anyone to do anything. The result was a feast which encouraged drinking, dancing, cross-dressing and the singing of bawdy songs. In particular, the participants mocked the behaviour of priests. They put on vestments backwards, danced and drank in churches, while the mock Bishop delivered nonsense prayers and sermons.

In the fifteenth century, Church leaders, appalled by the fact that young clergy were involved in profane activities, had attempted – without much success – to outlaw the celebration. Protestant and Catholic reformers in the sixteenth century had more success: the feast seems to have died out during the early seventeenth century.

Opposition to festivals

Criticisms of festivals and carnivals, invariably from the educated elites, are usually associated with the Reformation. In fact, they pre-dated it.

In the fifteenth century, some religious leaders opposed the overindulgence and immorality associated with festivals and carnival:

- A German lawyer, Sebastian Brant, considered drinking, gaming and dancing at church festivals the ruin of country people. His influential *Ship of Fools* (1495) included a bold attack on carnival.
- The great humanist scholar Erasmus regarded carnival as a remnant of ancient paganism and essentially unchristian.

Civic leaders often regarded carnivals and festivals with a degree of trepidation, recognising the potential for disruption, disorder and violence:

- May Day riots against foreigners occurred in London in 1517.
- Apprentices frequently caused trouble in many cities.
- Over twenty German carnivals in the 1520s and 1530s turned into anti-Catholic parades, reflecting and helping to promote the advance of the Lutheran movements.

Nevertheless, for most of the sixteenth century, urban elites were not afraid of carnival. On the contrary, they were often eager participants.

A safety valve?

Some scholars, for example Max Gluckman (1972), regard the rites of carnival in terms of a 'safety valve'. Arguably, the 'rituals of rebellion' (associated with the world turned upside down) allowed people not only an escape from everyday life but also an opportunity to express their resentment of authority without actually changing anything. In fact, it may be that the enjoyment of carnival served to strengthen support for the established social and political order. Some contemporaries thought the same. One metaphor used was the need to allow gas to escape from wine barrels periodically to prevent their exploding. This helps to explain why carnival was supported by many authorities.

Historian Natalie Zenon Davis, however, has claimed that carnival was more than just a safety valve (1975). While it could help to reinforce the existing order, it could also criticise it and that criticism could not always be safely contained. Riots and rebellion frequently did take place during the major festivities. Inhibitions against expressing hostility towards the authorities may have been weakened by the excesses of festivals and the consumption of large quantities of alcohol. If this combined with anger over bad harvests, tax increases or other calamities, the situation could get out of control. Symbolic violence could become real violence against the authorities or against foreigners or Jews, Catholics or Protestants.

Not all contemporaries saw carnival as a harmless 'safety valve':

- Moral reformers disapproved of the excesses and bawdy unruliness.
- Civil authorities, nervous of carnival's power to disrupt and subvert, did not take it for granted that the world once turned upside down would safely return to normal afterwards.
- Given the trouble often associated with carnival and festival, some members of the upper classes often suggested that particular festivals ought to be abolished.

Public humiliation

Diversions in most areas of Europe were provided by those who overstepped the bounds of accepted social practice. This frequently resulted in ritual – and humiliating – punishment.

The punishment of women

Those selected for public humiliation were often women. Women who were domineering, rebellious or unfaithful were perceived to be a threat to patriarchal society. Female misbehaviour might be dealt with by ecclesiastical or manorial courts. Those found guilty of scolding, adultery, prostitution or beating their husbands were forced to recite their crimes in the market place.

But sometimes the people of a locality would take matters into their own hands. A crowd would gather and then march in procession to the house of those who were thought to have exceeded the bounds of acceptable marital behaviour: domineering wives, hen-pecked husbands or old men who had married young women, or young men who had married old women. The crowd, often carrying effigies of the victims or with people dressed up to represent them, would gather outside the house of the offenders and beat pots and pans. (This was known as 'rough music'.) Sometimes the offenders were forced to join the rowdy parade. In

England, such ritual humiliations were known as **skimmingtons** (see Source B). In France, they were called *charivari*. Elsewhere in Europe, women who violated community standards were forced to parade through the streets bare-headed and bare-footed. Such rituals often ended in drunken revelry. But there was always the danger that they would degenerate into serious violence.

SOURCE B

A skimmington at Quemerford, near Calne, Wiltshire, in 1618. The main target, Agnes Mills, was beaten as well as humiliated. From Martin Ingram, 'Ridings, rough music and the "reform of popular culture" in Early Modern England', *Past and Present*, vol. 105, pp. 79–113, Oxford University Press, 1984.

[300–400 men came one day] some like soldiers … and a man riding upon a horse, having a white night cap upon his head, two shoeing horns hanging by his ears, a counterfeit beard upon his chin made of a deer's tail … [and outside the victims' house] the gunners shot off their pieces, pipes and horns were sounded together with lowbells and other smaller bells, … and rams' horns and bucks' horns, carried upon forks, were then and there lifted up and shown.

KEY TERM

Skimmingtons Public humiliations. The word is possibly derived from a ladle used in cheese-making, which women may have used to beat their husbands.

Study Source B. Does the source suggest that the skimmington was a very rare event or a relatively common practice?

Legal punishments

Misdemeanours of all kinds were harshly treated in the early modern period. Prisons were a rarity: they were mainly used for holding people awaiting trial. Public display and humiliation was the favoured method of law enforcement.

- Miscreants were often exposed in a specific public place in a restricting device, like the stocks or the pillory. Minor offenders might be tied in a chair and wheeled round a parish or left outside their homes for people to ridicule.
- Scolds and prostitutes might be subjected to the ducking stool, which became a common feature in many English towns in the early seventeenth century. The chair was operated rather like a see-saw or was on a pulley and victims were plunged into ponds, lakes or rivers before jeering crowds.
- Corporal punishment was inflicted, especially in Germany. People were forced to process through the streets before being whipped or birched.
- Offenders might be publicly branded.
- Serious crimes were punished by death: hanging, garrotting, beheading, burning or breaking on the wheel. Executions were elaborately orchestrated. Held at particular sites, they attracted large crowds. Men, women and children were there to enjoy themselves and hawkers sold refreshments and souvenirs.

Moral regeneration in the sixteenth century

The fear of the impending breakdown of society was widespread and intense in many parts of Europe in the early modern period. In England, for example, it has been commonly claimed that there was 'a crisis of order' in the period from 1540 to 1660. This is usually seen as related to religious divisions and the social and economic situation: population growth, inflation, land shortage, poverty and vagrancy. It should be said that not all historians are convinced. Peter Laslett, for example, stressed the stability of English society throughout the entire early modern period, dismissing the signs of tension as minor conflicts that exist in most smoothly functioning social systems (1972). Nevertheless, while the debate continues about the rebellious and disorderly nature of English – and European – society, there is no doubt that many contemporaries were concerned about the breakdown of order.

It does seem that the authorities had some cause to be worried:

- Most towns were violent places where the murder rate was much higher than in most present-day cities.
- There were serious peasant revolts in Germany in the early sixteenth century.
- Popular rebellions, riots and civil wars were a problem for most countries at some stage in the early modern period.
- There were a growing number of vagrants and vagabonds.

There was also growing concern at what was perceived to be ungodly behaviour: gambling, prostitution, sodomy and drunkenness. The authorities, at every level, from royal ministers to local magistrates and parish clergy, responded to the challenge. Some believe that the motivating force behind the attempts to control disorderly behaviour was puritanism – strong in many parts of Europe (notably Scotland, England and the Netherlands). But other historians note that the campaign against disorder and immorality occurred in many places in Europe where there was no strong puritan presence or pressure.

Protestant regeneration

Protestant reformers saw saints as successors to pagan gods. They thus sought to abolish the huge numbers of festivals, feasts and processions associated with Catholic saints (see page 41). Many Protestant leaders denounced festivals as relics of **popery**, distracting people from working or going to church.

Catholic regeneration

Such moral austerity found its echo in Catholic culture. The Council of Trent, set up by Pope Paul III in 1545, which met with several breaks over the next eighteen years, deplored the fact that 'the celebration of saints and the visitation of relics be perverted by the people into boisterous festivals and drunkenness' and took steps to prevent this. Such measures were only partially successful. They ran too far ahead of public opinion. To rein in excess was one thing: to attack the fundamentals of recreational culture was quite another thing, particularly when these were recreations enjoyed by the governing elites.

The role of magic in society

The violent tenor of life and scourges of famine and disease resulted in many people looking for safeguards against a world filled with catastrophes and

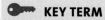

KEY TERM

Popery A derogatory term for Catholicism. It suggested that Catholics were part of an international conspiracy led by the pope against Protestantism.

unknown dangers. Most found these in religious observance. The Catholic Church had long seemed to offer a reservoir of magical assistance to people in their everyday lives. Its blessings in the form of prayers, exorcisms, holy water and charms were thought to ward off a variety of evils. The ringing of consecrated church bells might prevent storms, while priestly curses protected crops from the ravages of insects and weeds. The help of saints could also be sought. St Margaret was thought to help those suffering labour pains while prayers to St Job were thought to assist those suffering from the pox.

But many also believed that God and the Devil worked through nature in creating signs, wonders and portents. Some were convinced that men possessed the power and reason to understand the mysteries of nature and the universe. This helps to account for the widespread belief in magic, prophecy, astrology and alchemy.

Prophecy and astrology

Those who probed the workings of the heavens – astrologers – were regarded as particularly important in attempting to read the will of providence and predict the future.

The most popular book of prophecy in central Europe at the start of the sixteenth century was Lichtenberger's *Prognostications*. Written in 1488, it went through numerous editions. A variety of learned men read and discussed it. For Lichtenberger, the stars and planets were demonic powers, influencing the world of man for better and for worse. His studies – and imaginations – led him to compile a series of horoscopes which, in the short term, prophesied a series of catastrophes: wars, rebellions and plagues. But he ended by forecasting a golden age and universal peace.

Many early modern European monarchs had court astrologers who advised them on courses of action. By the seventeenth century, large numbers of ordinary men and women purchased horoscopes which predicted the future.

> ## The *Hermetica*
>
> Many scholars in the early sixteenth century attached great value to the *Hermetica* – a collection of treatises on philosophy, astrology, magic and other occult arts, rediscovered in the fifteenth century. The writings were attributed to Hermes Trismegistus, an Egyptian scholar who was thought to have lived at the time of Moses. (In fact, the writings were much later: they dated from the first to the fourth century AD.) Given the supposed age of the *Hermetica*, it was invested with a spurious aura of profundity. This helped to make magic, alchemy and astrology respectable and a source of inspiration for some of the greatest scientific minds of the sixteenth century. The book offered suggestions on how to exploit the hidden divine powers of minerals, plants and the planets.

Alchemy

Influenced by the *Hermetica*, many sixteenth-century scholars believed that ordinary minerals could be transformed into gold or cure diseases and prolong life. The search for the hidden powers was known as alchemy. Swiss physician Theophrastus Bombastus von Hohenheim, who called himself Paracelsus (1493–1541), was one of Europe's most influential alchemists. He believed that small doses of particular chemicals, especially sulphur and mercury, could cure diseases. Hoping to find one powerful agent – often called the 'philosopher's stone' or the 'elixir' of life – that was capable of healing all illnesses and transforming all less-perfect substances into more perfect ones, Paracelus experimented with ways to extract pure elements and divine essences. Other alchemists did likewise. While their work was rooted in ancient texts, they were innovative in their methods, advancing experimentation as the best way to discover the hidden properties of various substances. They were thus often the first to make extensive use of what was later called the 'scientific method' (see pages 165–8), in which a hypothesis to explain a phenomenon is developed and tested, the results are recorded and measured, and the hypothesis is confirmed, rejected or modified.

The mental world of the educated elite

Given that the scientific and medical world of the early modern period was infused with magic, it is easy to see how witchcraft was accepted there. Thomas and Macfarlane emphasised the importance of popular beliefs and of interpersonal tensions among the lower social status as the terrain from which witchcraft accusations were launched (see page 25). While this approach is of considerable importance, it does tend to obscure the extent to which witchcraft was a live issue for some members of Europe's political, social and religious elite until well into the seventeenth century. Clearly, some of the religious elite wrote treatises about witchcraft – treatises which mainly focused on the pact with the Devil (see pages 4–5). These treatises ensured that Europe's literate elite had some awareness of witchcraft, even if not all were convinced of its reality.

Common views of magic

The sophisticated discussions of magic, which formed such an integral part of the philosophic and scientific thinking of the sixteenth century, were incomprehensible to the ordinary man. But belief in magic powers and practices permeated early modern European society. There is ample evidence, for example, that people accepted the reality of ghosts, fairies and spirits of all sorts. Most people were also convinced that some individuals could perform incredible acts by harnessing the power of supernatural forces. Most had recourse to 'white' magic at some time in their lives in order to ensure the welfare of loved ones, livestock or crops. It was also understood that 'black' magic could equally be directed to do harm. Witches were perceived as a threat because they had the power to unleash harmful magic – *maleficium* – on a locality.

Ordinary Europeans did not necessarily initially attribute *maleficium* to the Devil. However, the evidence suggests that the diabolical nature of witchcraft, espoused by the elite, soon trickled down to illiterate villagers, who were able to assimilate the pact with the Devil into their own notions of witchcraft (see page 6). Belief in witchcraft – and the Devil – was, quite simply, part of the everyday popular culture of the period.

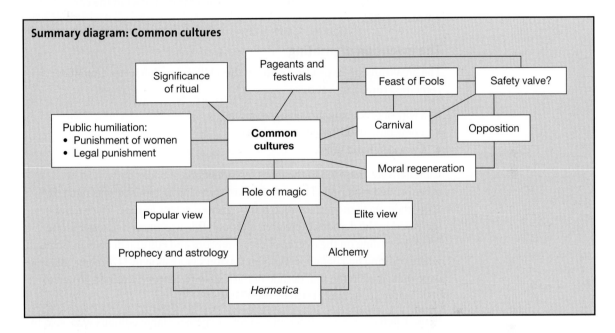

Summary diagram: Common cultures

3 Challenges to popular cultures

▶ *What were the main challenges to traditional popular culture in the early modern period?*

Cultures are always evolving, both internally and in response to outside pressures and influences. In the course of the early modern period, traditional popular cultures faced pressures from various directions. Peter Burke argued that the main threat came from the elites, who were determined to control society and popular culture for religious, social, economic and political reasons (2009). What may once have been regarded as useful safety valves for peasants and poor townsfolk to let off steam were no longer allowed. Given the sheer variety of cultures, Burke's view is rather too sweeping. Nevertheless, there is no doubt that some aspects of traditional popular culture were challenged by secular and religious authorities. These challenges are usually seen to have resulted from the impact of printing, religious change, political change, economic and social change, as well as the withdrawal of the elite from many aspects of traditional culture.

The impact of printing

Most Europeans were illiterate in 1500. For centuries the cultural world of the majority of people had rested on the spoken word. The young picked up skills from their parents or employers and absorbed values and beliefs from what they saw and heard in the home, at church and from their neighbours. Printing, invented in the fifteenth century, was to have a major impact in the early modern period.

The invention of printing

The breakthrough in printing came in the 1440s when Johannes Gutenberg combined three innovations:

- a way of producing movable metal type
- a new kind of oil-based printer's ink
- a wooden hand press.

Cumulatively, these led to the mass reproductions of books and a host of other printed materials. The expansion of the printing industry was rapid. By 1500, there were more than 1000 printing shops across Europe. Their number increased in the decades thereafter, although this was uneven across Europe, often depending on the degree of press freedom and cultural debate. In England, where printing had begun in William Caxton's workshop in 1476, some 400 titles were published in the first decade of the sixteenth century: this had grown to 6000 by the 1630s and 21,000 by the 1710s.

Books catered for many different markets. Expensive large editions were sold in bookshops, mainly for the social and learned elites. But most importantly, there was an astonishing growth of books in the middle-size range: school textbooks, popular histories, poetry, almanacs and books of prodigies and sensations. In the fifteenth century, a fine library was a status symbol of the highest social elites. By the late sixteenth century, libraries of several hundred books were something to which a relatively modest minister, lawyer or merchant could aspire. There were also cheap prints such as pamphlets, religious tracts and ballads that were sold by pedlars and achieved a wide dissemination. By the mid-seventeenth century, periodicals akin to newspapers had begun to appear. Many texts were illustrated with woodcuts which reinforced the message and made print more accessible to unlearned readers.

Was there a print revolution?

Some scholars claim that the revolution from a handwritten and oral culture to a print culture had a major impact on all aspects of European life, including popular culture. Elizabeth Eisenstein (1979), for example, claimed that the new 'print culture' changed the early modern world by shaping the processes we call the Renaissance, Reformation and scientific revolution. But others are not so certain.

The case against a print revolution

- Some historians are reluctant to place so much emphasis on one new technology. They perceive a wider communications revolution. An item of print only had impact once it was disseminated and that relied on improvements in marketing and even more fundamentally on the means of transport – better roads, ships, canals and postal services. Without developments in transport infrastructure the 'print revolution' would have had less impact.
- Workshops of medieval scribes had already created large numbers of books and manuscripts. Nor was scribal production suddenly replaced by printing. Handwritten copies of text continued to flourish until the late seventeenth century.
- Literacy rates improved only slowly, especially in southern Europe and among women. Rural areas lagged far behind cities. In many villages the local priest might be the only reader, even in the mid-seventeenth century. Probably only a third of Europeans were literate by 1700.
- Oral culture was not undermined by 'print culture'. Rather, print and oral culture existed in mutually reinforcing and stimulating ways. What was talked about found its way into print and what was printed was talked about.
- Far from verifying and establishing 'truth' and 'reason', print could be used to distort and invert them.
- Printing did not necessarily undermine the role of traditional authority. Indeed, it could support and strengthen the role of authoritarian governments and Church authorities which were able to control the printing presses. While printed texts did help to undermine the concept of a sacred monarchy and an unquestioned Church in some parts of Europe, elsewhere religious texts, schoolbooks, proclamations and government apologists served to defend the monarchy and the Catholic Church. In Catholic areas, scientific advance may have been hampered by the papal *Index Librorum Prohibitorium*. This listed titles forbidden to be printed or read by Catholics. It came to include many scientific books such as works by Galileo (see pages 165–6).

The case for a print revolution

- Printing reduced the cost of copying texts. This enabled more people to purchase books and pamphlets. In the first 50 years of the printed book, Europe's presses probably achieved a global output of some 10,000 editions. By the end of the sixteenth century, such totals were being published in Europe every year or eighteen months, and the numbers kept increasing in the seventeenth century. Printing thus greatly assisted the diffusion and dissemination of knowledge.
- Many scholars see the press as intrinsic to the Reformation. Pamphlets in Germany, Switzerland and the Netherlands played a vital role in spreading the Protestant message in the 1520s, undermining the authority of the Catholic Church.

- In some countries, for example, England, the printed press helped to undermine the established political order in the seventeenth century. Radical political movements would have been impossible without a large reading public ready to devour cheap pamphlets and early newspapers.
- More people became literate, albeit with significant social, regional and gender variations. (By 1630, it is estimated that a third of Englishmen were literate.) Thus, the printed word became widely accessible, assisting and reflecting an increase in literacy. This had a major impact on popular culture. As literacy increased, print became a form of entertainment as well as a means of disseminating information. Interestingly, many considered reading a sociable rather than a solitary affair for much of the early modern period.
- Reading became an essential skill for a wide variety of (mainly urban) jobs.
- The affordability of the book had a transforming effect on education and ultimately on the whole intellectual culture of the age. There was an increase in educational opportunities in towns across much of Europe in the early modern period. The German territory of Württemberg had 50 schools in 1534: by 1581 it had 2709.
- By the mid-sixteenth century, literacy was no longer the preserve and professional monopoly of the clerical estate that it had been for most of the Middle Ages.

The English antiquarian John Aubrey, writing in the late seventeenth century, thought that print had almost driven out the old world of oral folk tradition. He was exaggerating. Oral communication remained fundamental and printing did not necessarily pose a threat to the old order. Very often an 'oral tradition' can be shown to have originated in some printed ballad or story. Sometimes the process went in the other direction; and sometimes stories or songs moved to and fro between the oral and written traditions. Print could thus enrich as well as undermine traditional oral cultures.

The Bible

The great book of the early modern period was the Bible. The book had a huge influence in many fields. As well as being a book of faith it was a work of history, literature, poetry, prophecy (in an age obsessed by prophecy) and political thought. It provided role models for rulers and priests, for fathers and mothers, for soldiers and martyrs. The sixteenth century placed the Bible directly in the hands of unprecedented numbers of people. Many could afford a handy pocket-sized book in tiny print. Over 5000 whole or partial editions of the Bible were published across Europe – a total of at least 5 million copies. The Bible's many-sidedness made its impact unpredictable and extraordinarily various.

Religious change

The Reformation shattered the unity of the Church – with important cultural results. In the early modern period, Protestant and Catholic reformers attempted to change the attitudes and values of the rest of the population and to improve them (see page 23). The reform movement was far from monolithic.

- Protestant and Catholic reformers had very different aims. Protestant reformers were generally determined to eradicate what they saw as evils. Catholic reformers, by contrast, tended to favour reform and modification.
- Protestant reformers did not agree on precisely what reforms were necessary.

Protestant change

Protestant reformers supported vigorous action to control the many traditional forms of popular religion and the disorderly and unruly aspects of popular culture and recreation.

Their aim was to create a 'godly' society, reflecting proper Christian values of decency, diligence, gravity, modesty, orderliness and sobriety. Protestant clergy believed that religious festivals were relics of popery: they wanted to abolish feast days as well as feasting. Some Protestants attacked all holy days other than Sundays. Others were hostile to the very idea of a festival – to the idea that one time is holier than another. They attacked the rowdiness, drunkenness and sexual promiscuity that accompanied carnivals and festivals (see pages 42–3).

Protestant reformers went further. They saw many practices of the Catholic Church as pre-Christian survivals, comparing, for example, the cult of the Virgin Mary to the cult of Venus and the veneration of saints as similar to the veneration of pagan gods. Many Church rituals were denounced for being blasphemous, sacrilegious and profane.

But not all Protestants were united. Lutherans and Anglicans were generally more tolerant of popular traditions than Calvinists. Martin Luther himself did not object to saints' days or festivals, although many of his supporters did. Initially, the Lutheran Church kept many pre-Reformation practices and traditions.

But Calvinism from the start was different. It sought to end much of the traditional popular piety and ritual. The Christian world was thus turned upside down in Calvinist-controlled areas. Although traditional ritual did not have a role to play in Calvinist churches, Calvinists tried to install their own more 'godly' practices:

- A high priority was to make the Bible available to ordinary people in a language they could understand. The book was thus translated into virtually all European languages. This had a major cultural impact, influencing the language and literature of most countries.

- Sermons, interpreting the Bible, were an essential feature of Calvinist services.
- Psalms were frequently sung at funerals, weddings and meals, replacing folksongs and traditional hymns. Psalms were even sung as lullabies to young children.

Calvinist churches were also critical of many traditional aspects of popular culture including plays, lewd songs, dancing, playing cards, animal sports, fairs, and most – if not all – popular festivals and processions which were seen as pagan survivals. In Scotland, for example, from the mid-1570s, there were sustained attacks on the celebration of Christmas, Midsummer and other festivals with singing, dancing, bonfires and plays. English Puritan Philip Stubbs drew up a comprehensive list of popular recreations which he believed should be abolished, including Christian feasts, May games, bear-baiting, cockfighting, dancing and Lords of Misrule. Stubbs attacked what he called 'the horrible vice of pestiferous dancing' for providing participants with opportunities for 'filthy groping and unclean handling', and so acting 'as an introduction to whoredom, a preparative to wantonness, a provocation to uncleanness, and an [entry in] to all kinds of lewdness'.

Puritan pressure ensured that religious mystery plays had been abolished in virtually all English towns by 1600. Puritans, who held power in England between 1646 and 1660, despised the profane culture of the multitude who frequented alehouses and played football on the Sabbath. Many public amusements, such as theatre, dances, dice and card games were prohibited or restricted, because they could lead to immoral action or were perceived to be a waste of time. Maypoles, seen as phallic symbols, were chopped down.

Nevertheless, Calvinists did not always have their own way. Interestingly, in lands where Calvinist/Puritan authorities abolished traditional festivals and saints' days, the people often invented their own new occasions for bonfires, bell-ringing and feasting. In England, for example, these became commemorations of patriotic anniversaries associated with England's progress to Protestantism.

The impact of the Counter-Reformation

The Catholic Church, beginning with the Council of Trent (see page 46), initiated a number of reforms, aimed at purifying the Church:

- Religious ceremonies, which had also served as family and communal festivals, were subject to new regulations designed to emphasise their sacred nature. Clergy in Strasburg, for example, decreed that marriage was to be celebrated 'without tumult, mockery, taunts, scuffles, jokes and foul or immoderate speech which is customary at betrothals and weddings'.
- The Feast of Fools (see page 43), seen as a mockery of the ecclesiastical hierarchy, came to an end as the religious and political elite withdrew their support.

- Dances and fairs were forbidden on church grounds.
- The laity were forbidden to dress up as clergy in carnival and other festivals. This was seen as blasphemous given that clergy were seen as holy people.
- Catholic clergy were forbidden to participate in popular festivals in the traditional manner: for example, they were not allowed to dance, wear masks, watch plays or attend bullfights.

Catholic reformers were fighting on two fronts: against immorality and superstition; and against the excesses of Protestantism. Most wanted festivals reformed, not abolished. Within a stricter system of clerical control, popular piety and ritual was maintained. The cult of saints, for example, continued to flourish in Catholic-controlled areas, albeit it was more closely supervised. Various magical cures such as the use of holy water or amulets were retained. Nor did the Counter-Reformation abandon the Church's tradition of religious spectacle and visual display. Catholic leaders, well aware of the importance of ritual, used it convince ordinary people that Protestantism was wrong. Heretics and heretical books, for example, were burned in public at highly ritualised *autos-da-fé* in Spain.

> ## KEY TERM
>
> ***Auto-da-fé*** A ritualised public penance.

SOURCE C

A decree from The Council of Trent, a meeting of leading Catholic bishops, in 1563.

In the invocation of saints, the veneration of relics, and the sacred use of images, all superstition shall be removed, all filthy quest for gain eliminated, and all lasciviousness avoided, so that images shall not be painted or adorned with seductive charm, or the celebration of saints and the visitation of relics be perverted by the people into boisterous festivities and drunkenness, as if the festivals in honour of the saints are to be celebrated with revelry and with no sense of decency.

> Study Source C. Why might a Protestant have opposed this Catholic decree? **?**

According to Burke, the Catholic reformers wanted to reach the people and carry everyone with them. But in practice, things worked out differently. The reforms, in Burke's view, affected the educated minority more quickly and more thoroughly than they affected ordinary people and so cut the Catholic elite off more sharply from popular traditions.

Political change

Burke believes that the three centuries between 1500 and 1800 witnessed a 'politicisation' of popular culture and the spread of political consciousness. Ordinary people became more aware of affairs of state and displayed an increasing interest in the actions of government. Public opinion could impact on governments (although Burke accepts that it is very difficult to know what ordinary people actually thought).

- In the 1520s, Germany experienced major peasant revolt against clerical and lay landowners and the privileges they exacted.

- Rebellions and civil wars became commonplace in Europe, especially in the period from 1550 to 1650.
- Between 1618 and 1648 – the period of the Thirty Years' War – more western Europeans were interested in politics than ever before. In England and France, for example, there was a veritable flood of political pamphlets in the 1640s.
- In the late seventeenth century, political texts and images continued to be a part of everyday English life.

Nevertheless, the traditional secular elites, who feared popular political consciousness, generally retained power. (They lost it in England from 1642 to 1660.) Despite occasional outbursts, most people across Europe appear to have broadly accepted the political order. But it would be wrong to see popular political culture wholly in terms of deference and loyalty. Magistrates and tax officials often faced abuse and physical violence from ordinary men and women.

In many countries, governments allied with the Church in efforts to control the disorderliness of popular recreational culture and establish a godly state. Historian Robert Muchembled (1985), for example, claimed that in France there was an alliance between the Catholic Reformation Church and the state to root out profane, rowdy and superstitious practices and impose the culture and values of the elite upon the entire population. Arguably, much the same occurred in Calvinist Scotland.

Economic and social change

A number of economic factors had a major impact on European culture:

- Between 1500 and 1800, Europe's population grew from about 80 million to nearly 190 million.
- There was increasing urbanisation. In 1500, only three cities in Christian Europe – Naples, Venice and Paris – had populations of more than 100,000 people. In 1800, there were 23 such cities.
- There was a great expansion of trade within Europe and between Europe and the rest of the world. Certain towns and regions increasingly specialised in particular products.
- There was a communications revolution: more ships were built, more canals were dug and roads were improved.
- Agriculture was transformed, at least in the vicinity of large towns: there was a shift from subsistence farming to farming for the growing urban market.
- Most Europeans were better off by the eighteenth century than they had been 100 years earlier. They had better diets and more in the way of material possessions.

The scale of these economic changes should not be exaggerated. At the end of the eighteenth century, less than three per cent of Europe's population lived in towns of 100,000 people or more. Most Europeans continued to live in settlements of fewer than 5000 people – just as they had in 1500. The main form of industrial enterprise remained the small workshop, not the factory, and production was only beginning to be mechanised.

Nevertheless, as the economy changed, so did popular cultures, which tended to adapt to different occupational groups and regional ways of life. Entertainers, for example, adapted to the new economic conditions. If the decline of fairs was a blow to wandering entertainers, the growth of large towns provided them with compensating opportunities. In Britain, there was arguably a 'commercialisation of leisure' in the sense that:

- businessmen began to regard leisure activities as a good investment
- leisure facilities grew.

The withdrawal of the elite from traditional cultures

In 1500, according to Burke, popular culture was everyone's culture: a second culture for the educated, and the only culture for everyone else. By 1800, he argues, in most parts of Europe, the clergy, the nobility, the professional men, the scholarly elite – and their wives – had abandoned popular culture to the lower classes 'from whom they were now separated, as never before, by profound differences in world view'.

Burke overstretches his case. The movement was far from universal, nor was it necessarily unique. Arguably, the elites had always shunned many aspects of traditional culture. Burke, moreover, accepts that 'the withdrawal from popular culture did not take place in any one generation but at different times in different parts of Europe'. According to Burke, the process of withdrawal was more clear-cut and occurred earlier in France and Britain than elsewhere in Europe. In southern Europe, the process was slower. This is symbolically reflected in the survival of carnival, which remained popular in Mediterranean regions well into the eighteenth century.

Nevertheless, Burke makes a reasonable case for claiming that by the eighteenth century, the clergy, the nobility, the bourgeoisie and the learned elite, each for their own reasons, had withdrawn their support and involvement from many activities in which they had previously participated.

The clergy

In the case of clergymen, withdrawal was part of the Reformation and Counter-Reformation process. In 1500, the majority of the parish clergy were men of a similar social and cultural level to their parishioners. 'Godly' reformers – both Protestant and Catholic – were not satisfied with this situation and demanded a learned clergy. In Protestant areas, the clergy tended to be university graduates. In Catholic areas, after the Council of Trent, priests began to be trained at seminaries. In addition, Catholic reformers emphasised the dignity of the priesthood. The new style priest was thus better educated, higher in social status and considerably more remote from his flock.

Clergy, it should be said, generally had less control over people's lives than they had in earlier centuries. Education, for example, was no longer under the exclusive influence of the Church. The same was true of hospitals and poor relief.

The nobility

For the nobles, in Burke's view, the Reformation was less important than the Renaissance. Influenced by various texts, nobles adopted more polished manners and a more self-conscious style of behaviour. They exercised more self-control, behaved with a studied nonchalance, cultivated a sense of style and moved in a dignified manner. Treatises on dancing multiplied and court dancing quickly diverged from country dancing. Noblemen stopped eating in great halls with their retainers and withdrew into separate dining-rooms and drawing-rooms. They stopped wrestling with peasants and stopped killing bulls in public. They learned to speak and write 'correctly'. Their refined behaviour marked them as different from ordinary people.

The bourgeoisie

The polished manners of the nobility were imitated by officials, lawyers and merchants who wanted to pass for noblemen. So they too withdrew from popular culture, in the process abandoning local dialects and languages and adopting instead the 'ruling' language of the state.

The learned elite

Adopting ideas emanating from the scientific revolution (see pages 165–7), the scholarly elite abandoned the superstitions and belief in magic that were still held by ordinary people. The growing split between elite and popular culture was particularly evident in the case of witches. By the late seventeenth century, many if not most learned people had stopped believing in witchcraft (see pages 174–5).

Conclusion

Between 1500 and 1800, European popular culture evolved. While change came slowly, especially in more remote rural areas, the popular cultural world of 1750 differed considerably from that of 1500.

Religion exercised a weaker hold, at least in much of Protestant northern Europe. As church attendances dropped, ministers complained that Sundays and religious festivals were treated simply as holidays. However, religion maintained its grip in much of southern Europe, and even in northern Europe new movements such as Methodism proved that a religious spirit remained very much alive.

Belief in astrology, witchcraft and magic, which had formed part of the shared culture of the sixteenth century, had been abandoned by the elite and the middling sort by 1750, surviving only as a strand of popular culture, especially among women.

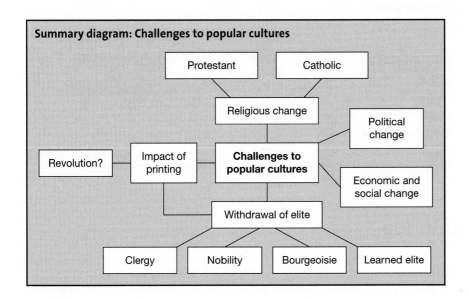

Summary diagram: Challenges to popular cultures

Chapter summary

Historian Peter Burke's notion of a binary division between 'popular' and 'elite' cultures has been challenged by many scholars who see a variety of ever-changing popular and elite cultures. Arguably, at the start of the sixteenth century many Europeans, rich and poor alike, did share some cultural practices and attitudes. These included the rituals and practices of the Church, involvement in festivals and carnivals, belief in the public humiliation of social outcasts and law-breakers, and belief in the power of magic and in witches.

In the early modern period, traditional popular cultures were challenged by secular and religious authorities who wished to establish a more orderly and godly society. The challenges are often regarded as resulting from the impact of printing, religious developments – especially the Reformation and Counter-Reformation – and political, economic and social change. Arguably, by the eighteenth century European elites – the clergy, nobility, bourgeoisie and the scholarly – had largely abandoned traditional popular cultures to the lower classes, whom the rich and educated elites increasingly saw as rowdy, unsophisticated and superstitious.

Refresher questions

Use these questions to remind yourself of the key material covered in this chapter.

1 To what extent did Europeans share a common culture in the early modern period?

2 Did women share the same culture as men?

3 Were the festivals of misrule and carnival useful safety valves?

4 Why did some authorities oppose festivals and carnivals in the sixteenth century?

5 How were people who overstepped the bounds of accepted social behaviour publicly humiliated?

6 Why was there action on moral regeneration in the sixteenth century?

7 To what extent did the elite and ordinary Europeans hold similar views on magic in the sixteenth century?

8 Why did popular cultures face challenges in the early modern period?

9 Was there a print revolution?

10 How did religious change affect popular cultures?

11 How did political, economic and social change affect popular cultures?

12 To what extent did the elites withdraw from traditional cultures in the early modern period?

 Question practice

ESSAY QUESTIONS

1 'In the period from 1560 to 1660 there was a host of popular and elite cultures.' How far do you agree with this view?

2 'During the period from 1560 to 1660, the elites gradually withdrew from participating in popular culture.' How far do you agree with this view?

3 'While carnival could help to reinforce the existing order, it could also criticise it and that criticism could be dangerous.' How far do you agree with this view in the period from 1560 to 1660?

4 'Catholic and Protestant reformers in the period from 1560 to 1660 had much in common in their approach to popular culture.' How far do you agree with this view?

CHAPTER 3

Witch-hunting in Europe

Witch-hunting on the continent of Europe was at its height in the period from 1560 to 1660. This chapter will examine some of the common features of witch-hunting and also some of the major witch-hunts that took place in early modern Europe. It will do so by focusing on the following:

★ The dynamics of European witch-hunting

★ Witch-hunts in Trier, Würzburg, Bamberg and Cologne

Key dates

1581–93	Trier witch-hunt	**1626–31**	Würzburg and Bamberg witch-hunts
1616–48	The Thirty Years' War	**1626–34**	Cologne witch-hunt

1 The dynamics of European witch-hunting

▶ *How did witch-hunting start and develop?*

Witch-hunts did not start spontaneously in those communities that were ideologically, legally, politically, socially and economically prepared to experience them. Combinations of circumstances – plague, famine, the preaching of clergy – which appear to have caused a hunt in one area, produced nothing in another. Essentially, someone, either an individual, a group of villagers or a magistrate, had to start proceedings by accusing or denouncing someone. In most cases what triggered the initial charge was a personal tragedy or misfortune that an individual interpreted as an act of maleficent magic. Sometimes, communal misfortune was responsible for the initial impetus to round up witches: for example, the destruction of a crop by unseasonal hailstorms. When villagers decided that a witch should be prosecuted, they denounced the suspect before a local court or asked members of the governing body of the village to take action.

Once judicial officials agreed to hear witchcraft charges, they assumed control. They were the gatekeepers of witch-hunts, deciding which cases to prosecute, which witnesses to call, whom to torture, and which alleged accomplices should be pursued. In most cases they determined the guilt or innocence of the accused. Thus, even though the impetus to prosecute came from below, the way in which hunts developed was determined mainly from above.

Witch-hunts

The most common witch-hunt involved the prosecution of one person or just a handful of people. However, some hunts claimed scores, even hundreds, of victims (see Table 3.1). Such large-scale hunts were most common in Germany but most European countries experienced at least one such episode. Many of these mass prosecutions were chain-reaction hunts in which suspected witches provided the names of accomplices.

Table 3.1 The largest witch-hunts in Europe 1420–1680

Number of victims	Former state	Religion	Dates	Country
2000	Duchy of Lorraine	Catholic	1580–1620	France
2000	Spanish Netherlands	Catholic	1580–1620	Belgium
2000	Electoral Cologne	Catholic	1626–35	Germany
2000	Mecklenburg	Lutheran	1570–1630	Germany
2000	Duchy of Milan	Pre-Reformation persecution	1480–1520	Italy
1800	Electoral Mainz	Catholic	1590–1630	Germany
1350	Scotland	Calvinist	1560–1670	UK
1200	Bishopric of Würzburg	Catholic	1616–30	Germany
1200	Vaud	Calvinist	1580–1620	Switzerland
1000	Denmark	Lutheran	1540–1680	Denmark
907	Vorderösterreich	Catholic	1560–1650	France/Germany
900	Bishopric of Bamberg	Catholic	1616–30	Germany
800	Kingdom of Hungary	Catholic	1710–50	Hungary
600	Pommern-Wolgast	Lutheran	1600–60	Germany
600	Pommern-Stettin	Lutheran	1600–60	Poland
600	Schleswig-Holstein	Lutheran	1600–60	Denmark/Germany
500	Duchy of Savoy	Pre-Reformation persecution	1428–36	Italy
500	Valais	Pre-Reformation persecution	1428–36	Switzerland
500	Dauphine	Pre-Reformation persecution	1420–50	France
450	Franche-Comté	Catholic	1600–61	France
450	Ellwangen	Catholic	1588–1627	Germany
400	Earldom of Nassau	Calvinist	1590–1660	Germany
387	Mergentheim	Catholic	1590–1665	Germany
358	Luxembourg	Catholic	1580–1630	Luxembourg
350	Electoral Trier	Catholic	1581–95	Germany
300	Earldom of Vaduz	Catholic	1648–80	Liechtenstein

From W. Behringer, *Witches and Witch Hunts*, Polity Press, 2004, p. 130.

Large hunts sometimes lacked the cohesion that they appear to have had. Not only did judges often hear cases from different areas within their jurisdiction but they did so over a long period of time. Hunts often occurred in waves, each rash of trials having its own dynamic. When a hunt spanned a two- or three-year period, marked by intervals when there were no trials at all, it is problematic to tell whether there was one large campaign or a succession of smaller operations conducted by the same court or judge. In the imperial city of Offenburg (in present-day Germany), for example, a hunt began in 1627 as an offshoot of a trial that took place in Ortenau, the larger territorial unit in which Offenburg was situated. Twelve witches were executed between November 1627 and January 1628. After a five-month respite, a new round of trials led to the execution of seven more witches and the death of another under torture. Then, four months later, there were more trials lasting until January 1630 which claimed 40 lives. The hunt thus comprised three distinct operations, each of which had its own dynamic.

Although many large hunts were composites of smaller hunts, the intensity of fears regarding witchcraft provided a unity to all the trials that occurred. Indeed, one of the main characteristics of large witch-hunts was the prevalence of a mood of profound fear while the hunt was going on. People were terrified that:

- their closest friends and neighbours were witches
- their communities would be the captive of diabolical power
- they would be falsely accused.

This terror led them to support the trials and to bring suspects to the authorities' attention. While it is wrong to apply a label such as 'witchcraze' to the entire European witch-hunt, within the context of specific witch-hunts it is legitimate to talk about mass hysteria. Without such collective behaviour the history of European witchcraft would have been less deadly.

The end of witch-hunts

Small hunts ended when the accused people were executed. Large hunts had the potential for indefinite extension, given that new accomplices were revealed every time someone was tortured. Authorities in the German town of Rottenburg, for example, worried that the 1585 hunt would eliminate all the women of the town. Their fears were not exaggerated: in that year, two villages were left with only one female inhabitant apiece in the aftermath of witch-hunts. But in most cases hunts ended before they took such a heavy toll. Few hunts lasted more than four years. Many ended rather abruptly and their termination often signalled the end of witch-hunting in that area for many years.

In most cases the hunts ended when judges or government officials became sceptical of the process. Once a higher percentage of wealthy and powerful individuals, children and males were named, this aroused suspicions that innocent persons were being accused. The most dramatic end to hunts came when conscious fraud or deceit was discovered. Once judges began acquitting suspects, this strengthened the conviction that at least some of the accusations were false. This encouraged greater judicial caution.

Sometimes popular pressure served as the main stimulus to ending the witch-hunt. Ordinary people had some power.

- They could refuse to denounce or testify against their neighbours.
- They could express their disapproval by boycotting executions.
- They could protest to the appropriate authorities.

Ironically, the high point of a nation's witch trials and their decline arrived together. Witch-panics encouraged accusations but also exposed the difficulty of proving them in a fair way. The two could not be reconciled and in the end doubt usually displaced enthusiasm.

Regional variations

Any attempt to establish chronological patterns of European witch-hunting is complicated by regional variations. Witch-hunting began, peaked and declined at different times and in different places. Moreover, the number of convictions and executions varied greatly in different states and regions.

The Holy Roman Empire

Large parts of Germany lay within the Holy Roman Empire (see Figure 3.1, page 65). In the sixteenth century, the Empire was a loose confederation containing seven prince-electorates, 43 secular principalities, 32 ecclesiastical principalities, 140 independent earldoms or lordships, about 70 imperial abbacies, about 75 imperial cities and hundreds of areas ruled by independent knights. There were thus more than 2000 territories with independent jurisdictions within the Empire's boundaries.

The Empire exercised very little control over the activities of the various judicial tribunals. While it supplied a legal code – the *Carolina* – for the Empire as a whole, it did not provide effective mechanisms for enforcing it. There were no:

- itinerant judges to ensure that the code was upheld
- procedures for regular appeals to the imperial supreme court at Speyer.

Although local courts could ignore imperial supervision, they were required to consult with the law faculty of neighbouring universities in witchcraft cases. This requirement was intended to help local judges deal with the complexities of procedure in an area of the law with which they were likely to be unfamiliar. Instead of leading to greater restraint in witchcraft prosecutions, this practice often had the opposite effect. Since the universities were the centres of dissemination of demonological theory, consultation with learned jurists helped to introduce diabolical ideas to local magistrates.

Figure 3.1 The Holy Roman Empire in the sixteenth century.

In most cases, therefore, the trial of witches in Germany was entrusted to courts which exercised jurisdiction over a relatively small area. German judges had a latitude in handling witchcraft cases 'that zealous witch-hunters in other parts of Europe would certainly have envied', says historian Brian Levack (2006). He believes the small size of jurisdictional units helps to explain why the largest witch-hunts took place in Germany.

With regard to witch-hunting, Germany can roughly be divided into two regions:

- The north and east, with the exception of the Duchy of Mecklenburg, experienced relatively little witch-hunting.
- Most witch-hunting occurred in the south and west.

The intensity of witch-hunting was particularly prominent in small ecclesiastical territories like Würzburg and Bamberg (see pages 75–9). Bavaria, a relatively large state with a population of 1.4 million, executed some 1000 witches in the entire period. By contrast, 1000 people died in the prince-bishopric of Trier between 1581 and 1593 (see page 74). There were severe witch-hunts in many small German territories between 1560 and 1630.

- A major persecution began in the prince-bishopric of Osnabruck in 1584.
- The prince-abbot Balthasar von Dernbach launched a witch-hunt in the ecclesiastical territory of Fulda between 1603 and 1605. Some 276 people were burned in a territory with fewer than 90,000 inhabitants. The persecution ended with the abbot's death in 1606.
- A major witchcraze began in the prince-electorate of Mainz, which had a population of some 400,000, under Archbishop Johann Adam von Bicken. His short reign (1601–4) saw some 650 burnings. Under his successor, Johann Schweikhard von Cronberg (reigned 1604–26), the persecution slowed down. Nevertheless, 361 people were executed as witches. Witch-hunting reached its zenith under Archbishop Georg Friedrich von Greffenklau (reigned 1626–9): 768 witches were killed in four years. Thus, some 1800 people were killed as witches under the rule of three prince-bishops.
- In the small Catholic principality of Ellwangen, some 400 suspected witches died between 1611 and 1618.
- In Eichstatt, a judge claimed the death of 274 witches in 1629.

In total, there were probably between 20,000 and 25,000 witch trials in the Holy Roman Empire. More than half of those tried were executed.

Economic conditions

Wolfgang Behringer (2004) believes that many of the witch-hunts were the result of severe economic conditions. He claims that the wave of witch-hunts around 1600, 1611 and between 1616 and 1618 were the result of extreme climatic events, crop failures, famine and diseases. Similar conditions prevailed in the late 1620s. In May 1626, there was unusually cold weather in **Franconia**. Rivers froze, and grapevines, rye and barley were destroyed. Local people blamed the unseasonal weather on the Devil and his agents. As late as 1630, witch suspects had to confess that they had been responsible for the weather. According to the confessions, Franconian witches had discovered how to make frost. Having prepared a special potion from children's fat, they flew through the air on the night of 27 May 1626, dropping the poison on the crops until everything was

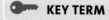

KEY TERM

Franconia A region of south-western Germany.

frozen. Since the climate remained unfavourable for several years, the demand for persecutions persisted.

Counter-Reformation zeal?

Nineteenth-century scholars often attributed the German persecutions to Counter-Reformation zeal and Catholicism in general. This attribution of responsibility is perhaps too simple. Not all Catholic states persecuted witches. Some burned far fewer than their Protestant neighbours. The Lutheran Duchy of Mecklenburg, for example, with only 200,000 people, executed some 2000 witches between 1560 and 1700. However, it remains true that the most terrible persecutions were conducted by Catholic prince-bishops and abbots (see below).

The impact of the Thirty Years' War

The early 1620s saw the Catholic reconquest of large parts of Germany. Some historians wonder whether it was a coincidence that the years 1626–31 saw the worst of all European witch persecutions.

The war also had serious economic effects:

- It resulted in the devastation of entire regions as various armies funded themselves by looting and exhorting **tribute**.
- It caused serious loss of life. Soldiers died in battle but also spread disease as they marched across Germany.
- The war had a depressing impact on trade and economic development generally.

This may have resulted in people attributing supernatural causes for their misery and a desire to find scapegoats.

 **KEY TERM**

Tribute Payment as an acknowledgement of submission.

The impact of individuals

With regard to witch-hunting, much depended on individuals. Johann Christoph von Westerstetten, for example, who represented the new fundamentalist type of Counter-Reformation ecclesiastical prince, was a determined witch-hunter. He initiated witch persecution in the prince-abbey of Ellwangen (where he ruled from 1603 to 1612). He continued to burn witches when he became prince-bishop of Eichstatt (reigned 1612–36). In both cases, the witch-hunts lasted exactly as long as Westerstetten was in power. Individual rulers, while not always responsible for starting witch-hunts, often grasped the chance to gain support from the populace.

Witch-commissioners

Persecutions were co-ordinated by a new type of judge, known eventually as a witch-commissioner. The prototype was the Fulda judge Balthasar Nuss. The prince-abbot's friend, Nuss by-passed district courts and even the central government, minimising outside interference and combining torture and denunciations to great effect. Other Franconian rulers adopted the Fulda model.

In the 1620s, there were political struggles in many territories over the question of whether witch-commissioners should be appointed. Bavarian politicians managed to avoid their appointment and thus escaped large-scale persecutions. The prince-elector of Cologne, on the other hand, deployed witch-commissioners and claimed the largest number of victims in German lands (see page 79).

Opposition to witch-hunting

Recent research suggests that strong governments in developed secular states tended to establish legal systems that prevented large-scale witch-hunts. The government of the Calvinist Electoral Palatinate at Heidelberg, for example, was sceptical about witchcraft. It held a strong grip on the lower courts. Thus, even though the Palatinate's subjects suffered from economic and climatic disasters, the government in Heidelberg avoided the execution of witches.

Popular pressure

Behringer believes the situation in the Alpine valley of Prättigau is instructive. The villages in the valley had repeatedly tried – and failed – to persuade the Tyrolian authorities to lead witch-hunts. In 1652, the valley liberated itself from Habsburg control and joined the Swiss canton of Graubünden. The Prättigau villages, which were now allowed to govern themselves, established three courts with judges elected by the villagers. Within a few years more than 100 witches were killed in the Prättigau.

France

France, with a population only slightly smaller than that of the Holy Roman Empire, saw some 3000 witch prosecutions and 1000 executions in the period 1500–1700. The areas in France most affected were situated on the frontiers of the kingdom: the north, the east, Languedoc, the south-west and Normandy. These areas were resistant to the efforts of the French monarchy to establish a centralised state. The courts in these regions operated with greater independence than those nearer Paris, a fact which may explain the more intense witch-hunting.

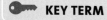 **KEY TERM**

Parlement A provincial high court in pre-revolutionary France for hearing appeals of local legal cases.

France's success in establishing a powerful monarchy in the early modern period helps to explain why far fewer witches were executed within its boundaries than in the Holy Roman Empire. Eight provincial *parlements*, staffed by men trained in law, undertook the regulation of local justice. The *parlement* of Paris, which exercised judicial power over most of northern France, was particularly important, refusing to sentence witches to death on the basis of confessions extracted under torture. Over a third of cases reviewed by the Paris *parlement* resulted in complete dismissal. Only a quarter of all cases were confirmed. The actions of the Paris *parlement* set the standards for the other *parlements*.

The nuns of Loudun

One of the most famous French witchcraft cases occurred in the 1630s. The supposed demonic possession of several nuns in a convent at Loudun and attempts to exorcise them attracted huge crowds. The possession led to the prosecution of Urbain Grandier, a local priest. Grandier probably became the target of witchcraft accusation because of his personal life: he had made pregnant the daughter of one of Loudun's leading officials, and apparently sympathised with the **Huguenots**. He had also incurred the enmity of the bishop of Poitiers and Jean Martin de Laubardemont, a counsellor of King Louis XIII. Grandier's enemies used the nuns' possession to destroy him. Under torture, Grandier confessed to having made a pact with the Devil and having caused the nuns' affliction. He was executed in 1634.

> **KEY TERM**
>
> **Huguenots** French Protestants.

SOURCE A

The execution of Urbain Grandier, 1634.

> Look at Source A. What appears to be taking place in the top left corner of the illustration?

SOURCE B

An account of a French contemporary of Urbain Grandier, des Niau, writing in 1634. Quoted in Edmund Goldsmid, editor, *The History of the Devils of Loudon*, Edinburgh, 1887–8.

A most convincing proof of Grandier's guilt is that one of the devils declared he had marked him in two parts of his body. His eyes were bandaged and he was examined by eight doctors, who reported they had found two marks in each place; that they had inserted a needle to the depth of an inch without the criminal having felt it, and that no blood had been drawn. Now this is the most

> Why did the author of Source B regard Grandier's guilt as certain?

decisive test. For however deeply a needle be buried in such marks no pain is caused and no blood can be extracted when they are magical signs …

What criminals could ever be condemned if such proofs were not deemed sufficient? The certainty of the possessions; the depositions of two priests who accused him of sacrilege; those of the nuns, declaring that they saw him day and night for four months, though the gates of the convent were kept locked; the two women who bore witness that he offered to make one of them Princess of the Magicians; the evidence of sixty other witnesses; his own embarrassment and confusion on so many occasions.

Switzerland

Ten thousand witches are estimated to have been executed in Switzerland. The various Swiss cantons, religiously, culturally and linguistically different, were jurisdictionally autonomous, a situation which encouraged a diversity in witch-hunting patterns. The severity of Swiss witch-hunting is best illustrated in the Calvinist Pays de Vaud, where over 3000 witches were executed between 1580 and 1620.

Franche-Comté, Lorraine, Luxembourg and the Spanish Netherlands

In these virtually autonomous areas, which were technically within the Holy Roman Empire, there was a lethal combination of central and local involvement in witch-hunting, with the King of Spain, the Holy Roman Emperor and the Archduke of Burgundy providing the legislation and sometimes the initial inspiration to witch-hunting, and the small duchies and states possessing the freedom to proceed as they saw fit.

- At least 400 witches were executed in the Franche-Comté before it became part of France in 1678.
- A large witch-hunt occurred in Lorraine (a duchy with some 400,000 people) under Duke Charles III (reigned 1552–1612). The *procureur generale*, Nicolas Remy, sent more than 800 witches to their deaths between 1586 and 1595 and continued to burn witches for ten further years. The burnings continued under his son Claude Remy. Historian Robin Briggs (1996) has estimated a total of 3000 witch trials in Lorraine, with 2000 victims.
- In Luxembourg, there were 358 executions between 1509 and 1687.
- Persecutions in the Spanish Netherlands during the reign of Philip II (reigned 1556–98) may have equalled the number of those in neighbouring Lorraine.

The Dutch Republic

The Dutch Republic had a population of over a million in the early modern period. Yet fewer than 150 witches were executed and witchcraft executions ended earlier than in any other part of Europe. In 1594, the central court in the province of Holland forbade the use of torture, a decision which contributed to the early decline in witchcraft prosecutions throughout the Republic. However, the main explanation for the liberal treatment of witches seems to be more rational than judicial. Dutch judges simply did not believe that witches were engaged in a diabolical conspiracy.

Denmark and Norway

Denmark was the first Scandinavian country to engage in witch-hunting. In the mid-1540s, 52 people were executed. In 1547, the Danish government declared that the testimony of those who had been convicted of infamous crimes, including sorcery, could not be used to convict another person. It also forbade the use of torture until after a death sentence had been pronounced. Despite these developments, there were some 2000 witchcraft trials and 1000 executions in Denmark. There were also about 350 executions in Norway, governed by Denmark throughout the early modern period.

Sweden

A law of 1593 requiring either the testimony of six witnesses or a confession for a capital conviction, together with a requirement (in 1614) that all death sentences be appealed to a royal court at Stockholm, ensured that witch-hunting was kept in check in Sweden. However, a large witch-hunt began in Dalarna in 1668 when children accused relatives, neighbours and older children of having taken part in a Swedish version of the sabbat. Between 1668 and 1676, some 200 people were executed in Sweden's northern provinces. The hunt ended in 1676 when:

- two commissions exercised a moderating influence on a panic-stricken population
- the Court of Appeals began to interrogate the children, many of whom admitted that their accusations had been false
- King Charles XI, who had been a minor when the witch-hunts began, stopped the hunts by decree. He also stopped witch trials in Finland and the Baltic states, then part of the Swedish empire.

Eastern Europe

Witch-hunting began much later in the lands to the east of the Holy Roman Empire than in western and central Europe. It also lasted longer – well into the mid-eighteenth century. The intensity varied from region to region.

- Prosecutions were most severe in Poland. At least 1000 suspected witches are thought to have been executed, mainly between 1676 and 1725. Most trials took place in municipal courts which were not under close central control.
- In Hungary some 1500 individuals were tried and about 500 executed for witchcraft.
- In Transylvania, Wallachia and Moldavia prosecutions were rare.

In general, those areas closest to Germany or populated by German-speaking people prosecuted far more witches than those that were Slavonic. Those regions which followed the rites of Orthodox Christianity (like Greece and Russia) did not engage in intensive hunting.

Southern Europe

After 1550, there were probably fewer than 500 executions for witchcraft in southern Europe. Most of these occurred in the Alpine regions of Italy. While the total number of prosecutions was fairly substantial, there were very few executions in Spain and Portugal – or in Spain and Portugal's American colonies. In Spain, for example, the Inquisition tried more than 3500 people for various types of magic and witchcraft. However, it was reluctant to put witches to death. Fewer than 100 witches were executed in Spain between 1580 and 1620.

Charges of collective devil-worship were very rare in southern Europe. Judges and inquisitors treated stories of night flights and sabbats with scepticism. They also adhered to fairly strict procedural rules. Torture was rarely employed. In the Basque witch-hunt of 1609–11, which involved hundreds of suspects (but only eleven deaths), the Spanish Inquisition tortured only two of the accused. Since the torture allowed their sentences to be commuted from death to banishment, it can be seen as an act of mercy.

Conclusion

Between 1500 and 1700, most European countries experienced witch-hunts. But witch panics, characterised by an unrestrained pursuit of hundreds of witches, really only took place in western-central Europe. The real centres were the Holy Roman Empire, Switzerland and the French-speaking duchies and principalities that bordered German territory. The reasons for this, thinks Levack, were fourfold:

- Wherever witchcraft was defined primarily as *maleficium* and not as Devil-worship, witch-hunts tended to remain limited in scope. There was far more stress on diabolism in German regions than elsewhere.
- Legal procedures, especially with regard to the use of torture, determined the number who died.
- The degree of judicial control over the trials was important. In most cases, local authorities were more determined to prosecute and execute witches than those who occupied higher positions of authority in Church or state and more likely to violate the procedural rules formulated by central governments while doing so.
- The degree of religious zeal manifested by the people, especially the leaders, of a particular region was often crucial. Those jurisdictions that executed witches in great numbers were known for their Christian militancy, their religious intolerance and their vigorous participation in either the Reformation or the Counter-Reformation.

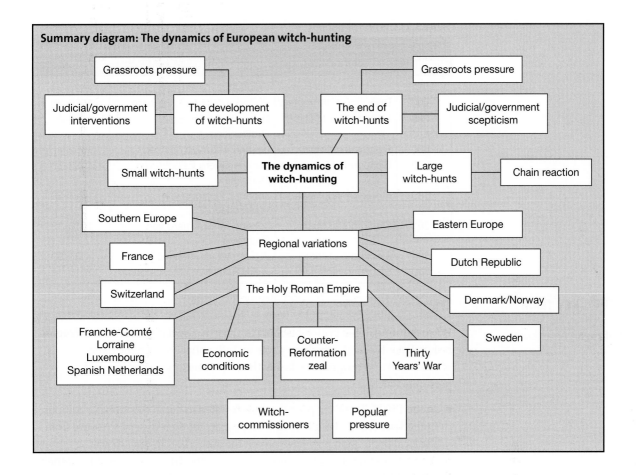

Summary diagram: The dynamics of European witch-hunting

2 Witch-hunts in Trier, Würzburg, Bamberg and Cologne

▶ *Why was witch-hunting so intense in southern Germany?*

Some 75 per cent of witchcraft prosecutions occurred in Germany, France, Switzerland and the Low Countries, an area comprising roughly half the population of Europe. During the sixteenth century, most prosecutions took place in France and Lorraine. But by the late sixteenth century, Germany had become the centre of prosecutions. This section will examine four of the greatest German witch-hunts: those in Trier (1581–93), Würzburg (1626–31), Bamberg (1626–31) and Cologne (1626–34).

Table 3.2 The prince-bishops

Victims	State	Ruling bishop	Persecution period
2,000	Electorate of Cologne	Ferdinand von Bayern	1624–34
900	Bishopric of Würzburg	Philipp Adolf von Ehrenberg	1626–30
768	Electorate of Mainz	Georg Friedrich von Greiffenklau	1626–9
650	Electorate of Mainz	Johann Adam von Bicken	1602–4
600	Bishopric of Bamberg	Johann Georg II Fuchs von Dornheim	1626–30
550	Ellwangen/Eichstatt	Johann Christoph von Westerstetten	1611–30
361	Electorate of Mainz	Johann Schweikhard von Cronberg	1616–18
350	Electorate of Trier	Johann VII von Schonenberg	1581–99
300	Bishopric of Würzburg	Julius Echter von Mespelbrunn	1616–18

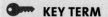
Trier

Witch-hunting in the prince-bishopric of Trier is associated with the **suffragan** bishop Peter Binsfeld, who later wrote an influential book on the danger of witchcraft and how best to deal with it. Three factors helped Binsfeld to persecute witches:

- In the 1580s, a series of poor harvests resulted in harsh economic conditions in the Trier region. People sought scapegoats for their misery. Pressure from the local population may have driven the authorities in Trier to act.
- A long-standing struggle for power between the Trier town council and the prince-bishop was decided in favour of the prince-bishop.
- A newly established Jesuit College enthusiastically supported Binsfeld's campaign against witchcraft. From 1585, the Jesuits kept in custody young boys who claimed that they had attended sabbats and were able to recognise witches. Jesuit leaders used this source of information for their own political and religious ends.

Most of the witches convicted initially conformed to the usual stereotype: female, old and relatively poor. But as the witch-hunt gathered momentum, not even the noble and rich were safe. In 1587, Dr Dietrich Flade was accused by one of the Jesuit boys of presiding at a sabbat. Flade had served as councillor to the prince-bishop, as chancellor of the university and as chief-prosecutor. It is possible that he had opposed the witch persecutions and was thus regarded by the Jesuits as an enemy. Flade, tortured until he confessed, was burned in 1589. In addition to Flade, the Trier persecution resulted in the burning of former lord mayors, councillors and scores of parish priests. Accusations of witchcraft could be turned into an instrument for political and social revenge. It may be that the Trier authorities also wished to make money by confiscating the possessions of their rich victims.

The Trier witch-hunt, including the actions of nearby independent monasteries, led to more than 1000 deaths.

Würzburg

Witch-hunting in Würzburg reached its climax during the reign of Prince-Bishop Philipp Adolf von Ehrenberg (reigned 1623–31). Between 1626 and 1631, some 900 people were executed. Victims came from all sections of society, regardless of age, profession or gender. Those burned included nobles and mayors, Ehrenberg's own nephew, nineteen Catholic priests and children of seven who were said to have had intercourse with demons. In 1631, Philipp Adolf died. When Würzburg was taken by King Gustavus Adolphus of Sweden in the same year, the witch trials came to an end.

Friedrich Spee von Langenfeld, a Jesuit, was a confessor of condemned witches in Würzburg. The experience turned his hair prematurely white. He was convinced that not a single witch whom he had led to the stake had been guilty. Since he could not utter his thoughts – he feared suffering the witches' fate – he wrote a book, *Cautio Criminalis*, condemning the activities in Würzburg. The book was printed anonymously in the Protestant city of Hamelin in 1631. It had considerable effect in halting witchcraft persecution in many parts of Germany.

Bamberg

Bamberg was a small, independent Catholic bishopric in the Franconia region of Germany. Witch-hunting began in Bamberg under Prince-Bishop Johann Gottfried von Aschhausen (reigned 1609–22). Determined to re-Catholicise his diocese, he invited Jesuits into Bamberg, founded new schools and tried to remove any taint of Protestantism. He also burned about 300 suspected witches, including 102 in 1617. Witch-hunting resumed on an even greater scale under Prince-Bishop Johann Georg II Fuchs von Dornheim (reigned 1623–33). Earning the nickname 'Witch-bishop', he took a leading role in the persecutions which resulted in the deaths of some 600 victims. He even built a special 'witch-house' with room for 30 or 40 prisoners, complete with a torture chamber. He was aided by his suffragan Bishop Friedrich Forner, several witch-commissioners, some recruited from other German territories, and a council of doctors of law. Forner, a leader of the Counter-Reformation in Germany, was an avid witch-hunter and author of a sermon collection, *A Display of the Weaponry against all Superstition, Divinations, Enchantments and Devil-Worship* (1626).

In the mid-1620s, the Bamberg area of southern Germany had been devastated by war as well as a series of crop failures, famines and plagues. People looked for supernatural explanations and accusations of witchcraft proliferated.

The vice-chancellor of Bamberg, Dr George Haan, had served the bishops of Bamberg loyally for many years. But his relative leniency as a judge made him suspect as a witch sympathiser. His wife Ursula and daughter Maria were

Johann Georg Fuchs von Dornheim

1586	Born in Wiesentheid in Germany
1623	Elected prince-bishop of Bamberg
1626–31	Presided over the Bamberg witch trials
1632	Advance of Swedish and Saxon armies forced him to flee from Bamberg
1633	Died in exile in Spital am Pyhrn

Dornheim, who held near absolute power, on both the ecclesiastical and secular fronts, in the prince-bishopric of Bamberg, played a crucial role in the persecution of witches. He oversaw the establishment of a network of informers and built the notorious Drudenhaus witches' prison in 1627 to house a special torture chamber. Those brought in for investigation could suffer torture only with the personal consent of the prince-bishop, consent which was usually freely given. In part, Dornheim might have been reacting to pressure from the people who blamed witches for their economic distress. But his own religious zeal was certainly a factor in encouraging persecution. An ardent Catholic reformer, he was determined to create a godly state in Bamberg. Convinced that the Devil was at work in his lands, he was also determined to pursue witches. Many rich and powerful people, who were executed for witchcraft, had their property and assets confiscated. This made Dornheim very rich and may have encouraged his passion for witch-hunting. Anyone who questioned his actions was likely to be arrested, tortured and burned alive.

arrested in 1627. Haan and his son Adam fled to the imperial court in Speyer and obtained an injunction forbidding the prince-bishop proceeding against Ursula and Maria. By the time they returned to Bamberg, Haan's wife and daughter had been tortured, confessed to witchcraft and already burned. Father and son were now arrested and forced to confess that they too were witches. Both men were burned in 1628. During the course of torture, George Haan confessed to having seen five councillors at a sabbat: they too were burned.

Johannes Junius, who had been lord mayor of Bamberg, was one of the men denounced by Haan. Junius, who was 55, was tortured so extensively that he eventually agreed to confess to whatever the witch-commissioners wanted. Accordingly, he admitted to the Devil's pact, having sex with a succubus and dancing at a sabbat. He also named fellow-witches, including relatives and friends. He and all his family, except one daughter, were executed in 1628. Junius himself was beheaded with a sword before his body was burned.

SOURCE C

Part of a letter written by Johannes Junius which was supposedly smuggled out of prison and given to his daughter. Quoted in G.L. Burr, editor, *The Witch Persecutions*, Philadelphia, 1902.

Many hundred thousand good-nights, dearly beloved daughter Veronica. Innocent have I come into prison, innocent have I been tortured, innocent must I die. For whoever comes into the witch prison must become a witch or be tortured until he invents something out of his head and – God pity me – bethinks him of something …

? According to Source C, how did Junius justify his confession?

The executioner put the thumb-screws on me, both hands bound together, so that the blood ran out of the nails and everywhere, so that for four weeks I could not use my hands, as you can see from the writing. Thereafter they first stripped me, bound my hands behind me, and drew me up in the torture. Then I thought heaven and earth were at an end; eight times did they draw me up and let me fall again, so that I suffered terrible agony ... When at last the executioner led me back into the prison, he said to me: 'Sir, I beg you, for God's sake confess something, whether it be true or not. Invent something for you cannot endure the torture which you will be put to; and even if you bear it all, yet you will not escape, not even if you were an earl, but one torture will follow after another until you say you are a witch.' ... As so I made my confession ... but it was all a lie.

As the burnings increased, some prominent people fled to Rome, Prague or the imperial court at Regensburg to plead for intervention. But the prince-bishop, who benefited hugely from the confiscated property of those condemned, cared little for Emperor Ferdinand II.

The speed of the trials was amazing. For example, the **calendar** of Frau Anna Hansen in 1629 reads as follows:

KEY TERM

Calendar A list of events.

- 17 June   imprisoned on suspicion of witchcraft
- 18 June   refused to confess: scourged.
- 20 June   tortured with the thumbscrews: confessed
- 28 June   her confession read to her
- 30 June   voluntarily confirmed her confession: sentenced
- 4 July   informed of the date of her execution
- 7 July   beheaded and burned.

Methods of torture

Most Bamberg witches were kept in the Drudenhaus prison in Bamberg, which contained a special torture chamber. The walls of the prison were covered in biblical texts, either for the edification of the prisoners or for the protection of the warders against the spells of the prisoners. Bamberg witch-hunting became synonymous with torture. Among the devices routinely employed in extracting confessions were:

- thumbscrews
- leg vices
- scourging
- the stocks, furnished with iron spikes
- the strappado (see page 17)
- burning feathers held under the arms and groin
- the prayer stool, a kneeling board with sharp wooden pegs
- forcible feeding on herring cooked in salt and denial of water

- scalding water baths to which lime had been added (in 1630, six people were killed at Zeil by this method)
- the Linsten Chamber – a small room with small pyramids covering the floor, leaving nowhere for the accused to sit, stand or sleep without being impaled on one of the pyramids.

After sentencing and on the way to being burned, additional punishment could be imposed, including cutting off the right hand and tearing the breasts of women with red-hot pincers. Victims were usually burned alive without the mercy of preliminary strangulation.

The chain-reaction

The practice of torturing suspects to name their accomplices had a cumulative effect, driving up the number of accused. As this occurred, the witches conformed less and less to the traditional stereotype and a host of prominent citizens were arrested, tortured and burned. The victims' assets were confiscated by the prince-bishop and their families were responsible for all the costs of their imprisonment and executions, including paying for the fees of the torturers, executioners and even the wood used at the stake.

Although Dornheim fiercely opposed Protestantism, there was no correlation, positive or negative, between the areas of substantial Protestant presence in Bamberg and the areas of intensive witch-hunting.

Imperial opposition

The imperial court attempted to restrain Dornheim's zeal. Emperor Ferdinand II (reigned 1616–37) had ordered the release of George Haan on the grounds that 'the arrest was a violation of the law of the Empire not to be tolerated'. Dornheim ignored the emperor.

The emperor was also forced to intercede in the case of Dorothea Flock, an accused witch. Her husband, a Bamberg official, managed to escape to the imperial city of Nuremberg. From here, he appealed to both the emperor and the pope. In April 1630, Ferdinand II issued a directive calling on Dornheim to account for the charges against him. Again the prince-bishop paid little heed to the emperor. A stronger imperial directive forbidding all future proceedings against Dorothea was issued and the pope also seemed prepared to intervene. Before official messages from the emperor and the pope arrived, Dornheim had Dorothea executed (May 1630), enraging imperial officials.

As the situation in Bamberg deteriorated, Emperor Ferdinand II was under increased pressure to do something. His Jesuit confessor told him: 'It was horrifying what prominent men everywhere were thinking and saying about the procedure in the courts.' Another Jesuit questioned whether 'the numerous persons who perished in the flames were really guilty and deserved so horrible a death'.

Dornheim sent representatives to a **diet** of the empire at Regensburg at which the Bamberg witchcraft situation was due to be discussed. They pleaded in vain. The imperial court condemned the prince-bishop's actions. Other refugees from Bamberg continued to add their complaints. One man who had escaped from the witches' prison presented a written petition from Barbara Schwarz, tortured eight times without confessing and confined for three years in a dungeon. In September 1630, Ferdinand's confessor told the emperor that if he continued to ignore the lawlessness of the Bamberg courts, he could hardly give him absolution. In September 1630 and June 1631, Ferdinand issued strong directives opposing the persecution in Bamberg. The emperor ordered that in future trials the basis for accusations be made public, legal counsel be allowed to the defendants and confiscation of property cease. He also appointed an official, known to be opposed to the witch-hunts, as head of the Bamberg witch commission.

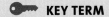

KEY TERM

Diet A meeting of the states that made up the Holy Roman Empire.

The end of the Bamberg terror

The terror in Bamberg receded in the summer of 1631, owing partly to the opposition of Emperor Ferdinand II, partly to the death of Bishop Forner in December 1630, and partly to the threats of Swedish King Gustavus, who entered Leipzig in September. In February 1632, Swedish and Saxon troops occupied Bamberg, forcing Fuchs von Dornheim to flee. He died in exile in 1633. With his death and that of his cousin, the Bishop of Würzburg in 1631, two of the fiercest promoters of persecution were gone.

Cologne

In the Duchy of Westphalia, subject to Prince-Elector Ferdinand, Archbishop of Cologne (reigned 1612–50), about 2000 people were burned for witchcraft between 1626 and 1634. Ferdinand had been educated in Trier during the witch-hunt of the 1590s. However, during the first fifteen years of his rule there were few witchcraft prosecutions. A series of devastating crop failures seem to have led to the Cologne witch-hunt. Only after the persecution of witches had gathered momentum at local level did Ferdinand intervene, appointing witch-commissioners to establish control over the situation. The commissioners soon got out of control, implementing their own policies and terrorising whole regions.

The witchcraze in southern Germany: conclusion

Witchcraft was not a major source of concern in the principal Catholic states in the Holy Roman Empire. Bavarian politicians, for example, stopped the witch persecutions which threatened to take off and ensured the maintenance of regular legal procedure. In Bohemia and Austria, where governments had a firm grip on the lower criminal courts, there were no major witch-hunts. The Habsburg capitals Prague and Vienna, centres of the Counter-Reformation, became a refuge for witch suspects from the prince-bishoprics.

Moreover, not all small Catholic ecclesiastical territories were affected by witch-hunts:

- The majority of the imperial abbacies avoided persecutions.
- There were only a few trials in some of the prince-bishoprics, for example, Passau, Regensburg and Münster.

But the fact remains that Catholic prince-electorates, prince-bishoprics and prince-abbacies within the empire were particularly susceptible to witch-hunts. Nine Catholic prince-bishops (see Table 3.2, page 74) were responsible for over 6000 deaths – a quarter of all those who died in Germany in this period. Some made a career out of witch-hunting. Johann Christoph von Westerstetten, who cut his teeth in the witch-hunts in Ellwangen, went on to preside over a major persecution as Bishop of Eichstatt (see page 67). Much depended on the personality and religious zeal of the ruler. Friedrich Spee von Langenfeld (see page 75), writing around 1630, interpreted the hunts as 'the disastrous consequence of Germany's religious zeal'.

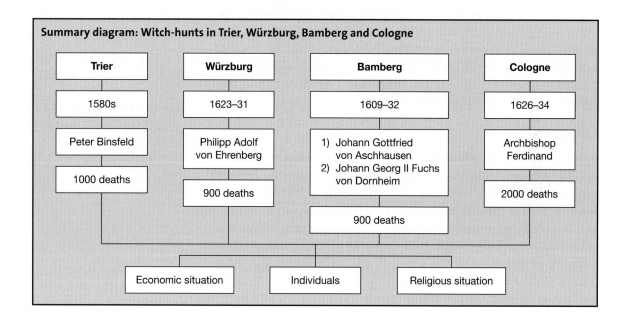

Summary diagram: Witch-hunts in Trier, Würzburg, Bamberg and Cologne

Trier	Würzburg	Bamberg	Cologne
1580s	1623–31	1609–32	1626–34
Peter Binsfeld	Philipp Adolf von Ehrenberg	1) Johann Gottfried von Aschhausen 2) Johann Georg II Fuchs von Dornheim	Archbishop Ferdinand
1000 deaths	900 deaths	900 deaths	2000 deaths

Economic situation Individuals Religious situation

Chapter summary

Some areas saw only small-scale witch-hunts; others large scale. There were great regional variations. The Holy Roman Empire saw major witch-hunting: economic conditions and specific individuals seem to have been determining factors. Witch-hunting was also strong on the borders of the Holy Roman Empire, especially Switzerland. It was far less strong in the Dutch Republic and in southern Europe (after 1520). The major witch-hunts were in southern Germany – in Trier, Würzburg, Bamberg and Cologne – where the use of torture was crucially important.

 ## Refresher questions

Use these questions to remind yourself of the key material covered in this chapter.

1 How did witch-hunting develop?

2 What were the main features of large witch-hunts?

3 Why was there so much witch-hunting in the Holy Roman Empire?

4 Where else, apart from the Holy Roman Empire, did witch-hunting occur on a large scale?

5 Which countries saw relatively little witch-hunting?

6 Why was witch-hunting so intense in southern Germany?

7 What were the main features of the Trier witch-hunt?

8 What were the main features of the Bamberg witch-hunt?

9 What were the main features of the Würzburg and Cologne witch-hunts?

 ## Question practice

ESSAY QUESTIONS

1 How accurate is it to say that the European witch-hunt mainly occurred in southern Germany in the years from 1623 to 1632?

2 How accurate is to say that there would have been no witch persecutions in Bamberg had it not been for the Counter-Revolution?

3 How far was the religious zeal of Johann Georg Fuchs von Dornheim responsible for the persecution of witchcraft in Bamberg in the years 1626 to 1631?

4 To what extent was the European witch-hunt essentially a German phenomenon in the period from 1560 to 1660?

5 How significant was the Bamberg witch-hunt within Germany in terms of the overall persecution of witches in the period 1623–32?

INTERPRETATION QUESTION

1 Read the two passages and then answer the question. Evaluate the interpretations in both of the passages and explain which you think is more convincing as an explanation of the reasons for the persecution of witches in Bamberg in Germany.

PASSAGE I

From R. Rapley, *Witch Hunts: From Salem to Guantanamo Bay*, McGill-Queen's University Press, 2007, pp. 25–6.

What went wrong in Bamberg? Underlying everything that happened was a desperate fear of the power of the Devil, combined with a general belief that this power was being exercised through the witches. Without this fear, the overriding impulse to stamp out the contagion would not have been present. What triggered a fear of the Devil in this case seems to have been a crop failure, a local disaster during a period of disaster. Witches were assumed to be the cause. Fear was a prerequisite because it gave the rulers of Bamberg and Würzburg the support of the elite, at least initially, to create a witch hunt. A passionate fear is a common accompaniment to witch hunts – both then and now.

Another factor that made the events possible was that the prince-bishops had, at least temporarily, unrestricted powers. Once each decided that the good of the state demanded an overwhelming response against the enemy, there were no limits to the extremes of the actions that it could take. Their excessive actions were abuses of power. We know this because the emperor made it clear to them and demanded that they stop. …

All of these ills were performed by men who in large part believed themselves to be doing good. Anything was justified to stamp out the Devil and the witches because it served the interests of God and the Godly state.

PASSAGE 2

From B.A. Pavlac, *Witch Hunts in the Western World: Persecution and Punishment from the Inquisition through the Salem Trials*, Greenwood Press, 2009, p. 66.

Rampaging armies inflated enormous suffering on the Germans, seizing food and supplies, forcefully recruiting men and boys, waging destructive battles, and plundering ruthlessly. Adding to the natural fragility of the agricultural system were crop failures due to bad weather, since the 1620s were notorious for being cold, wet and rainy. People later remembered 1628 as 'the year without a summer'. Crop failures drove up prices and created food shortages. The demands of armies, whether paid for by taxes or by plundering an enemy, fuelled inflationary crises. The horrors of a long war only amplified the usual fears and panics of people attributing their misfortune to witches. Although the decisions and failures of the territorial princes were actually at fault for most of the suffering, blaming witches was more convenient.

The heightened enthusiasm of Counter-Reformation Catholics to fight for their version of Christianity added to the fanaticism. Any deviation from perceived Roman Catholic orthodoxy was heresy, and heresy had long become associated with diabolic activity. The Protestant attack on the celibacy of Roman Catholic priests carried over into an overheated concern about sexual temptations of all kinds. Anyone whose sexuality deviated from approved norms ran the danger of being drawn into witch hunts.

SOURCE ANALYSIS QUESTION

1 Study Source 1 before you answer the question. Assess the value of the source for revealing popular attitudes to witches and the way that confessions were extracted from those accused of witchcraft in Bamberg in the 1620s. Explain your answer, using the source, the information given about its origin and your own knowledge about the historical context.

SOURCE 1

Part of the record of the interrogation of Johannes Junius, accused of witchcraft in Bamberg in 1628. Junius was mayor of Bamberg. Quoted in G.L. Burr, editor, *The Witch Persecutions*, Philadelphia, 1902.

On Wednesday, June 28, 1628, was examined without torture Johannes Junius, Burgomaster at Bamberg, on the charge of witchcraft: how and in what fashion he had fallen into that vice. Is fifty-five years old … Says he is wholly innocent, knows nothing of the crime, has never in his life renounced God, says that he is wronged before God and the world, would like to hear of a single human being who has seen him at such gatherings [as the witches' sabbats].

Confrontation of Dr. Georg Adam Haan. Tells him to his face that he will stake his life on it, that he saw him, Junius, a year and a half ago at a witch-gathering in the electoral council-room, where they ate and drank. Accused denies the same wholly.

Confronted with Hopffens Elsse. Tells him likewise that he was on Haupts-moor at a witch-dance; but first the holy water was desecrated. Junius denies. Hereupon he was told that his accomplices had confessed against him, and was given time for thought.

On Friday, June 30, 1628, the aforesaid Junius was again without torture exhorted to confess, but again confessed nothing, whereupon, … since he would confess nothing, he was put to the torture.

Thumb screws were applied. Says he has never denied God his Saviour nor suffered himself to be otherwise baptised; will again stake his life on it; feels no pain in the thumbscrews.

Leg screws. Will confess absolutely nothing; knows nothing about it. He has never renounced God; will never do such a thing; has never been guilty of this vice; feels likewise no pain.

Is stripped and examined; on his right side is found a bluish mark, like a clover leaf, is thrice pricked therein, but feels no pain and no blood flows out.

Strappado. He has never renounced God; God will not forsake him … He knows nothing about witchcraft …

On July 5, the above named Junius is without torture, but with urgent persuasions, exhorted to confess, and at last begins and confesses.

CHAPTER 4

Witch-hunting in England

In some ways, witch-hunting in early modern England was similar to that in continental Europe. But in other ways it was markedly different. This chapter will examine the similarities and differences by focusing on the following issues:

★ Witchcraft in early modern England

★ English witch-hunting 1560–1612

★ The Lancashire witches 1612

★ Matthew Hopkins and the East Anglian witch-hunt 1645–7

The key debate on *page 115* of this chapter asks the question: To what extent was English witchcraft distinct from continental European witchcraft?

Key dates

1563	Witchcraft Act		1604	Witchcraft Act
1584	Publication of *The Discoverie of Witchcraft*		1612	Pendle witches
			1645–7	East Anglia witch-hunt

1 Witchcraft in early modern England

▶ *What were the main features of English witch persecutions?*

It is likely that some 500 witches were executed in England between 1500 and 1700. There was only one mass witch-hunt: that associated with Matthew Hopkins in East Anglia between 1645 and 1647 (see pages 106–13). Witchcraft in England, according to historian James Sharpe (2002), was 'an endemic, rather than an epidemic problem, where witch trials were sporadic and few … and where the acquittal rate was high'.

The sources

Contemporary sources of witch activities are patchy.

Trial records

Most trial records have been lost. The only area where **indictments** against witches survive in bulk, but not in their entirety, is in the south-eastern counties of Essex, Hertfordshire, Kent, Surrey and Sussex. These records indicate that witchcraft charges rose steadily in number from the 1560s, peaked at a total of more than 180 in the 1580s, stayed high in the 1590s and then fell away with fewer than twenty indictments in the 1630s. There were some 130 indictments in the 1640s and 1650s, largely attributable to Hopkins' witch-hunt (see pages 106–13). After 1660, indictments returned to their 1620s' level. The last-known trial in the south-east was in Hertfordshire in 1712. Essex, with 464 indictments, had the highest number of indictments. Sussex, by contrast, had only 36 indictments and one execution. The trial records suggest that witchcraft indictments formed only a tiny fraction of the courts' criminal business.

Pamphlets

Pamphlets were often published after witchcraft executions. Some 140, varying in length from about 100 pages to just a handful, have survived. They tended to take the form of sensational moralising tales based loosely on the evidence found in trial reports. The pursuit of truth tended to take second place to the writer's desire to spin a good yarn or teach a clear moral lesson. Given that most trial records have been lost, the pamphlets are often the only surviving contemporary accounts of many witch trials.

Witchcraft in England pre-1542

Prior to 1542, Church courts dealt with most cases concerning witchcraft, cunning folk and sorcerers. Sanctions were directed more to penance and atonement than to harsh punishment. Often, the guilty party was ordered to attend the parish church, wearing a white sheet and carrying a wand, and swear to lead a reformed life. The surviving records suggest there were relatively few witchcraft cases.

Where fraud, treason, murder or injury were involved, witchcraft could be dealt with in secular courts. From the fourteenth century, most English monarchs faced combined treason/sorcery plots, in which those planning their downfall sought magical assistance. In the reign of Henry VI, for example, Margery Jourdemayne was burned at the stake for conspiring to bring about the king's death through sorcery. One of her co-conspirators, Eleanor, Duchess of Gloucester, escaped death, but after performing a public penance, spent the rest of her life as a prisoner.

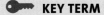

KEY TERM

Indictments The formal charges on which suspects stand trial.

The 1542 Act

By the 1542 statute it became a capital offence to conjure spirits or to practise witchcraft, enchantment or sorcery in order to find lost treasure, destroy a person's body, members or goods, or for any other unlawful intent or purpose. There is no evidence that this Act, the harshest of all English witchcraft statutes, was ever enforced: it was repealed, for reasons which are unclear, in 1547.

The 1563 Act

The 1563 Act, passed in the reign of Queen Elizabeth I (reigned 1558–1603), re-established witchcraft as a felony. Under this Act:

- Killing people by witchcraft was punishable by death.
- Injuring people or animals or damaging goods by witchcraft, attempting to do the same, using witchcraft to find lost or stolen money, goods or treasure, or using witchcraft to provoke love or for any other purpose, was punishable by a year's imprisonment for the first offence, and death on the second.

The statute was once thought to have been inspired by Protestant clergy who had fled abroad during the reign of the Catholic Mary Tudor (reigned 1553–8) and who had been influenced by continental witchcraft ideas. However, it now seems that the 1563 Act was passed because a group of Catholic plotters were discovered using sorcery against Elizabeth's Protestant regime and the authorities realised that there was no law in existence to try them. The government apparently pushed for new laws against Catholics and witches. While the 1563 statute may well have been the product of a particular situation, it is likely that the Elizabethan regime, emulating most other European governments of the period, would have enacted witchcraft legislation. While ecclesiastical courts retained a role in the determination of witchcraft accusations, after 1563 secular law dominated, with punitive displacing reformative justice.

The 1604 Act

The 1604 statute made injuring people a capital offence on the first conviction. It added and made capital the offence of using dead bodies or parts of them for witchcraft or sorcery. It also imposed the death penalty for anyone who 'shall consult covenant with entertain employ feed or reward any evil and wicked spirit to or for any intent or purpose'.

Reginald Scot

Oddly, the first major book on witchcraft published in England, Reginald Scot's *The Discoverie of Witchcraft* (1584), was an attack on witchcraft persecution. An educated layman of deep Calvinist convictions, Scot was sceptical of the notion of witchcraft for two reasons:

- He believed in the sovereignty of God: it was thus wrong to attribute supernatural power to witches.
- He could find no biblical foundation for witch-hunting.

Using philosophy and science, Scot established the impossibility of the deeds confessed by witches.

SOURCE A

From Reginald Scot's *The Discoverie of Witchcraft*, first published in 1584. Reprinted by Elliot Stock, 1886, pp. 5–6.

One sort of such as are said to bee witches, are women which be commonly old, lame, bleare-eied, pale, fowle, and full of wrinkles; poore, sullen, superstitious, and papists; or such as knowe no religion: in whose drousie minds the divell hath goten a fine seat; so as, what mischeefe, mischance, calamitie, or slaughter is brought to passe, they are easilie persuaded the same is doone by themselves; inprinting in their minds an earnest and constant imagination hereof. They are leane and deformed, shewing melancholie in their faces, to the horror of all that see them. They are doting, scolds, mad, divelish; and not much differing from them that are thought to be possessed with spirits; so firme and stedfast in their opinions, as whosoever shall onelie have respect to the constancie of their words uttered, would easilie beleeve they were true indeed.

These miserable wretches are so odious unto all their neighbors, and so feared, as few dare offend them, or denie them anie thing they aske: whereby they take upon them; yea, and sometimes thinke, that they can doo such things as are beyond the abilitie of humane nature.

> What type of people, according to Source A, were likely to be accused of witchcraft? **?**

Pro-witchcraft texts

A number of texts which perceived witchcraft to be a serious threat were written by Englishmen in the late sixteenth and early seventeenth centuries. Published works included:

- *A Treatise against Witchcraft* (1590), written by a Cambridge-educated clergyman, Henry Holland.
- *Discourse of the Damned Art of Witchcraft* (1608), written by William Perkins, the leading Puritan theologian of his day. This work remained influential throughout the seventeenth century.
- *A Guide to Grand Jury Men with Respect to Witches* (1627), written by Richard Bernard, a Puritan clergyman.

Most English demonologists hoped to see the establishment of a godly **commonwealth**. Extirpating witchcraft was only one aspect of this process and was not the most important one. More significant for most witchcraft writers was the need to eradicate 'superstitious' beliefs and practices. Their prime targets were the rituals of the Catholic Church as well as a host of popular beliefs and customs, including resorting to cunning folk.

🔑 KEY TERM

Commonwealth A term used in the early modern period to describe the public or the nation.

Sharpe stresses that there was 'no single hegemonic attitude to witchcraft among educated men and women in England but rather a plurality of possible positions'. Some believed in the threat of witchcraft. Others were sceptical. Probably most were somewhere in the middle: they were willing to accept witchcraft as a potential threat but cautious about persecuting people who were simply disliked in their communities.

The role of the Devil

English witchcraft beliefs have often been portrayed as being less concerned with the demonic pact than continental beliefs. Nevertheless, by the early seventeenth century, there was a growing awareness of the idea of the pact. While few people read the serious demonological texts, many read (or had read to them) the pamphlets which described witch trials. These conveyed a clear warning of the danger of Satan's snares and stressed that witches were his agents. Several of those executed in Lancaster in 1612 (see pages 101–4) confessed to entering into a diabolical pact. By the time of Hopkins' witch-hunt (see pages 106–13) between 1645 and 1647, such ideas were firmly implanted.

However, the sabbat was a phenomenon rarely alluded to in sources dealing with English witchcraft. There does not seem to have been much concern about it at popular or theoretical level.

Familiars and the witch's mark

When it came to witchcraft accusations, the Devil generally had, 'at best, a walk-on part', writes historian Malcolm Gaskill (2010). Instead, familiars – or imps – in the shape of animals, birds and insects took centre stage. Familiars, half-animal and half-demonic beings that most witches were thought to own, were a uniquely English phenomenon. Some familiars were described as fearsome beasts. Others seemed to be like pets. A 1566 pamphlet recounting the trial of three Chelmsford women includes the confession of Elizabeth Francis, aged twelve. She was initiated into witchcraft by her grandmother, who gave her a familiar in the shape of a cat called Satan. Elizabeth was assured she would be rewarded in return for her renunciation of God and her giving her soul to the cat in return for a few drops of blood.

Familiars were supposed to suck blood from witches and the English version of the witch's mark was regarded as the place from which the blood was sucked. The mark was usually identified as a teat or similar protuberance. The identification of this mark became one of the most definite proofs of witchcraft. By the seventeenth century the mark was normally found in the anus of female witches, possibly adding a sexual dimension to the witch's relationship with her familiar. Contemporary notions of modesty meant that teams of women, usually including a midwife, were appointed as searchers.

Cunning folk

Alan Macfarlane (1970) demonstrated that in the Elizabethan period no village in Essex was more than ten miles from a 'cunning' person, of whom a high proportion were male. Cunning folk carried out a number services including:

- providing medicine for the sick
- helping people to identify those who were bewitching them
- giving advice about how to deal with witches.

Given that cunning folk were considered a 'good thing' by the bulk of the population, they were unlikely to be reported to the authorities. Nevertheless, many preachers and writers argued, as did Richard Bernard (see page 87): 'All witches, in truth, are bad witches and none are good.'

Witchcraft, magic and educated culture

The tendency for recent historians to focus on the witchcraft beliefs of the masses has tended to obscure the importance of magic and the occult in educated culture.

Alchemy and astrology

Throughout the early modern period educated men dabbled in alchemy, attempting to turn base metals into gold by occult means. Belief in astrology was also widespread:

- John Dee, an English intellectual and skilled mathematician, established himself as Elizabeth I's court astrologer, one of his first tasks being to help establish the best date for her coronation.
- In the 1640s, the parliamentary regime sought the advice of William Lilly, an astrologer, seeking predictions about its military plans.
- Doctors used horoscopes to aid their diagnosis and treatment.
- Charts and almanacs that set out the various astronomical events of the coming year, and the best time for action, were very popular.

It is likely that the widespread acceptance of the reality of magical and occult influences helped to convince the educated elite that malefic witchcraft existed.

The impact of classical culture

Classical culture helped to reinforce the acceptance of witchcraft among the scholarly. Education for those destined to become clergymen was largely restricted to training in Latin and Greek and immersion in classical texts. These texts contained overt references to witchcraft and magic. Dramatists of the period, anxious to display their learning to their audiences, made use of witches and the occult. The best known example is the witch scene in Shakespeare's *Macbeth*, probably first staged in 1606. These cultural and intellectual currents

KEY TERM

Justice of the peace
A person commissioned to perform certain judicial and other functions within a specified locality in England and Wales.

were present in the minds of judges, **justices of the peace** (JPs) and the gentlemen who sat on grand juries and screened witchcraft accusations.

The impact of the Reformation

Historians once assumed that witch-hunting in England was the result of the Reformation. In the eyes of many Protestants, the dividing line between Catholicism and magic was blurred. At the heart of Catholicism was the belief in the power of rituals and relics, which were not far removed from the spells and potions peddled by cunning folk. A raft of methods were employed by the Catholic Church to invoke God's power or ward off evil spirits. These included rituals for blessing people, houses and crops. Holy water was routinely scattered on fields to ensure good harvests. The use of talismans, amulets and crosses was also commonplace. Protestant theologians wanted to rid society of such superstitious practices. They also sought to extirpate witchcraft.

The impact of Puritanism

By the seventeenth century, many English radical Protestants – Puritans – were at odds with the Anglican Church, which they saw as too 'papist'. Influenced by the ideas of John Calvin (see pages 21–2), Puritans wished to establish a godly commonwealth on earth. In the Civil War (1642–6) the Puritans succeeded in defeating King Charles I. Oliver Cromwell, who effectively ruled England from the late 1640s until his death in 1658, was a Puritan.

Historians have generally regarded Puritans as more likely than Anglicans to persecute witches. Certainly the most serious witch-hunt in England, in 1645–7, occurred in an area dominated by Puritans and was undertaken by Puritans. However, recent thinking has questioned the connection between Puritanism and a desire to prosecute witches. While some Puritans, notably William Perkins (see page 87), argued for the extirpation of witches, others, while not denying witchcraft's reality, were cautious about how to approach the issue. Some accepted the views of Reginald Scot (see pages 86–7) and believed that many of the misfortunes which were ascribed to the Devil were in fact due to the providence of God. Macfarlane, analysing witchcraft prosecutions in Essex, could find little evidence of the influence of a persecuting Puritan clergy. 'At the very least', writes Sharpe (2002), 'among English Puritans, witchcraft was a contested issue, rather than a phenomenon which was likely to engender a persecutory knee-jerk reaction'. It is perhaps noteworthy that Oliver Cromwell's speeches and letters of the Civil War period contain no mention of witchcraft.

Socio-economic influences

Alan Macfarlane (1970) and Keith Thomas (1971) provided an approach to witchcraft which focused on ideas about witchcraft on a popular level and concentrated on the connections between witchcraft accusations and socio-economic change.

The quality of life in England's village communities in the early modern period remains problematic. The 10,000 or so English parishes varied in extent, in density of population and in their economic life. The heavily populated and economically advanced villages of south-eastern England were markedly different from the thinly populated northern parishes. It is thus hard to generalise. Nevertheless, there is evidence of marked if gradual socio-economic change. The key was population growth. From 1530 to 1630, England's population rose from 2.5 million to 5 million. This created a flooded labour market resulting in a substantial proportion of the population being wholly or partially dependent on wage labour. Many found it hard to get work and received less in terms of real wages. The result was increased poverty and serious social strains at the base of society.

However, rising bread prices brought enhanced profits for those with a surplus of grain to sell. Thus, many villages were increasingly divided between the poor and a loose oligarchy of gentry and prosperous **yeomen** farmers, tradesmen and craftsmen who exercised control as employers and through the holding of local offices.

Macfarlane regarded the socio-economic changes that were occurring as crucial to the understanding of witch persecutions in Essex. He claimed that the widening gap between rich and poor resulted in altercations and deteriorating relations between people at local village level. He believed that between *c.*1560 and 1660 richer villagers were concerned about how to deal with the growing number of poor whom they saw as an increasing nuisance. He claimed that they felt guilt at not helping them and that they transferred this guilt to the transgressors of the community norms – particularly those who begged and mumbled threats against those who refused to give them charity.

Macfarlane's Essex model, however, does not fit Kent, Hertfordshire, Middlesex and Surrey. These counties saw similar socio-economic change to that occurring in Essex but witnessed relatively little in the way of witchcraft persecution. Nor is the transference of guilt theory convincing. Most of those who brought witchcraft accusations did so because they felt personally threatened by witches. There is little evidence to suggest that they felt consciously or subconsciously guilty.

The English legal process

English legal procedures were different from those across most of Europe. In England, the determination of guilt was left to a trial jury. The judge remained in theory, although not necessarily in practice, an impartial arbitrator who presided over the judicial process rather than an official who was entrusted with the investigation, prosecution and conviction of the crime.

KEY TERM

Yeomen Farmers who owned a relatively small amount of land, on which they themselves usually worked.

Accusations

Most of the accusations in England were rooted in rural communities, where the presence of an undesirable person could less easily be ignored than in a town. Macfarlane calculated that in 410 of 460 cases in Essex, the witch and his or her victim came from the same village. In many cases, the 'victim' had probably made some effort to counter the perceived witchcraft. He or she may have visited a cunning person to seek advice. The victim may also have taken direct action. Drawing blood from a witch by scratching (often her forehead) or burning something belonging to a witch (especially her hair) was thought to be effective. Assuming none of this worked, the victim might eventually take the matter to court.

The process of bringing a suspected witch to trial was relatively simple. In rural communities, a complaint would be made to the village constable, who would pass it on to the local JP. The latter would then question both the accused and the accuser. In doing so, he would try to draw out information which would be useful at the court of assize. All this was written down in a pre-trial document. On the basis of the evidence, the JP would commit the suspect for trial or let her go free. If she was sent for trial, she would pass the period of waiting in gaol. This could be up to six months, depending on when in the court cycle arrest had taken place. The input of JPs was of great importance in many witchcraft cases, not least those of Pendle in 1612 and East Anglia between 1645 and 1647.

The assizes

Judges of the three common-law courts at Westminster, appointed by the Crown, heard criminal cases at the assizes: a generally effective way of bringing centrally directed justice to the localities. England's counties were grouped into six circuits, and twice a year, in January and mid-summer, two judges were allocated to each of the assize circuits and sent out from Westminster to try cases. In England, therefore, witch trials were presided over by experienced judges who were culturally distanced from the world of village squabbles that so often formed the context of witchcraft accusations. This distancing process was enhanced by a convention that assize judges could not ride the circuit in a county in which they lived.

The assize process

Evidence was first presented to a grand jury to determine whether a person should go to trial. If a majority of the twelve jurors thought there was a case to answer, the accused was indicted. If the suspect pleaded not guilty, she was tried before a trial jury which determined her guilt or innocence. It was customary that there was no defence lawyer for those accused of felony. The truth was expected to emerge from the written testimonies that had been taken before the trial. Because the assizes only happened twice a year, there was always a great deal of business to get through. Routine trials lasted just 15–20 minutes. Even complex ones rarely lasted 30 minutes. In contrast to modern times, the defendant was effectively presumed guilty unless proved otherwise.

Legal evidence

Evidence for witchcraft cases was questionable because by its very nature witchcraft was secret. English courts, like those on the Continent, were thus forced to rely on indirect evidence. Juries were not bound by the strict laws of evidence that prevailed on the Continent and could convict a witch on the basis of either reputation or circumstantial evidence. Given that witchcraft was supernatural, courts had to admit evidence of a supernatural or quasi-magical kind:

- The suspect's association with an animal or insect could be interpreted as the entertaining of a familiar spirit.
- If some contact with the suspected witch were followed by a mishap, a causal connection could be imputed.
- Various categories of physical evidence were accepted. These might include a waxen image of the victim found in the accused's possession after a misfortune had been suffered. Witches' marks were accepted as evidence. If the accused's alleged crime was to have committed murder by witchcraft and the corpse bled at her touch, this was also regarded as evidence of guilt. If a witch was unable to recite the Lord's Prayer in court without faltering, this suggested guilt.
- On occasion, spectral evidence relating to demonic apparitions (see page 108) was accepted as admissible.

Sub-inquisitorial trial

Historian C.R. Unsworth accepts that English legal practice was 'distinctly more moderate' (2001) than continental practice, especially with regard to torture. However, he points out that in many respects, English criminal proceedings developed tendencies which led them to resemble the inquisitorial process:

- Judges often acted oppressively towards accused witches in an effort to secure a confession or otherwise managed trials in such a way as to promote the chances of conviction.
- Zealous clergyman put pressure on the accused to confess.
- Those who searched for the Devil's mark were effectively professional witnesses, equivalent to those who provide forensic evidence in court today. If Devil's marks were discovered, the accused was likely to be found guilty. The search itself, an examination in private prior to the court proceedings, can be seen as akin to inquisitorial procedures in Europe.
- As in Europe, rules relating to the giving of evidence were modified for witchcraft cases. Children below the normal age of competence (fourteen years of age) often gave evidence, sometimes against their parents (see page 103).
- Magistrates, in presenting evidence from the initial inquiry to the trial court, were in a strong position to prejudice the latter.

- In an exceptional situation in 1645, during the Civil War, when central justices failed to supervise the conduct of prosecutions, self-proclaimed witch-finders Matthew Hopkins and John Stearne succeeded in using forms of torture (see page 111).

Given these procedures, it is legitimate, thinks Unsworth, to classify English witch trials as 'sub-inquisitorial in character'.

Acquittal

The evidence suggests that opinion about witchcraft accusations within local communities could be divided. While some people might identify women as witches, others were cautious or felt moved by ties of kinship or friendship to support the accused. Therefore, a suspected witch was not destined automatically to face trial and execution. Local enmities and friendship groupings might work as effectively against the accuser as against the witch. Thus, in 1623, Edward Fairfax, member of an important gentry family in Yorkshire, concerned about the bewitchment of his daughters, had the women he suspected tried. But Fairfax was unable to secure a conviction in the face of a rallying of community support for the alleged witches.

The evidence suggests that acquittal rates for witch suspects in England were high. On the south-eastern counties circuit of the assizes only 104 of 474 (22 per cent) accused were sentenced to death. This suggests that judges and juries handled witchcraft cases with caution and some scepticism.

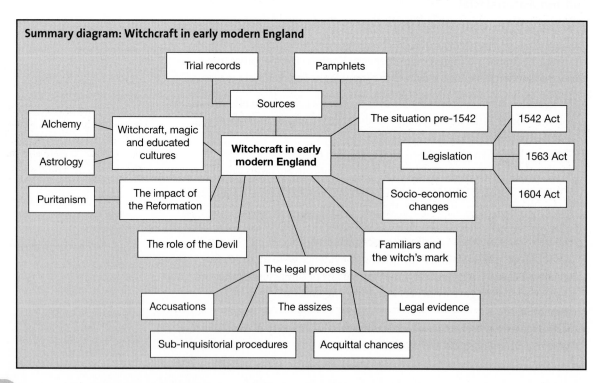

Summary diagram: Witchcraft in early modern England

2 English witch-hunting 1560–1612

▶ *How did English witch-hunting develop in the period 1560–1612?*

On the basis of the criminal charges, most people were worried about *maleficium*, not the Satanic pact. People taking witches to court were selective about what harms witches were meant to have caused. Between 1560 and 1680 in Essex, they were accused of causing the death of 233 humans, the illness of a further 108, while in 80 cases they were accused of harming or killing animals. A further six were charged with harming property by witchcraft: burning barns, hindering the brewing of beer and preventing cream from becoming butter. Most of those tried as witches found themselves in court as a result of actions levelled against them by their neighbours – in Thomas's words, the 'tyranny of local opinion'.

The village community

Witchcraft was a rural phenomenon largely because most people lived in the countryside. London, with 150,000 people in 1550 and 500,000 by 1700, was easily England's largest town. Few other towns had more than 10,000 people. Norwich, England's second largest town, had a population of 30,000 by 1700. Although there is evidence of cases of witchcraft in towns it was less common. Most people lived in village communities. Few historians now believe that pre-industrial villages were harmonious, cooperative places where people lived happier lives than those of later industrial workers.

In village communities, most people knew everyone else. Those who stood out as troublemakers were swiftly punished, either by the Church courts or by the community. Community-led punishments included the **ducking-stool**, putting the offender in a cage or leading them around the streets by a metal bridle. The most frequent offenders were 'scolds', legally defined as 'a troublesome and angry woman who, by her brawling and wrangling amongst her neighbours, doth break the public peace and beget, cherish and increase public discord'. There was a close association between scolding and witchcraft. Reginald Scot (see pages 86–7) claimed that the 'chief fault' of witches 'is that they are scolds'.

Gossip was a major pastime in most villages. The conduct of individuals was constantly subjected to neighbourhood evaluation, with an awareness of past reputation for good or ill constantly being brought into play. Thus, when misfortune occurred and a natural explanation seemed insufficient, memories of past acts of witchcraft could be raked up. An enormous range of antagonisms, personal feuds and areas of competitiveness underlay a witchcraft accusation. In Thomas's view, a local reputation for deviance fuelled the process which led to 'the making of the witch'.

 KEY TERM

Ducking-stool A stool or chair in which people who had committed a not very serious offence were tied and ducked in a pond or river.

Macfarlane's evidence from Essex suggests that those accused of witchcraft were most likely to be the wives of labourers while those accusing them were more likely to be members of yeomen families. This may have been because taking a witch to court was expensive: poor people who thought themselves bewitched may therefore have been dissuaded from taking their tormentors to court. Usually it took many years for the pressure of suspicion to build before it exploded into an accusation. Plaintiffs, says Sharpe, 'had to be unusually confident or foolhardy, or unusually afraid or angry'.

The female stereotype

As on the Continent, the powers of malefic witchcraft in England were overwhelmingly ascribed to women. Given Macfarlane's research in Essex, it is likely that 90 per cent of those accused of witchcraft were female. They were also generally elderly. John Gaule, writing in 1646, could castigate the attitude by which 'Every old woman, with a wrinkled face, a furrowed brow, a hairy lip, a goober [prominent] tooth, a squint eye, a squeaking voice, or a scolding tongue, having a ragged coat on her back; a skull cap on her head, a spindle in her hand, and a dog or cat at her side; is not only suspected, but pronounced for a witch.' Single women were particularly vulnerable because it was believed that without the guidance of a husband they did not have the willpower to resist the Devil's wiles.

Most suspected witches were relatively poor. The notion that older members of society were looked after by their children or relatives seems to have had little basis in fact. There were far more women than men at the bottom of the social scale.

As well as being the most vulnerable and dispensable members of society, elderly women were prone to eccentric behaviour, refusing to conform to social norms, including regular attendance at church. Their neighbours often felt uncomfortable in their presence. The likelihood of senility also increased with age, which made it easier for interrogators to extract confessions of Devil worship or other evil practices.

Suspects had often requested something at the door of one their more substantial neighbours: food, money, work. This would be refused and the woman would either curse the refuser or go away mumbling threats. Soon afterwards a misfortune might befall the refuser's household. The misfortune would be ascribed to witchcraft, especially if the curser already had the reputation of being a witch.

Male witches

Male witches were sometimes the husbands or offspring of female witches, dragged in by association. William Perkins (see page 87) said 'witches are wont to communicate their skill to others by tradition, to teach and instruct their children and posterity, and to initiate them in the grounds and practices of their own trade'. But men were also accused for independent acts of witchcraft and broader forms of sorcery for which women were rarely indicted.

Female involvement in witch accusations

While women were usually the victims, they often played a key role in generating accusations of witchcraft:

- Inter-female rivalries were a common feature of rural life. Far from there being a sense of sisterhood, hostilities between women could be more intense than those involving men.
- Witchcraft accusations became one of the most effective means by which women could exercise power in a male-dominated society.
- At the centre of many of the accusations was concern over children at a time when childcare was regarded as an overwhelmingly female activity.
- Evidence from the south-eastern English counties assize circuit suggests that women were up to fifteen times more likely to give evidence in witchcraft trials than in other felony cases. It may be that women were giving evidence at their husband's instigation. But it is just as likely that many of the men who bore testimony did so at the prompting of their wives.

Elizabethan witch-hunts

The first English witch trial resulting in a hanging took place in 1566 at Chelmsford in Essex. A rush of similar trials followed. The witch panic was accentuated by the discovery in 1578 of a plot to kill Queen Elizabeth and two of her advisers by maleficent magic. A full-scale investigation was launched by the **Privy Council**. The panic felt at the heart of the government may have filtered down to the rest of society. Cases of witchcraft increased significantly in the 1580s and 1590s, particularly in Essex – the 'home of English witch-hunting', says Sharpe (see Source B, page 98).

However, by the end of Elizabeth's reign, the number of witchcraft trials had declined significantly. Late in Elizabeth's reign, the ascendancy of Whitgift as Archbishop of Canterbury led to the development of a religious style which eschewed both 'popery' and extreme Protestantism. This style, usually described as Arminianism, was continued by Richard Bancroft, who succeeded Whitgift in 1605. By the 1590s, the Anglican hierarchy was sceptical about demonic possession and the threat posed by witches.

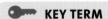 **KEY TERM**

Privy Council The central governing body convened by royal summons.

SOURCE B

? Look at Source B. Why has the artist placed the small animals in the foreground?

The hanging of Chelmsford witches, Essex, 1589.

The Boy of Burton

In 1596, Robert Toone of Burton in Staffordshire went hunting in local woods with his thirteen-year-old nephew, Thomas Darling. Separated for a short time, they were soon reunited and returned home. Thomas then became ill. Confined to bed, he complained that a green cat was tracking him and that he could see green angels. He also began to have fits. Darling's family suspected that he was bewitched, a notion that seemed to be confirmed when Thomas claimed that while alone in the woods he had met an old woman who had cursed him. From Thomas's description, the woman was first identified as Elizabeth Wright, known to neighbours as the Witch of Stapenhill. But others declared that she was too old to go wandering about the woods and that the woman was more likely to be her 60-year-old daughter Alice Gooderidge.

Local JPs arrested both women, inspected them for witches' marks – duly found – and then took them to visit Thomas. In Alice's presence, he fell into a serious fit. This seemed to prove that she was the witch and she was imprisoned. Eventually, she confessed that she was a witch, had summoned the Devil and asked him to torment Thomas. Thomas's family now called on the assistance of John Darrell, a lawyer turned Puritan preacher, who had already established a reputation for relieving those who were 'possessed'. Darrell claimed that Thomas was possessed by two evil spirits whom he proceeded to drive from his body. Thomas recovered. Alice died in prison before she could be brought to trial.

The case made Darrell famous and he was called on to perform other exorcisms, including one in Nottingham in which he apparently cured William Somers. Somers declared that his affliction had been caused by witchcraft and named thirteen women as witches. However, in 1598, Somers admitted to feigning being possessed. As a result, Darrell was arrested and found guilty of fraud by a Church commission in 1599. He was soon released from prison but his career as an exorcist was over.

The influence of Samuel Harsnett

Samuel Harsnett, chaplain to Bishop Bancroft of London, sat on the commission which investigated Darrell's activities. Harsnett had previously spearheaded a campaign to discredit a rash of exorcisms performed by Jesuit priests in England in 1585–6, the purpose of which had been to promote Catholicism by demonstrating that they, not the Anglican clergy, were the Devil's true opponents. The fact that Puritans, like Darrell, were now conducting their own exorcisms was of concern to the Anglican clerical establishment, which was keen to discredit Puritanism, Catholicism and exorcism.

In 1599, Harsnett published *A Survey of Certain Dialogical Discourses,* which condemned Darrell's exorcist practices. The treatise also questioned the belief in demons and came close to denying the reality of witchcraft. Later, by order of the Privy Council, Harsnett wrote another attack on exorcism, *A Declaration of Egregious Popish Impostures* (1603). In this work, he scoffed openly at witchcraft superstition, and declared there were natural explanations for most apparent supernatural phenomena, including exorcisms. In 1603, the Anglican Church prohibited ministers from casting out devils, except by special licence from a bishop. Harsnett continued to rise in the Church, becoming Archbishop of York in 1628.

The impact of James I

James I became king of England in 1603. Previously he had been James VI of Scotland. In Scotland, he had supported major witch-hunts after 1590 (see pages 125–34) and written a book – *Daemonologie* – about the dangers of witchcraft. Initially, it seemed that he intended to take stronger action against witches. The Witchcraft Act of 1604 was a harsher version of the 1563 Act (see page 86), making hanging mandatory for the first offence of witchcraft. However, James's policies and attitudes towards witchcraft after 1603 are not clear or consistent. He was certainly not the avid witch-hunter of historical myth.

The Gunter case

In 1604, Anne Gunter, the fourteen-year-old daughter of Brian Gunter, a gentleman from North Moreton, Berkshire, displayed many of the symptoms that had become common in cases of possession. She experienced convulsive fits, became temporarily deaf and blind, sneezed up, voided and vomited pins, foamed at the mouth, went as many as twelve days without eating and physically assaulted those around her. Anne alleged that three women, Elizabeth Gregory, Mary Pepwell and Agnes Pepwell, were responsible for her condition. Not everyone was convinced, particularly as the Gunter family had long been at odds with the families of the accused women.

Elizabeth Gregory and Agnes Pepwell were tried in March 1605 (Mary Pepwell had fled). The jury decided on a verdict of not guilty. This was largely because Thomas Hinton exposed Anne's fits as counterfeit, and assize judge David Williams was sympathetic to the two women, appointing three sceptical JPs (including Hinton) to the jury.

Anne's fits attracted the attention of King James and he interviewed her on several occasions between August and October 1605. At some point, he referred the case to Richard Bancroft, now Archbishop of Canterbury. Bancroft, in turn, placed Anne in the custody of Samuel Harsnett, who extracted a confession from her. She admitted that her father had made her fake being possessed in order to accuse Gregory and the Pepwells of witchcraft. Harsnett reported this to James who now took legal action against the Gunters. The prosecution took place in February 1606 in the Court of Star Chamber, a court which was, in effect, the Privy Council acting in a judicial capacity. The record of the court's decision has been lost but it seems Gunter was convicted and fined. The Gunter trial was the first attempt by an English government to bring the accusers of witches to trial. It is striking that the process of counteraction began only two years after the passage of the severe 1604 witchcraft statute.

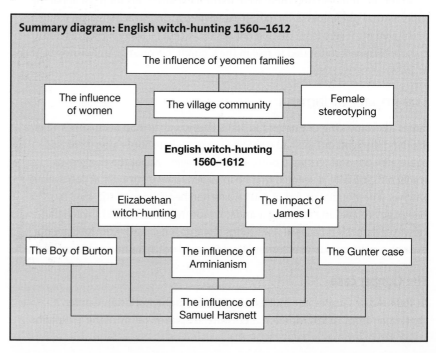

Summary diagram: English witch-hunting 1560–1612

The Lancashire witches 1612

▶ *Why are the Pendle witches' trials in Lancaster in 1612 so important in English witch-hunting history?*

The trials of the Pendle witches in Lancaster in August 1612 are among the most famous witch hearings in English history. The accused lived in the area around Pendle Hill in Lancashire.

The socio-economic situation

Lancashire at the time was regarded as a wild and lawless region. The Pendle area was experiencing poverty at the base of society. However, it is difficult to link economic pressures directly to the witchcraft accusations in 1612. Many parts of England were experiencing similar economic problems without subsequent witch trials. Moreover, a much greater economic crisis in the Pendle area in the 1620s did not produce a major witch-hunt.

Historian John Swain (2002) thinks it likely that there were people in the Pendle area (including some of those charged) who, in an effort to earn more money, cultivated a reputation for witchcraft. It may be, says Swain, that for some of the Pendle witches 'witchcraft was a business, albeit a very risky one, for which several paid the ultimate price'.

Events leading up to the trials

On 21 March 1612, John Law, a pedlar, encountered Alizon Device, who asked him for some pins. Law refused. A few minutes later he stumbled and fell. Managing to regain his feet, he reached a nearby inn. Initially, Law made no accusation against Alizon. But she appears to have been convinced of her own powers. When Abraham Law took her to visit his father, John, a few days after the incident, Alizon reportedly confessed to bewitching him and asked for his forgiveness.

Alizon, her mother Elizabeth and her brother James were summoned to appear before Roger Nowell, an experienced JP, on 30 March. It is unclear whether Nowell encouraged what now happened or just happened to get sucked into an ever-growing mass of accusations and confessions. Alizon admitted to Nowell that she had sold her soul to the Devil and that she had told him to lame John Law. James stated that his sister had also confessed to bewitching a local child. Elizabeth was more reticent, admitting only that her mother Elizabeth Southerns (alias 'Old Demdike') had a suspicious mark on her body.

Questioned about Anne Whittle (alias 'Chattox'), the matriarch of another family reputedly involved in witchcraft in the Pendle area, Alizon accused Chattox of murdering four men by witchcraft and of killing her father in 1601. There seems to have been bad blood between the two families, possibly because they were in competition, both trying to make a living from healing and extortion.

On 2 April, Demdike, Chattox and Chattox's daughter, Anne Redferne, were summoned to appear before Nowell. Both Demdike and Chattox were by then blind and in their eighties. Both provided Nowell with damaging confessions. Demdike claimed that she had given her soul to the Devil twenty years previously while Chattox said that she had given her soul to 'a Thing like a Christian man', on his promise that 'she would not lack anything and would get any revenge she desired'. Although Anne Redferne made no confession, Demdike said that she had seen her making clay figures. Margaret Crooke, another witness, claimed that her brother had died after having had a disagreement with Redferne. Based on the evidence and confessions he had obtained, Nowell committed Demdike, Chattox, Redferne and Alizon Device to prison in Lancaster Castle, to be tried for causing harm by witchcraft at the next assizes.

The meeting at Malkin Tower

On 10 April, Elizabeth Device organised a meeting at Malkin Tower, the home of the Demdikes. Friends and others sympathetic to the family attended. When word of the meeting reached Nowell, he decided to investigate. On 27 April, an inquiry was held before Nowell and another magistrate, Nicholas Bannister, to determine the meeting's purpose, who had attended and what had happened. Evidence emerged that those at the meeting had plotted further acts of witchcraft and considered trying to blow up Lancaster Castle to secure the release of their imprisoned family members. As a result of the inquiry, eight more people – Elizabeth and James Device, Alice Nutter, Katherine Hewitt, John Bulcock, Jane Bulcock, Alice Gray and Jennet Preston – were accused of witchcraft and committed for trial. Preston lived at Gisburn, then in Yorkshire, so she was sent for trial at York; the others were sent to Lancaster.

Nowell and his fellow JPs were now convinced that they were confronting a major outbreak of witchcraft. This seemed to be confirmed on 19 May when Chattox confessed to making a pact with the Devil and James Device confessed to being a witch. Moreover, neighbours came forward in large numbers to tell the authorities of acts of witchcraft which had occurred over many years.

The York assizes

Jennet Preston was tried at York assizes on 27 July. Her judges were Sir James Altham and Sir Edward Bromley. She was charged with the murder by witchcraft of a local landowner, Thomas Lister, four years previously. She had already appeared before Bromley accused of murdering a child by witchcraft but had been found not guilty. Evidence against Preston was sent from Lancashire to York, not least that she had attended the Malkin Tower meeting. She was found guilty and executed on 29 July.

The Lancaster assizes

The judges Altham and Bromley now travelled to Lancaster to try the rest of the Pendle witches. Old Demdike had already died in prison while awaiting trial. A number of other suspected witches were also tried at Lancaster, including:

- the Samlesbury witches, Jane Southworth, Jennet Brierly and Ellen Brierly, the charges against whom included child murder and cannibalism
- Margaret Pearson, who was facing her third trial for witchcraft, this time for killing a horse
- Isobel Robey, accused of using witchcraft to cause sickness.

Thomas Potts

Almost everything that is known about the Lancaster trials comes from *The Wonderful Discoverie of Witches*, written by Thomas Potts, clerk to the Lancaster assizes. Potts was instructed to write his account by the trial judges. He completed his work in mid-November 1612. Bromley revised and corrected the manuscript before its publication in 1613, declaring it to be 'truly reported'. Potts seems to have relied heavily on witness depositions and accounts of what happened in court. But he also edited and dramatised the materials to give an impression of an unfolding succession of dreadful revelations. Essentially, he was intent on displaying that justice had been done.

The importance of Jennet Device

Nine-year-old Jennet Device was a key witness for the prosecution, something that would have been permitted in few other seventeenth-century criminal trials. However, King James had made a case for suspending the normal rules of evidence for witchcraft trials in *Daemonologie*. As well as identifying those who had attended the Malkin Tower meeting, Jennet gave evidence against her mother, brother and sister. She must have harboured a deep-seated hatred of her family or been pressured and intimidated by members of the judiciary.

18 August

Anne Whittle (Chattox) was accused of the murder of Robert Nutter. She pleaded not guilty but the confession she had made to Nowell was read out in court and evidence against her was presented by a witness who had lived with the Chattox family twenty years earlier. Chattox broke down and admitted her guilt, calling on God for forgiveness and the judges to be merciful to her daughter Anne Redferne.

Elizabeth Device was charged with three murders. When Jennet stood up to give evidence, Elizabeth screamed and cursed her daughter, forcing the judges to have her removed from the courtroom. Jennet then stated that she believed her mother to be a witch. James Device also gave evidence against his mother and Elizabeth Device was found guilty.

James Device pleaded not guilty to two murders by witchcraft. However, the confession he had made to Nowell was read out in court. This, and the evidence presented against him by his sister Jennet, persuaded the jury to find him guilty.

19 August

Anne Redferne, who had been found not guilty of one charge of murder the previous day, was now found guilty of another. Jane Bulcock and her son John, identified as attending the Malkin Tower meeting by Jennet Device, were found guilty of murder by witchcraft. Alice Nutter was unusual among the accused in being comparatively wealthy, the widow of a yeoman farmer. She made no statement either before or during her trial, except to enter her plea of not guilty to the charge of murdering Henry Milton by witchcraft. Jennet Device claimed that Alice had been present at the Malkin Tower meeting. It is possible that Alice called in at the meeting on her way to a secret Catholic service and refused to speak for fear of incriminating her fellow Catholics. Alice was found guilty.

Katherine Hewitt and Alice Grey were charged with murder and with attending the meeting at Malkin Tower. Hewitt was found guilty. Grey was found not guilty.

Alizon Device, whose action against Law had prompted the trials, was charged with causing harm by witchcraft. She seems genuinely to have believed in her own guilt. When Law came into court, she fell to her knees and confessed.

Execution

The ten Pendle witches who had been found guilty were hanged in Lancaster on 20 August.

The other witches

Concentration on the Pendle witches has tended to divert attention from the trial of the other five witches at Lancaster:

- Margaret Pearson, convicted for non-capital witchcraft, was sentenced to stand on the pillory in Lancaster, Clitheroe, Whalley and Padiham on four market days, where she had to make public confession of her offence, followed by a year's imprisonment.
- The accusations against the three Samlesbury witches were thrown out.
- Isobel Robey was acquitted.

The judges

Before 1612, no English judge had condemned so many witches at one assize. As Stephen Pumfrey (2002) points out, judges were briefed on royal policy before riding out on circuit so Bromley and Altham presumably believed they were acting in accordance with James's wishes. Pumfrey argues that they commissioned Potts to write *The Wonderful Discoverie* to show that they were following James's guidelines. Interestingly, the book was dedicated to Sir Thomas Knyvet, a powerful courtier, who was very much aware of James's thinking. Moreover, it seems that James approved their actions. Bromley was promoted to the Midlands circuit in 1616.

The last years of James's reign

Towards the end of his reign, James seemed to grow increasingly sceptical of witchcraft accusations, preferring to display his knowledge of witchcraft through exposing fraudulent accusations rather than discovering nests of malefic witches. In 1616, he castigated two judges for finding a large number of accused witches in Leicestershire guilty. Five were pardoned as a result of James's intervention – an intervention with important consequences in an age when ambitious men kept an ear cocked to catch every royal hint. According to historian Malcolm Gaskill (2010), by this time James was 'more passionate about deer-hunting than ever he had been about witch-hunting'. Given to intense but short-term attachments to both people and causes, James seems to have lost interest in demonology.

A decline in official concern

By the mid-1620s, English authorities had become sceptical about witchcraft accusations. Few witches came before the courts after Charles I became king in 1625 and those that did were invariably acquitted, usually for insufficient evidence.

An incident in 1633–4 indicates the government's hostility to witch-hunting. In 1633, eleven-year-old Edmund Robinson, who lived near Pendle, claimed to have been taken to a sabbat by a witch and to have seen a number of local women there whom, on his father's suggestion, he identified as witches. The judge, who tried the first few cases arising from Robinson's statements, became alarmed when he realised that the number of accused was rising sharply. He thus invoked the aid of central government. The Bishop of Chester, who was instructed to investigate the matter, was soon convinced the affair was a fraud. Robinson, his father and five of the suspects were then taken to London. William Harvey, the eminent royal physician, was ordered to examine the five women. Assisted by a team of surgeons and midwives, Harvey found little by way of witches' marks on the women. Robinson then confessed that he had made up the story and that the names had been suggested by his father 'for envy, revenge and hope of gain'. On this admission, all of those who had been convicted were acquitted. What is striking is how the government acted quickly and decisively to prevent what could have been an outbreak of witch-hunting far larger than the 1612 trials.

By 1640, witchcraft had become marginalised as a source of concern for central government and as a subject of intellectual and theological debate. In the 1630s, playwrights did not regard witchcraft as a serious subject. Nor were any major demonological texts published. However, despite the sceptical attitude of the elite, it may be that popular anxiety about witchcraft increased during the 1620s and 1630s because the law no longer offered protection against witches.

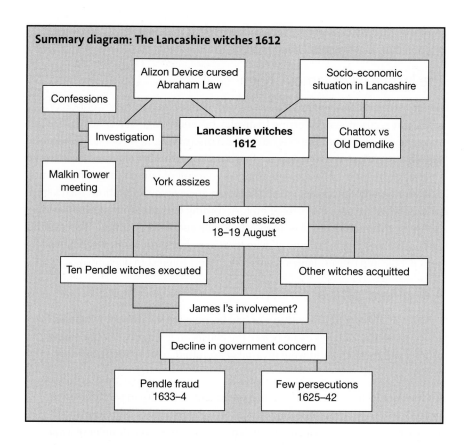

Summary diagram: The Lancashire witches 1612

 4 # Matthew Hopkins and the East Anglian witch-hunt 1645–7

▶ *To what extent were Matthew Hopkins and John Stearne responsible for the East Anglian witch-hunt?*

The East Anglian witch-hunt between 1645 and 1647 is usually associated with Matthew Hopkins. In reality, however, Hopkins worked closely with John Stearne. The two men were to become England's most notorious witch-finders.

The impact of the Civil War

By 1642, Charles I and Parliament were at odds. Civil War convulsed England for the next four years. Each side had a different religious perspective. The king's most aggressive opponents were the Puritans – strict Calvinists who had urged further reformation of religion before the war. By the 1640s, many Puritan clerics feared that the Devil was everywhere: some even believed that Charles I was Satan's agent.

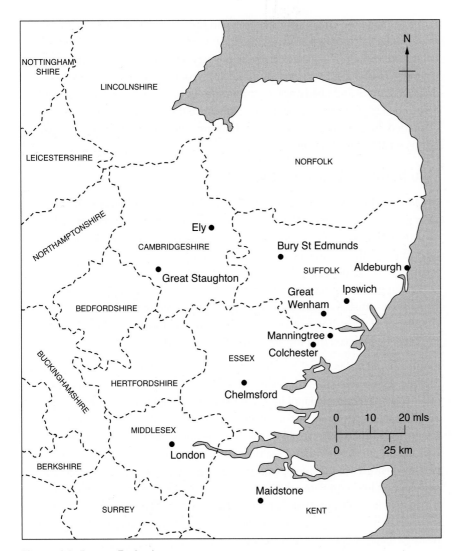

Figure 4.1 Eastern England.

The Civil War saw the collapse of traditional authority and traditional institutions. Parliament legislated without royal assent, excluded bishops from the House of Lords, executed William Laud, the Archbishop of Canterbury, and dismantled the Church courts. In parliamentary-held areas religious images in churches were destroyed. Some Puritan activists came to regard witches as they did devotional art: as something that needed to be rooted out and destroyed.

The situation in East Anglia in 1645

By early 1645, the eastern counties of England, the heartland of the parliamentarian and Puritan cause, were in a state of crisis. The outcome of the Civil War was far from certain. (It did not become so until parliamentary forces defeated the king's army at Naseby in June 1645.) It seemed possible that royalist forces might advance into East Anglia. People were fearful and overtaxed. Inflation had led to growing poverty. The principal concerns of the County Committees that ruled parliamentary-controlled areas were money, order, resources and obedience. Communities fighting for their lives also seemed threatened from within – by witches. 'The sense that victory on the battlefield depended on godliness at home made hunting witches feel like part of the war effort', writes Malcolm Gaskill (2005).

Witchcraft in Essex in 1645

In March 1645, in the small town of Manningtree near Colchester in Essex, John Rivet accused Elizabeth Clarke of being a witch. Some townsmen, who confronted Clarke, were shocked – but also pleased – to hear her admit an association with several witches. Her confession was entrusted to John Stearne. Stearne, in his mid-thirties, had grown up in Suffolk but was now resident in Manningtree. A staunch Puritan, he had the ear of local magistrate Sir Harbottle Grimston. Grimston was a highly principled man with half a century's experience of defending truth – as he saw it – in religion and politics. Like many Puritans, he believed that the witchcraft threat was real.

Grimston and his assistant Sir Thomas Bowes received Clarke's confession from Stearne. They then gave him a warrant to discover from Clarke the names of other witches. Matthew Hopkins volunteered to assist Stearne. Like Stearne, Hopkins was a devout Puritan, anxious to serve the parliamentary cause and concerned about witchcraft. Hopkins, Stearne and several other local people sat with Clarke for several nights, waiting for her familiars to appear. Eventually, various creatures put in an appearance – a creature like a cat, an imp like a dog, another dog like a greyhound, followed by an imp like a ferret and another like a toad. Clarke now admitted that she had allowed the Devil the use of her body six or seven years before and implicated Anne West, a suspected witch from the nearby village of Lawford, in her confession.

After Clarke's testimonies, other women were arrested – Anne and her daughter Rebecca West, Elizabeth Gooding, Anne Leech and Helen Clarke. They were imprisoned in Colchester awaiting trial. Hopkins knew that confessions did not guarantee conviction. A first-hand account of a sabbat from a witness was necessary to satisfy a judge that the case fell within the law's compass. He eventually persuaded Rebecca West to become an informer. Her life would be spared in return for her revealing her attendance at the sabbat and the full extent of the witches' conspiracy.

Meanwhile, more women from the Colchester area were accused. For example, Margaret Moone was blamed for deaths of livestock, spoiling food and beer, and the murder of a child. She was examined and three teats were found in her 'secret parts'. In April 1645, she confessed that she had twelve imp-disciples.

Matthew Hopkins

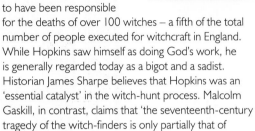

c.1620	Born in Great Wenham, Suffolk; his father was a Puritan clergyman
c.1643	Moved to Manningtree
1644	Became interested in witchcraft after overhearing various women discussing meetings with the Devil
1645–6	With John Stearne, conducted a series of witch-hunts in East Anglia
1647	Published *The Discovery of Witches*
1647	Died in Manningtree, probably of consumption

Very little is known about Hopkins apart from his witch-hunting activities. During a two-year period, he and Stearne are thought to have been responsible for the deaths of over 100 witches – a fifth of the total number of people executed for witchcraft in England. While Hopkins saw himself as doing God's work, he is generally regarded today as a bigot and a sadist. Historian James Sharpe believes that Hopkins was an 'essential catalyst' in the witch-hunt process. Malcolm Gaskill, in contrast, claims that 'the seventeenth-century tragedy of the witch-finders is only partially that of Matthew Hopkins'.

The situation in the summer of 1645

Hopkins and Stearne, accompanied by two search-women, continued the witch-hunt without initially straying far beyond the territory over which Grimston and Bowes presided. By June, there were at least 30 suspected women in Colchester gaol, where conditions were unspeakable. By mid-June, four suspects had died in prison.

The Chelmsford trial 1645

On 17 July 1645, 29 women accused of witchcraft were tried at Chelmsford. With the Civil War in progress, the trial was conducted not by assize judges but by JPs presided over by the Earl of Warwick, Lord Lieutenant of Essex. Warwick did not possess much legal expertise. According to Gaskill, he was happier directing a sea-battle than he was debating theory.

The trials were short. Batches of women were brought forward together. Most were found guilty. Only one was fully acquitted. However, concerned magistrates and a clergyman approached Warwick to beg reprieves for nine women. The request was granted. Application was made to Parliament stating that the court was not fully satisfied with the evidence given against the women and that they were deemed 'fit for mercy and pardon'.

Fifteen of the condemned were executed at Chelmsford on 18 July. The remaining four were hanged at Manningtree on 1 August.

Witch-hunting in Suffolk

By July 1645, Hopkins and Stearne had moved their witch-finding to Suffolk, Hopkins operating in the east of the county, Stearne in the west. Most contemporaries believed – wrongly – that they had been given a commission

SOURCE C

What point was the
illustration in Source C
trying to convey?

Hopkins interrogates Elizabeth Clarke and Rebecca West: a woodcut from 1647.

by Parliament to discover witches. The witch-finders chose their destinations carefully. While they preferred a written invitation, local knowledge did much to ensure they received a warm reception. Communities noted for their godly enthusiasm were most likely to find their way on to their itinerary, especially those where there had been much destruction of church images in 1643–4. More than any other single factor, the fate of a witch suspect was determined by the politics and religion of the prevailing local authority, usually the lord of the manor. Over the summer as many as 150 Suffolk men and women from some 50 small towns and villages were identified as witches.

Confessions

Hopkins and Stearne made obtaining admissions of guilt their business. Their interrogations could last several days. The confessions, recorded by Suffolk magistrates, indicate that suspects were invariably starved of sleep. This, coupled with confinement, isolation and intimidation, caused the mental health of all but the most resilient to deteriorate. After several nights awake, suspects entered a void between waking and sleep, their eyes open but their brains dreaming. The accused thus had no idea what they were admitting to. Fact fused with fantasy.

The usual routines of searching and watching were also implemented. Hopkins would sometimes cut the arm of the accused with a blunt knife and if she did not bleed, she was said to be a witch. It is also possible that some suspects were 'swum' (see page 18). Finding the so-called witch's mark remained crucial.

The Suffolk trials

Some 90 Suffolk witches were tried at Bury St Edmunds on 26 August. The grand jury approved 60 or so for trial. At least sixteen were rejected. The rest may have been carried over to the next assizes. By the end of 26 August, half the accused presented by the grand jury had been tried, of whom sixteen women and two men were sentenced to death, including John Lowesan, an unpopular Anglican vicar. Lowesan and the rest of the Suffolk witches were executed the following day.

SOURCE D

John Gaule describes Hopkins' and Stearne's methods in 1646. Quoted in Tracy Borman, *Witches: A Tale of Sorcery, Scandal and Seduction*, Jonathan Cape, 2013, pp. 155–6.

Having taken the suspected witch, she is placed in the middle of a room upon a stool or table, cross-legged, or in some other uneasy posture, to which she submits not, she is then bound with cords: there is she watched and kept without meat or sleep for the space of 24 hours for (they say) within that time they shall see her imp come and suck. A little hole is likewise made in the door for the imp to come in at; and lest it might come in some less discernible shape, they that watch are taught to be ever and anon sweeping the room, and if they see any spiders or flies, to kill them. And if they cannot kill them, then they may be sure they are her imps.

According to Source D, what methods were used against suspected witches to ensure they were found guilty?

The witch-hunt continues

In 1645–6, Hopkins and Stearne travelled over other eastern counties – Norfolk, Huntingdonshire, Northamptonshire, Cambridgeshire and Bedfordshire. The executions continued with Hopkins now giving evidence against suspected witches in court. In Aldeburgh in January 1646, seven women were tried for witchcraft. All were found guilty and hanged. The last serious witch-hunting came on the Isle of Ely. Hopkins may have visited the area briefly in early 1647 but he was already seriously ill. (He died, aged 27, later in 1647.) The final phase of the hunt was left to Stearne.

Gaskill claims that Hopkins and Stearne had the potential to earn more in a week than most people earned in a year. It has been suggested that this motivated their actions. But it remains likely that they were spurred on by religious conviction. The costs to the local community of Hopkins' work were such that in 1645 a special local tax rate had to be levied in Ipswich. The Aldeburgh witch-hunt was a severe drain on the town, costing a seventh of its annual expenses. Costs included the following:

- Matthew Hopkins' fees (£8)
- the fees of the searcher Mary Phillips (£2)
- Hopkins' and Phillips' expenses in Aldeburgh (over £4)
- the gaoler's fees (over £2)
- the fees of the guards at the trial (15 shillings 6 pence; 77.5p)
- food and drink during the trial (£15)
- the carpenter's fee for the gallows (£1)
- the roper's fee for making the nooses (8 shillings; 40p)
- the executioner's fee (11 shillings; 55p)
- burial costs (6 shillings; 30p).

Opposition to the witch-finders

In July 1645, a report was delivered to Parliament raising concerns about the number of confessed witches in Suffolk. In September 1645, the *Moderate Intelligencer*, a parliamentary newspaper, expressed unease at the state of affairs. In March 1646, pardons for the nine reprieved Essex witches were finally granted by Parliament: criticism of the evidence on which they had been convicted was implicit in the judgment.

Meanwhile, at Great Staughton in Huntingdon, a minister named John Gaule launched a preaching campaign against the witch-finders, declaring them to be no better than Catholic Inquisitors. He proceeded to publish his sermons in a book, *Select Cases of Conscience Touching Witches and Witchcrafts*. Gaule's criticisms had some impact. At the Norfolk assizes, Hopkins and Stearne were questioned about their interrogation methods and their fees. They were also asked whether their success as witch-finders suggested that they themselves were in league with the Devil.

Hopkins' and Stearne's defence

Hopkins published his response – *The Discovery of Witches* – as did Stearne in *A Confirmation and Discovery of Witch Craft*. Both men insisted that witches posed a threat to society and that they themselves only visited places to which they had been invited and applied their expertise to suspects identified by local people. There was much truth in this. Victims of witchcraft chose whether to go to law. JPs decided whether there were grounds to prosecute. Thereafter, the progress of a prosecution depended on grand and trial juries under the guidance of a judge. Hopkins and Stearne were not the commanders-in-chief of the witch-hunt. 'They were catalysts who gave accusers confidence by confirming their suspicions and beliefs', says Gaskill. Essentially, they were working within society, not against it. They received active cooperation and encouragement from large sections of the local population. Hopkins was a man of his time, thinks Gaskill, 'no more ruthless than his contemporaries and, above all, driven by a messianic desire to purify'. By contrast, Oliver Cromwell, who was also driven by a desire to purify (a process that he called 'a reformation of manners'), chose to do it more through clemency and conciliation, appealing for 'liberty of conscience'.

Conclusion

Between 1645 and 1647, at least 250 people were tried as witches or at least subjected to preliminary investigation, of whom at least 100 – and possibly many more – were executed. (The exact number is unknown: the records do not survive.) The East Anglian witch-hunt was thus a tragedy. But it needs to be seen as part of something even more terrible – a Civil War characterised by bigotry, brutality and bloodshed. The conflict is thought to have killed 190,000 Englishmen out of a population of 5 million – 3.7 per cent – a greater proportion than those who died during the First World War.

Most of those executed were thought to have committed the usual types of *maleficium*. What was new was the widespread presence of the Devil in the witches' confessions, with details of the pact and accounts of sexual intercourse between the witch and the Devil, although even in these confessions familiars appeared more frequently than did Satan. Much of this was probably attributable to Hopkins' and Stearne's interrogation methods, particularly sleep deprivation. Many of those questioned presented signs of inner turmoil, secret doubts and desires surfacing from the depths of consciousness. Some felt guilty and confessed. A desire for the alleviation of suffering probably also lay behind confessions.

There were several factors at work in East Anglia which probably encouraged witch-hunting in the mid-1640s:

- East Anglia was very much affected by the strains of warfare.
- The local administration was concerned with maintaining the war effort. Hence, local JPs who might otherwise have helped to defuse witchcraft accusations at an early stage were preoccupied, allowing local pressure to get out of hand.
- People in East Anglia had been exposed to preaching from Puritan ministers and parliamentary propaganda that had stressed the threat posed by the Devil and his agents to the creation of a godly commonwealth. Popular Puritanism, reinforced by the Civil War, helped to fuel the East Anglia witch-hunts.

Witch-hunting 1647–60

Partly because of the vivid reporting of the events of 1645–7, concern about witchcraft continued through the 1650s. There were a number of outbreaks of witch-hunting:

- The most serious came in Newcastle in 1650 when the town's Puritan administration called in a Scottish witch-pricker to help them hunt witches. Fifteen people were executed.
- In 1652 at the Maidstone assizes in Kent, eighteen people were tried, a third of whom were hanged.

After the restoration of Charles II in 1660, witchcraft received only half-hearted support from the ruling elite. As a result, witch trials declined sharply after 1660 (see pages 171–4).

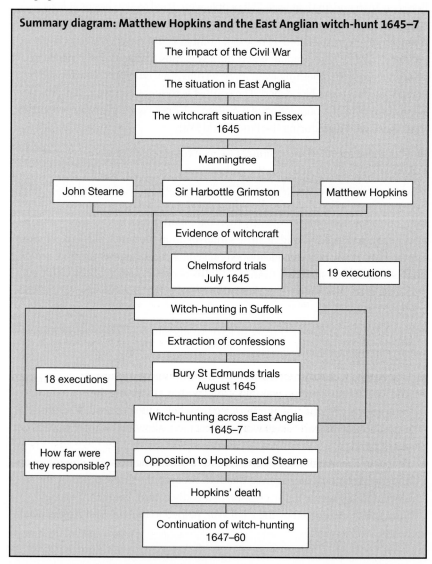

Summary diagram: Matthew Hopkins and the East Anglian witch-hunt 1645–7

The impact of the Civil War

The situation in East Anglia

The witchcraft situation in Essex 1645

Manningtree

John Stearne — Sir Harbottle Grimston — Matthew Hopkins

Evidence of witchcraft

Chelmsford trials July 1645 — 19 executions

Witch-hunting in Suffolk

Extraction of confessions

18 executions — Bury St Edmunds trials August 1645

Witch-hunting across East Anglia 1645–7

How far were they responsible? — Opposition to Hopkins and Stearne

Hopkins' death

Continuation of witch-hunting 1647–60

Key debate

> ▶ *To what extent was English witchcraft distinct from continental European witchcraft?*

The idea that English witch-hunting was different from continental European witchcraft has long been central to writing on English witchcraft. Those, like Macfarlane and Thomas, who believe that English witch accusations were unique, generally stress the following points:

- English witch-hunting was tame in comparison with continental witch-hunts. Only 500 witches were executed.
- English trials were free of some of the more bizarre elements found in continental witch trials: there is little by way of the sabbat or of sexual intercourse with incubi or succubi. Mention of a broomstick occurs only once in an account of an English trial.
- English witch-hunts remained preoccupied with *maleficium* rather than with the demonic pact.
- The demand for prosecutions arose essentially from local communities rather than being stoked up by the elite or the government.
- In England, the fact that witches were hung rather than burned reflects the lesser link with heresy.
- The concept of the witch's familiar was uniquely prominent in England.

However, the English experience of witchcraft and witch-hunting may not have been unique. Arguably, it was simply a variation on a number of themes which can be found across Europe. There was actually no such thing as a unified 'continental' witchcraft model.

- The 'English' pattern of isolated accusations against individual or small numbers of witches occurred in many European regions.
- English demonological writers were familiar with the works of continental demonologists, while continental peasants seem to have shared the same concerns over *maleficium*.
- The East Anglian trials (1645–7) suggest that by the 1640s a wide range of – continental – ideas about witchcraft were present in England.
- The German chain-reaction hunts of the early seventeenth century, regarded as typical of the 'continental' situation, were in fact atypical.
- Unsworth has shown that with regard to witchcraft the English legal process had similarities with continental practice.
- The East Anglian trials (1645–7) show that England had as great a potential for mounting large-scale witchcrazes as any European nation.

Evaluate the interpretations in Extracts 1 and 2. Explain which you think is a more convincing explanation of the nature of English witchcraft in the early modern period.

EXTRACT 1

From G. Scarre and J. Callow, *Witchcraft and Magic in Sixteenth- and Seventeenth-century Europe*, Palgrave, 2001, pp. 26–7.

England's experience of witch prosecution was, in several important respects, quite different from that of the greater part of Continental Europe. In English trials, the emphasis of the charge normally fell on the maleficia *allegedly performed by the supposed witch, rather than on any contract with the Devil … The sabbat at which the Devil was held to preside was virtually unheard of before the Essex trials of 1645 promoted by the witch-finder Matthew Hopkins and his colleague John Stearne … In a similar manner, there was less emphasis on weather magic – the raising of storms and the destruction of crops – than on the Continent … But a common charge against English witches, though much less often raised against their European counterparts, was that they kept 'familiars' – imps or demons, usually in the form of small animals such as dogs, cats, mice and toads, which did their bidding in return for nourishment from a special nipple concealed on the witch's body, and known as her 'witch-mark'. (This witch-mark is not to be confused with the 'Devil's mark' of Continental witches, an insensitive point in the body produced by Satan as a sign of compact.) … Multiple trials were considerably less common in England than in mainland Europe, probably because of the absence of the notion of witches gathering in large sociable groups at the sabbats, and the non-employment of torture to extract from accused people the names of accomplices.*

EXTRACT 2

From W. Behringer, *Witches and Witch-Hunts*, Polity Press, 2004, pp. 133–4.

The Hopkins persecutions pose a major challenge to current interpretations of English witchcraft, not just because of the large numbers of the persecuted, but also because the records demonstrate that fantasies of demonic witchcraft were anything but absent from England. Clearly, for the witch-finders the witches' 'League and Covenant with the Devil' was central to the crime, including sexual intercourse, and the stigma diabolic, the Devil's mark. The familiar spirits in animal shape, or imps, a speciality of English witchcraft, were also a token of their alignment to the Devil. According to their confessions, the witches did not restrict their activities to simple maleficent magic, but gave details of their pact and of their witches' assemblies … Furthermore the treatment the suspects received from their persecutors included general maltreatment, sleep deprivation and the use of leading questions … Sharpe concludes that the events in East Anglia 'show clearly that England has as great a potential for mounting large-scale witch crazes as any other European nation'.

There were earlier occasions, which had the potential for a large-scale persecution in England, for instance the Lancashire trials of 1633–4 where at least nineteen witches were executed, while another sixty were under suspicion

… The confessions show the fully developed fantasy of a witches' sabbat, revealing ideas about a permanent meeting point 'at Harestones in the forest of Pendle' where the witches flew for feasting and dancing, shape-shifting and having sexual intercourse, where they adored the devil and practised harmful magic.

Chapter summary

Some 500 witches were executed in England under the Witchcraft Acts of 1563 and 1604. This number, small by continental European standards, reflects a degree of scepticism about witchcraft, displayed, for example, in Reginald Scot's *The Discoverie of Witchcraft*. Most English people were concerned with *maleficia* rather than with the Devil. The precise impact of Puritanism and socio-economic factors on witchcraft remain debatable. The English legal process was different from that on the Continent but it did have some continental tendencies. Most condemned witches were relatively old and poor women. Witch-hunting seriously began in the reign of Elizabeth but there was some scepticism in the Anglican Church by the early seventeenth century. James I, despite his reputation, was not as fierce a witch-hunter in England as in Scotland. Nevertheless, the Pendle witch trials resulted in the execution of ten witches on one day in 1612. Witch-hunting declined in the 1620s and 1630s but revived in East Anglia in 1645. This witch-hunt, associated with Matthew Hopkins, was partly the result of the situation arising from the Civil War. Debate continues about the extent to which English witch-hunting differed from that on the Continent.

Refresher questions

Use these questions to remind yourself of the key material covered in this chapter.

1. What were the main features of English witch persecution?

2. What are the main sources for English witch-hunting?

3. What were the main English witch treatises in the period 1560–1630?

4. How important was Puritanism with regard to witch-hunting?

5. How were English legal processes different from continental European legal procedures?

6. How did English witch-hunting develop in the period 1560–1660?

7. What were the main features of Elizabethan witch-hunting?

8. How far was James I an avid witch-hunter?

9. What caused the Pendle witch trials?

10. To what extent was Matthew Hopkins responsible for the East Anglian witch-hunt?

11. In what respects was English witch-hunting distinct from continental witch-hunting?

Question practice

ESSAY QUESTIONS

1 To what extent were the Lancashire witch trials of 1612 the result of the socio-economic situation in the Pendle area?

2 'Puritanism was largely responsible for the East Anglia witch-hunts in the years 1645 to 1647.' How far do you agree with this statement?

3 'The East Anglia witch-trials were not brought about purely by the influence of Matthew Hopkins and John Stearne.' How far do you agree with this statement about witch-hunting in the years 1645–7?

4 'The East Anglian witch-hunt was the result of the breakdown of traditional authority.' How far do you agree with this explanation?

5 How accurate is it to say that the case of the Boy of Burton was the primary turning point in popular perceptions of witchcraft in England in the period c.1580–c.1750?

INTERPRETATION QUESTION

1 Read the two passages and then answer the question. Evaluate the interpretations in both of the passages and explain which you think is more convincing as an explanation of the reasons for the persecution of witches in East Anglia.

PASSAGE A

From Tracy Borman, *Witches: James I and the English Witch-hunts*, Vintage, 2014, p. 234.

An even more shocking expression of this new brutality was the massive wave of witch hunting in East Anglia in 1645–7, during the brief and brutal ascendancy of the Witch-finder General, Matthew Hopkins. A petty gentleman living in Manningtree, Essex, Hopkins claimed to have become greatly troubled by the presence of witches during the winter of 1644–5. He initiated a series of investigations and extracted his first confession – from an elderly and disabled widow named Elizabeth Clarke – in March 1645. This set the pattern for a rush of similar interrogations and convictions, which spread with terrifying speed across Essex and into Suffolk, Norfolk and Huntingdonshire. A total of 184 women were tried in the two years of Hopkins's activity, at least 100 of whom were executed. This was comparable to the worst excesses of the continental trials. The renewed fervour for witch hunting continued after Hopkins's sudden disappearance (and probable death) in 1647.

PASSAGE B

From M. Gaskill, *Witchfinders: A Seventeenth-century English Tragedy*, John Murray, 2006, pp. 273–4 and 283–9.

And yet Hopkins and Stearne were not commanders-in-chief of the witch-hunt: they were catalysts who gave accusers confidence by confirming their suspicions and beliefs. In their books they were emphatic that they had never accused anyone of anything: they went only to places where they were invited, and applied their expertise to suspects identified by the inhabitants. There was truth in this. It was for the searchers and watchers appointed by their own parishes to decide whether there were grounds to prosecute, and for victims and their allies to choose whether to go to law. Thereafter the progress of a prosecution depended on the consideration of a godly magistrate… and even then proceedings might still be thwarted by a grand jury, after that by a trial jury under the guidance of a judge …

No one knows exactly how many suffered in the witch-craze of 1645 to 1647: as many as three hundred women and men were interrogated, of whom more than a hundred were put to death … If one discounts the sensational, the particular and the judgemental, one is left with a different kind of Matthew Hopkins: an intransigent and dangerous figure, for sure, but a charismatic man of his time, no more ruthless than his contemporaries and, above all, driven by a 'messianic desire to purify'. In this the witch-finders resembled most puritans, believers with little breadth of mind but considerable depth of spirit, even if they did mistake their own passions for the word of God … Nor should the other witch-finders be forgotten, for without them Hopkins would have remained the obscure younger son of a country clergyman.

SOURCE ANALYSIS QUESTIONS

1 Assess the value of Source 1 for revealing popular attitudes to witchcraft and the approaches of magistrates to gathering evidence to be used against suspected witches in early seventeenth-century England. Explain your answer, using the source, the information given about its origin and your own knowledge about the historical context.

2 Assess the value of Source 2 for revealing judicial fears about witch-hunting in East Anglia in 1647, and for revealing Hopkins' defence of his actions. Explain your answer, using the source, the information given about its origin and your own knowledge about the historical context.

SOURCE I

From Thomas Potts, *The Wonderfull Discoverie of Witches in the Countie of Lancaster*, published in 1613. Potts was clerk of the court during the trial of the witches. He was instructed to write this account by the two presiding judges. One of them, Sir Edward Bromley, checked and revised it before publication.

The Confession and Examination of Anne Whittle alias Chattox being prisoner at Lancaster; taken the 19 day of May 1612; before William Sandes, Mayor of the borough town of Lancaster, James Anderton of Clayton, one of his Majesty's Justices of Peace within the same county, and Thomas Cowell, one of his Majesty's Coroners in the said county of Lancaster.

First, the said Anne Whittle, alias Chattox, sayeth, that about fourteen years past she entered, through the wicked persuasions and counsel of Elizabeth Southerns, alias Demdike, and was seduced to condescend and agree to become subject into that devilish abominable profession of witchcraft. Soon after which, the Devil appeared unto her in the likeness of a man, about midnight, at the house of the said Demdike; and thereupon the said Demdike and she, went forth of the said house unto him; whereupon the said Spirit moved this examinate [person under examination], that she would become his subject, and give her soul unto him; the which at first she refused to assent into; but after, by the great persuasions made by the said Demdike, she yielded to be at his commandment and appointment; whereupon the said wicked Spirit then said unto her, that he must have one part of her body for him to suck upon, the which she denied to grant unto him; and withal asked him, what part of her body he would have for that use; who said he would have a place of her right side near to her ribs, for him to suck upon; whereunto she assented.

And she further sayth. That at the same time, there was a thing in the likeness of a spotted bitch that came with the said Spirit unto the said Demdike, which then did speak unto her in this examinates hearing, and said that she should have gold, silver and worldly wealth, at her will …

And being further examined how many sundry persons had been bewitched to death, and by whom they were so bewitched: she sayth, that one Robert Nutter, late of the Greenhead in Pendle, was bewitched by this examinate, the said Demdike, and widow Lomshawe (Late of Burnley), now deceased.

And she further sayth, that the said Demdike showed her, that she had bewitched to death, Richard Ashton, son of Richard Ashton of Downeham Esquire.

SOURCE 2

From a tract, written by Matthew Hopkins and published in 1647, 'in answer to several queries' about his investigative techniques which had been raised with the assize judges in Norfolk. Quoted in Matthew Hopkins, *The Discovery of Witches*, published in 1647 (available at: www.gutenberg.org/files/14015/ 14015-h/14015-h.htm).

Quest. 13
How can any possibility believe that the Devil and the Witch joining together, should have such power, as the Witches confesse to kill such such a man, child, horse, cow, the like; if we believe they can do what they will, then we derogate from God's power, who for certain limits the Devil and the Witch and I cannot believe they have any power at all.

Answer
God suffers the Devil many times to do much hurt, and the Devil doth play many times the deluder and imposter with these Witches, in persuading them that they are the cause of such and such a murder wrought by him with their consents, when and indeed neither he nor they had any hand in it, as this. We must needs argue, he is of a long standing, above 6,000 years: then he must needs be the best scholar in all knowledge of arts and tongues, and so have the … best knowledge of what disease is reigning in this or that man's body, by reason of his long experience. This subtle tempter knowing such a man liable to some sudden disease (as by experience I have found) as Plurisie, Imposthume etc, he resorts to divers Witches.

Quest. 14
All that the witch-finder doth is to fleece the country of their money, and therefore rides and goes to towns to have employment, and promiseth them fair promises, and it may be doth nothing for it, and possesseth many men that they have so many wizards and so many witches in their town, and so hartens them on to entertain him.

Answer
You doe him a great deale of wrong in every of these particulars. For, first,

1 *He never went to any towne or place, but they rode, writ, or sent often for him, and were (for ought he knew) glad of him.*
2 *He is a man that doth disclaime that ever he detected a witch, or said, 'Thou art a witch'; only after her tyall by search, and their owne confessions, he as others may judge.*
3 *Lastly, judge how he fleeceth the country, and inriches himself, by considering the vast summe he takes of every towne, he demands 20.s. a town, and doth sometimes ride 20 miles for that, & hath no more for his all his charges thither and back again (& it may be stayes a weeke there) and find there 3 or 4 witches, or if it be but one, cheap enough, and this is the great summe he takes to maintain his companie with 3 horses.*

CHAPTER 5

Witchcraft in Scotland and New England

Between 1590 and 1707, some 1500 people are thought to have been executed for witchcraft in Scotland. In the late 1690s, a major witch-hunt occurred at Salem in Massachusetts in North America. Witch-hunting in both areas was associated with the Calvinist Church. This chapter will examine witch-hunting in Scotland and Salem by focusing on the following issues:

★   The North Berwick witch-hunt

★   Witch-hunting in Scotland 1591–1670

★   The Salem witch trials

The key debate on *page 153* of this chapter asks the question: Why did the Salem witch trials occur?

Key dates

1590–1	North Berwick witch-hunt		1649–50	Scottish witch-hunt
1590–7	National Scottish witch-hunt		1661–2	The last major Scottish witch-hunt
1597	Publication of *Daemonologie*		1692–3	Salem witch trials

1 The North Berwick witch-hunt

▶   *What caused the North Berwick witch-hunt?*

In 1590–1, there was a major witch-hunt in Scotland. The hunt is associated with the East Lothian town of North Berwick although, ironically, none of the witches actually came from there. King James VI's involvement in the witch-hunt makes it particularly important.

Witchcraft in Scotland before 1590

Before 1563, witchcraft in Scotland was usually dealt with in ecclesiastical courts. A Witchcraft Act passed in 1563 criminalised witchcraft. The Act was just one of a number of measures passed by a new Protestant government dealing with misbelief and misbehaviour. Nevertheless, the 1563 statute, which called for death in all cases of witchcraft, was more severe than that passed in England in the same year (see page 86).

The religious situation in Scotland in the late sixteenth century

Witch-hunting in Scotland can only be fully understood in relation to the Reformation. In the 1560s, zealous Calvinists seized power and began to sweep away Catholic institutions. Catholicism did not immediately crumble. Many Scots opposed the religious changes. Thus, in many areas there was an uneasy coexistence of Catholicism and Protestantism.

The Scottish Reformation was a long process of change and conflict. Nevertheless, by the late 1580s, the Scottish clergy had more power to influence the secular government than its English counterparts. The influence of **presbyteries** increased at the expense of bishops. Bishops drew much of their authority from being appointed by the Crown and were one means by which the government exerted its will on the Church (or Kirk). Presbyteries, on the other hand, looked to God and the body of the Kirk for their authority. By the late sixteenth century, religious and secular authority overlapped in **lowland Scotland**.

The Kirk's attitude to witchcraft and magic fluctuated considerably in the decades before 1590. While it saw both as evils to be stamped out, it was by no means always obsessed with them. Nevertheless, by the late 1580s, the **General Assembly** of the Kirk put pressure on the government to establish a godly state by prosecuting witches.

The Scottish legal system

An accusation of witchcraft in early modern Scotland was usually brought against a woman by someone living in her neighbourhood. As elsewhere, what began with an insult could end in a burning. There were three main types of secular courts where witches could be tried:

- The Court of Judiciary, which sat in Edinburgh, was the highest court.
- Circuit courts were held in various shires and presided over by judges from the central court. However, these courts did not function with regularity.
- Regality courts exercised judicial powers devolved from the Crown to try serious crimes. They were effectively independent jurisdictions with powers equivalent to the circuit courts. These courts were presided over by local landowners and not staffed by trained judges.

The Scottish legal system was not dissimilar to that of England. It was based more on the common law than on Roman law and had a jury system. But there were differences from the English system – differences that impacted on the prosecution of witches.

- The Regality courts, which did not exist in England, had far higher conviction and execution rates than those of the Court of Judiciary or the circuit courts.

- The Scottish Privy Council routinely performed legal functions, intervening at every level of the judicial structure, as is evident in the North Berwick cases (see pages 125–9).
- Officially, torture was only legal in Scotland if authorised by the Privy Council or Parliament. In witchcraft cases, only two Privy Council warrants for torture were issued: one in 1591 and the other in 1610. But there is abundant evidence that torture was used – illegally – in the pre-trial investigation of witches to obtain confessions. At local level it might include beating, sleep deprivation and pricking for the Devil's mark. Pricking involved sticking a pin into several places of the body until a place was found which was insensible to pain. This was supposedly where the Devil had sealed the pact with the witch by inflicting a wound which, when healed, would not register pain. Pricking could turn into a form of torture in which suspects were repeatedly stabbed until they confessed.

The socio-economic context

Scotland in the early modern period was largely a rural society, with only a fifth of its population living in small and scattered towns. Edinburgh was the largest town, with some 18,000 people in 1600. Most people outside the towns were engaged in **subsistence farming**, many living their lives on the verge of poverty, vulnerable to the effects of a poor harvest. There is some evidence that in the late sixteenth century there was a succession of harvest failures and resultant famine. According to historian Brian Levack (2007), this led to 'a general sense of anxiety'.

Witchcraft cases 1563–90

There seems to have been no major increase in witchcraft cases following the 1563 Witchcraft Act. Incomplete records suggest that there were about 60 cases in the 1560s, six in the 1570s and fourteen in the 1580s. The General Assembly's attitude to those who consulted witches – a capital offence – was often lenient. It was regarded as a moral failing but not necessarily a sign of a pact with the Devil. Its prescription was public repentance.

Before 1590, suspected witches were invariably accused of *maleficium*, not with making pacts with the Devil or meeting at sabbats. Historian Christina Larner (1981) claims that the differences between the witchcraft trials before 1590 and the North Berwick witch-hunt are 'clear cut'.

The impact of King James VI

James VI had been proclaimed king of Scotland at the age of one in 1567. He had a lonely and often dangerous childhood, narrowly escaping several assassination attempts. The problems of James's childhood may account for his fearful and

KEY TERM

Subsistence farming
Farming in which land will yield just enough to support the farmer and his family, leaving little or nothing to be sold.

suspicious nature. Trained by Protestant scholars, he grew up with a strong aversion to Catholicism. Because the latter was closely entwined with sorcery in the eyes of many Calvinist Scots, it was perhaps understandable that he developed a deep-seated suspicion of witchcraft.

James's position in Scotland in the late 1580s and early 1590s was far from secure. In 1589, the Catholic Earl of Huntly led a rebellion. He was supported by Francis Stewart, Earl of Bothwell, who hated James's chancellor, Sir John Maitland. James quashed the rebellion and briefly imprisoned Huntly and Bothwell. Both men were released in September 1589.

James's marriage to Anne of Denmark

By 1589, James was under some pressure to marry and produce an heir. The fact that he had not married earlier had damaged his reputation (as had the fact that he had a number of male 'favourites'). His eventual choice was Princess Anne of Denmark. The Danish fleet bringing Anne to Scotland left Denmark in September 1589 but gales forced the fleet to seek shelter in Norway, then under Danish rule. James now decided to sail to Norway. His fleet reached Oslo in mid-November. On 23 November, James and Anne married. The royal party then travelled to Denmark.

James remained in Denmark for six months. While he was there he met the theologian Niels Hemmingsen, author of a book on witchcraft. It was once thought that this meeting introduced James to continental demonological ideas. However, recent research suggests that the two men did not talk about demonology. Moreover, Hemmingsen's notion of witchcraft was less 'continental' than once supposed: for example, he denied the reality of the sabbat. It remains unclear what James might have learned about witchcraft from Denmark. Danish authorities were not preoccupied with witchcraft. Moreover, most Danes were concerned with *maleficium*, not pacts with the Devil. It is thus unlikely that James's stay in Denmark helped to sow the seeds of his own witch-hunting fervour or brought him, for the first time, into contact with continental theories. Indeed, it is likely that he was already familiar with such ideas.

James and Anne sailed to Scotland in April. The royal fleet was battered by storms and one ship was lost. However, the royal couple arrived safely at Leith in May.

In May 1590, a Danish witch confessed that she had used sorcery to hinder Anne's crossing to Scotland in 1589 and accused several others of involvement. All were executed. News of the first Danish witch's execution did not reach Scotland until July 1590. When the Danish court made a reciprocal visit to Scotland in the summer of 1590, it is likely that witchcraft was a topic of conversation.

The situation in Scotland in 1590

There is no indication from James's actions in the months after his return to Scotland that he had been profoundly affected by continental theories of witchcraft while in Denmark. Papists, Jesuits, pirates and quarrelsome lords took up much of his attention. His relationship with Bothwell between May and November 1590 is significant. In May, they were friendly. Then Bothwell left the court. In June, he returned, quarrelled and departed again. In July, he was involved in intrigue against Maitland but later the two seem to have been reconciled. In September, Bothwell was appointed Lord Lieutenant of the Borders.

Gilly Duncan

In November 1590, a young maid servant, Gilly (or Geillis) Duncan from Tranent, near Edinburgh (see Figure 5.1), was arrested for suspected witchcraft. David Seaton, a deputy bailiff, for whom she worked, was suspicious of the fact that she was frequently absent overnight from his house. Duncan, who had a reputation as a local healer, was interrogated. After protracted torture, using the 'pilliwinks' (a device similar to thumbscrews), and after the discovery of a 'Devil's mark' on her neck, she confessed to having sold her soul to the Devil. Under further torture, she claimed to be one of over 200 witches who had gathered in the Auld Kirk at North Berwick on All Hallows Eve (Halloween) in 1590. She named some 70 accomplices, including Dr John Fian, a local schoolmaster, Agnes Sampson, a midwife and healer, Barbara Napier, wife of Earl Archebald of Angus, and Euphane MacCalzean, daughter of Lord

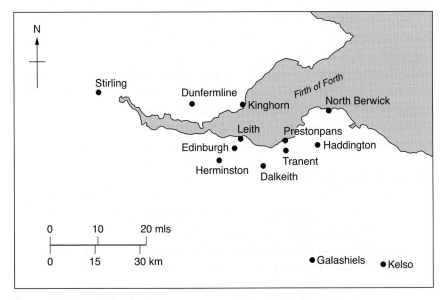

Figure 5.1 Central Scotland.

Cliftonhall. Two other names also surfaced as particularly significant, those of Richard Graham and the Earl of Bothwell. Duncan claimed that both men had plotted James's death and tried to raise storms at sea to sink his ship returning from Denmark. They had later made attempts to kill the king by means of witchcraft and poison.

The East Lothian trials, autumn 1590

The North Berwick trials seem to have emerged from a local witch-hunt in East Lothian. At least three accused witches were executed before James and the Privy Council became involved. Accordingly, James was not responsible for starting the 1590–1 witch-hunt. But his interest was certainly influenced by:

- stories of scores of witches gathering together to plot his death
- the allegations against Bothwell.

In late November, James ordered the main suspects – Sampson, Fian, Napier, MacCalzean and Duncan – to be brought to Edinburgh to be questioned before members of the Privy Council. According to *Newes from Scotland*, printed in 1591 (see page 132) James also 'took great delight to be present at their examinations'. Witchcraft had become entangled with treason, which increasingly became the central issue. By late 1590, James was convinced that Scottish witches were plotting to kill him.

Agnes Sampson

The Kirk, not the state, had first taken action against Agnes Sampson. She had a long-established career as a healer, fortune-teller and midwife. In May 1590, she had been investigated by the synod of Haddington on an accusation of witchcraft. Sampson was among the first to be examined by James and his Privy Council at Holyroodhouse in Edinburgh in November 1590. She faced 53 witchcraft charges including making a wax image of the king to destroy him and also conspiring to raise the storm that sank a ship returning from Denmark to Scotland. At one stage, Sampson apparently took James to one side and shocked him when she told him the intimate words he had exchanged with Anne on their wedding night. Sampson finally confessed to the indictments against her, including meetings with the Devil.

Torture and execution

Sampson's confessions were extracted by torture. Dr Fian was tortured even more extensively (see Source A, page 127). Crippled and blooded, he eventually signed a confession. The torture applied to Sampson, Fian and other accused witches in 1590–1 was not covered by a warrant; it presumably took place simply by order of the king.

SOURCE A

From *Newes from Scotland*, published in 1591. Quoted in L. Normand and G. Roberts, *Witchcraft in Early Modern Scotland*, University of Exeter Press, 2000, p. 322.

Whereupon the King's Majesty, perceiving [Dr Fian's] stubborn wilfulness, conceived and imagined that in the time of his absence he had entered into new conference and league with the devil his master … yet for more trial of him to make him confess, he was commanded to have a most strange torment which was done in this manner following. His nails upon all his fingers were riven and pulled off with … a pair of pincers, and under every nail there was thrust in two needles even up to their heads. At all which torments notwithstanding the doctor never shrunk any whit, neither would he then confess it the sooner for all the tortures inflicted upon him. Then was he with all convenient speed, by commandment, conveyed again to the torment of the boots, wherein he continued a long time and did abide so many blows in them that his legs were crushed and beaten together as small as might be, and the bones and flesh so bruised that the blood and marrow spouted forth in great abundance, whereby they were made unserviceable for ever. And notwithstanding all these grievous pains and cruel torments he would not confess anything; so deeply had the devil entered into his heart, that he utterly denied all that which he had before avouched.

Why might Source A have described the tortures in so much detail?

Having confessed to a variety of crimes, Sampson and Fian were tried. Sampson was found guilty on 27 January 1591 and executed the next day. Dr Fian, convicted on 26 December, was not executed until late January. Facing execution, he denied everything to which he had confessed.

The trials of MacCalzean and Napier

Euphane MacCalzean was a wealthy, married lady – an atypical witch. Some suspect she was Catholic and a supporter of Bothwell but there is no evidence for either view. She was charged with treasonable witchcraft against James and with attending four witches' sabbats. Found guilty on 15 June 1591, she had to wait until 25 June for execution. Witches were usually strangled and then burned. The sentence against MacCalzean stated specifically that she should be burned alive.

In 1591, James showed particular interest in the trial of Barbara Napier, wife of Archibald Douglas, brother of the Lord of Carschogill. In May, she was convicted on charges of consulting with witches to harm the king, but acquitted of attending the convention of witches on All Hallows Eve 1590. The court's verdict was then overridden by James. He ordered the jury members to be charged with wilful error for arriving at a verdict which flew in the face of the evidence. On 7 June, he forgave the jurors but declared that witches were odious to the laws of God and man, and it was his special duty as king to pursue them. Napier escaped immediate execution because she claimed to be pregnant. But she was probably executed later in 1591.

Conclusion

Dozens of suspected witches confessed to having met with the Devil in North Berwick churchyard in 1590 and devoting themselves to doing evil, including attempts to sink the king's ships. However, the exact number of witches executed in 1590–1 is unclear: few of the records have survived. It is known that eight witches were burned in Haddington, one in Dalkeith and one in Dumfries in February 1591. Gilly Duncan, whose confession seems to have initiated the trials, was finally executed in December 1591. She declared moments before she was executed that everything she had said about Napier and MacCalzean had been lies.

The cases of Fian, Sampson, Napier and MacCalzean followed procedures that were unprecedented and never repeated. The involvement of the king and council, and the use of torture, meant that the system was akin to the inquisitorial system. James seems to have been particularly concerned about the activities of MacCalzean and Napier, who were not typical witches and who seem to have had some connection with Bothwell. James may well have believed that they were involved in a high-level plot to kill him. This would explain MacCalzean being burned alive and James's determination to ensure that Napier was found guilty.

Bothwell's role

The complexity of the North Berwick situation is increased by the fact that a politically motivated accusation was brought against Francis Stewart, Earl of Bothwell. Bothwell, James's first cousin, was not averse to using violence. In 1584, he had killed three members of the Hume family with whom he was at odds. His dislike of the chancellor, John Maitland, intensified the factionalism at court. Although Bothwell had led a rebellion in 1589, James had trusted him sufficiently to appoint him second in command of the government while he was in Denmark in 1589–90.

Bothwell was accused by Duncan of plotting against James's person and ordering witches to use magic against the king. Richard Graham, a student of magic, was similarly accused. Under examination, Graham stated that Bothwell had urged him to devise James's end. Bothwell was called to answer the accusations before the Privy Council on 15 April 1591. He denied the charges but was imprisoned in Edinburgh Castle.

It seems possible that some kind of arrangement had been made between Graham and a person or persons unknown to say what he did. Bothwell blamed his enemy, Chancellor Maitland. It is possible that Maitland exploited the accusations in order to ruin Bothwell. It is even possible that the 1590–1 witch-hunt was essentially a plot by Maitland and other lords to destroy Bothwell's power to their own advantage. Charges of witchcraft against political enemies had long been familiar in Scottish politics.

James seems to have been in two minds about Bothwell's implication. Having listened to what Graham had to say, he kept him imprisoned while the Privy Council pursued its investigations into Bothwell's treasonable activities. Bothwell's trial, set for 6 May, was postponed because the evidence against him was thin. On 19 June, arrangements were made to release Bothwell and grant him liberty on condition that he went into exile. Two days later, Bothwell escaped from Edinburgh Castle and fled south. On 25 June, he was denounced by the Privy Council for giving himself 'over altogether in the hands of Satan'. According to the council's proclamation, he had used witchcraft for deadly political ends.

But Bothwell had influential defenders who recognised the witchcraft charges against him for what they were: the product of factional politics. He was thus given protection and became a focus of opposition to the king's policies. At the same time, he tried – unsuccessfully – to rebuild relations with James. In December 1591, Bothwell broke into Holyroodhouse and attempted to seize James and kill Maitland. He failed on both scores. Bothwell and witchcraft were kept to the fore by the execution of Richard Graham in February 1592. At his death, Graham maintained he had spoken the truth about Bothwell. But it may be that fear of torture or a slow death determined what he said.

Bothwell continued to pose a danger to James. In July 1593, he staged a successful coup and effectively took control of the government. Shrinking from regicide, he set about trying to clear his name. In August 1593, he was acquitted of the charges of witchcraft. At the trial, 'diverse honest men of Edinburgh … deposed that Richie Graham said to them that he must either accuse the Earl Bothwell falsely, or else endure such torments as no man were able to adide'. But James eventually came out on top in the power struggle. In 1595, Bothwell was exiled, his lands granted to his enemies. He died in Italy in 1612.

Conclusion

Witchcraft beliefs permeated every social and cultural level of late sixteenth-century Scotland. According to Levack, witch-hunts prompted from above tended to be driven by ideological and religious factors. Those started from below tended to be more the result of social and economic factors. The events suggest a movement from local – East Lothian – accusations towards accusations at the centre by the Crown and its agents. The North Berwick witch-hunt offers a striking example of James's ideas being influenced by interviews with witchcraft suspects. The suspects' confessions were directed into accounts of conspiracy and treason that suited the Scottish government's power politics.

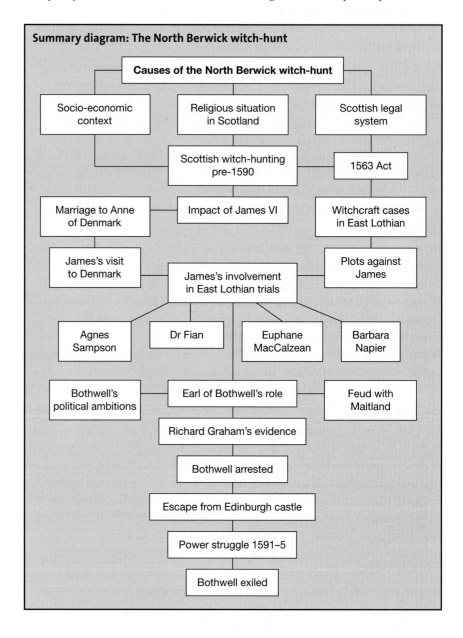

Summary diagram: The North Berwick witch-hunt

Causes of the North Berwick witch-hunt

- Socio-economic context
- Religious situation in Scotland
- Scottish legal system

Scottish witch-hunting pre-1590 — 1563 Act

Marriage to Anne of Denmark — Impact of James VI — Witchcraft cases in East Lothian

James's visit to Denmark — James's involvement in East Lothian trials — Plots against James

Agnes Sampson · Dr Fian · Euphane MacCalzean · Barbara Napier

Bothwell's political ambitions — Earl of Bothwell's role — Feud with Maitland

Richard Graham's evidence

Bothwell arrested

Escape from Edinburgh castle

Power struggle 1591–5

Bothwell exiled

2 Witch-hunting in Scotland 1591–1670

▶ *Why was witch-hunting so severe in Scotland in the 1590s?*

The high-profile witch-hunts in 1590–1 reinforced existing anti-witch sentiments and resulted in a wave of trials which continued until 1597. Serious witch-hunts also broke out in the seventeenth century.

Witchcraft persecution 1591–7

The North Berwick trials seem to have made a deep impression on James. Convinced that the Devil hated him, he determined to do battle with the Devil and his supporters. He thus set about convincing his subjects of the evil in their midst:

- He commissioned *Newes from Scotland,* a pamphlet informing Scots of the events of 1590–1. This was designed to whip up popular fear of witches.
- In 1591, James declared that evidence from witnesses usually assumed to be unfit to provide reliable evidence, namely women and partners in crime, could be accepted in heresy, witchcraft and treason cases.
- He set up a commission to hunt out witches.

SOURCE B

Look at Source B. What seems to be going on in the woodcut illustration? **?**

A woodcut from *Newes from Scotland,* 1591.

> ### *Newes from Scotland*
>
> Published in late 1591, *Newes from Scotland* was the first work printed about Scottish witchcraft. More sensational and violent than sixteenth-century English pamphlets, it was essentially government propaganda, the authorities' attempt to define and interpret to their advantage the disparate events of the 1590–1 witch-hunt. Its writer or writers are unknown but many think James Carmichael, the minister of Haddington, may have been involved. Interestingly, no mention of Bothwell is made in the *Newes*.

The 1591 commission

In October 1591, the Privy Council established a special commission to inquire into witchcraft cases, using torture if necessary. Historians are divided over the commission's significance. Christina Larner (1981) viewed it as the most decisive instrument in the maintenance of prosecutions and 'the licence for an indiscriminate witch-hunt'. She regards the commission as evidence of the government's wish to maintain anxiety about witchcraft and control of the direction of prosecutions. Levack thinks differently. He claims 'it would be misleading to see the government as the inspiration of the large rash of witchcraft trials that took place between 1591 and 1597'. He argues that:

- the Privy Council action came about in response to requests to prosecute from particular areas
- the commission was limited in extent: it gave power to only six commissioners.

Given that all evidence of its deliberations has disappeared, the commission's effect on witch-hunting is hard to determine. Evidence from the Judiciary Court suggests that the commission may have been used to wind down the trials in and around Edinburgh. Moreover, if the central authorities were indeed trying to control prosecutions, in 1592 that central control was lost.

The Kirk–state commission 1592

In June 1592, the Privy Council set up a joint body consisting of commissioners from the Kirk and government to tour the country and address a number of social and religious issues – including witchcraft. With the Church in the ascendant in 1592 and the king weak, this measure was passed in response to Kirk pressure. The Act undoubtedly promoted witch-hunting as it sent commissioners round Scotland with the authority to empower local leaders to investigate witchcraft. It was this commission, not that of 1591, that was the licence for an indiscriminate witch-hunt.

The national witch-hunt 1592–7

A nationwide witch-hunt took place between 1592 and 1597. In this period, the Crown and the Presbyterian party in the Kirk found common cause in suppressing witchcraft. Kirk leaders were a major driving force behind the witch-hunt. In the view of historian Robin Briggs (1996), 'without the intellectual underpinning the Kirk provided there might well have been no witch-hunt of any significance in Scotland' in this period.

Scots were encouraged to inform on those whom they believed to be witches. Inside every church was a box into which anyone could post the name of a person they suspected, together with a few details of their crime. The system tempted people to make accusations not just against suspected witches but against their enemies. Not surprisingly, hundreds of people were accused and tried as witches and many executed on the flimsiest of evidence. The result was a climate of fear and suspicion.

In many respects, the 'long' witch-hunt from 1592 to 1597 was a composite of a number of hunts which took place across Scotland. The Privy Council did not give proper consideration to the petitions for local trials. In local courts, those accused of witchcraft were unlikely to be acquitted since the local community had already judged them guilty.

Between 1591 and 1597, King James wrote an 80-page book, *Daemonologie*, about the menace that witches posed to society. The book, printed in 1597, showed that James was acquainted with continental theories of witchcraft.

SOURCE C

From a passage of King James's *Daemonologie*. Quoted in L. Normand and G. Roberts, *Witchcraft in Early Modern Scotland*, University of Exeter Press, 2000, pp. 353–4.

The fearful abounding at this time in this country of these detestable slaves of the devil, the witches or enchanters, has moved me (beloved reader) to dispatch in post [to write quickly] this following treatise of mine. Not in any wise, as I protest, to serve for a show of my learning, but only, moved of conscience, to press thereby so far as I can to resolve the doubting hearts of many, both that such assaults of Satan are most certainly practised, and that the instruments thereof merit most severely to be punished – against the damnable opinions of two principally in our own age, whereof the one, called [Reginald] Scot, an Englishman, is not ashamed in public print to deny that there can be such a thing as witchcraft … The other called [Johann] Weyer, a German physician, sets out in public apology for all these craftsfolk, whereby, procuring for their impunity, he plainly betrays himself to have been one of that profession.

According to Source C, why did James write *Daemonologie*?

The 1597 witch-hunt

The climax to the witch-hunts came between March and October 1597. At least 400 people were tried and probably 200 executed. The first recorded case in March 1597 came from north of Aberdeen. This was followed by a large witch trial in Aberdeen against Janet Wishart and her accomplices. Wishart was alleged to have raised storms and used 'nightmare cats' to inflict horrible dreams. She was burned. Witch-hunts occurred thereafter in Fife, Perthshire, Glasgow and Stirlingshire.

The best known case was that of Margaret Aitken. Arrested in Fife in April 1597, she pleaded guilty under torture. She offered to help the commission to identify witches elsewhere in Scotland in exchange for her life. For four months the Aitken commission toured Scotland. Many people were arrested, tried and executed after having been picked out by Aitken. Eventually she was discredited after having identified some people as witches whom she had previously cleared.

The Privy Council order 1597

The Aitken scandal may have prompted James to change policy. In August 1597, the Privy Council recalled all the commissions of justiciary it had granted to local authorities. Thereafter, the Privy Council:

- considered each request for a commission to hold a witchcraft trial
- issued commissions only to groups of three or four men to prevent individuals acting prejudicially.

The withdrawal of the standing commissions put a stop to the witch-hunting that had been raging across Scotland. According to Larner, witchcraft now became 'a centrally managed crime'. Her view may attribute more power to the government than it actually had. Its control over large parts of Scotland was limited. Moreover, it was still responsive to pressure from the Kirk and many Calvinists were still determined to extirpate witchcraft. Nor did Scotland have a sufficiently large central judicial establishment to ensure that all witchcraft cases could be heard in either the Court of Judiciary or the circuit courts. Thus, the Privy Council still granted commissions of judiciary to local magistrates, who were often determined to execute witches.

Witch-hunting in the seventeenth century

Witchcraft beliefs remained strong in Scotland throughout much of the seventeenth century. Although there were no major witch-hunts, there were still some twenty witch trials a year between 1603 and 1625 involving some 450 people. Half the accused were probably executed.

The 1649–50 witch-hunt

There was another great witch-hunt in 1649–50. The hunt followed a poor harvest in 1649. There was also political and religious turmoil resulting from the defeat of the Scottish Army in the Second English Civil War and the rise to power of the radical Kirk Party, which attempted to create a 'godly society', rooting out witches and other offenders. A new Witch Act (1649) encouraged local presbyteries to seek out witches. The intense period of hunting continued into 1650. Some 600 people were accused of witchcraft and over 300 were executed. Most of these were tried in temporary courts.

The Kirk Party's rule ended when Oliver Cromwell marched into Scotland, eventually winning a decisive victory at Dunbar in September 1650. The new Scottish government supervised witch trials more closely and there was a huge reduction in the number of trials.

The witch-hunt of 1661–2

At least 660 people were tried in another major witch-hunt in 1661–2. The number executed is unknown but probably amounted to several hundred. These prosecutions were not completely divorced from each other.

- The Privy Council or Parliament approved all of the trials.
- Many cases were heard before the same judges.
- The same men were often hired to search for the Devil's marks.

But for the most part, the hunts were discrete operations, separate manifestations of a national panic regarding witchcraft. They ended when the Privy Council again limited commissions of judiciary and cracked down on torture. Two witch-hunters were prosecuted by the council for fraud in their work of pricking witches.

Conclusion

Historians once thought some 4000 witches in Scotland were executed. More likely the figure was around 1500. Even accepting the lower figure, three Scottish witches were executed for every one in England, and England (with 5 million people) had a population five times greater than Scotland. Scotland is an example of a relatively weak government, with a small judicial establishment, having difficulty guaranteeing due legal process. It is also an example of a state where witch-hunts were strongly supported by the Church.

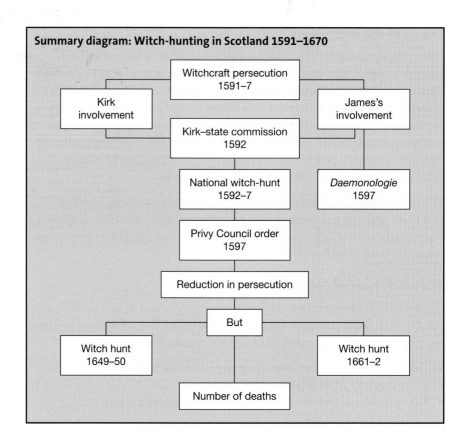

Summary diagram: Witch-hunting in Scotland 1591–1670

- Witchcraft persecution 1591–7
- Kirk involvement
- James's involvement
- Kirk–state commission 1592
- National witch-hunt 1592–7
- *Daemonologie* 1597
- Privy Council order 1597
- Reduction in persecution
- But
- Witch hunt 1649–50
- Witch hunt 1661–2
- Number of deaths

3 The Salem witch trials

▶ *What caused the Salem witch trials?*

There were 234 New Englanders indicted for witchcraft between 1647 and 1693 and there were 36 executions. Given that the population of New England by the 1690s was only about 100,000, the scale of witch-hunting was intensive – at least by English standards. One large witch-hunt in and around Salem in Massachusetts in 1692–3 claimed more than half the victims. (Less than a third of those accused actually came from Salem Village – now the town of Danvers – or Salem Town.) Given that the records are particularly good, the Salem witch trials are among the best researched episodes in witchcraft's history.

Background to the Salem witch-hunt

English colonists settled in North America in the course of the seventeenth century. They took their religion and witchcraft beliefs with them.

The religious situation in Massachusetts

Witch-hunting in America mainly occurred in the Puritan New England colonies (see Figure 5.2). In the colonies further south, predominantly Anglican, only one woman was executed for witchcraft. The New England colonies, at least in inception, were theocratic institutions, led by fervent Puritans. The urge to create a godly state that was evident in Scotland thus developed in New England.

Witch-hunting pre-1692

A witchcraft law was introduced in Massachusetts in 1641. It simply stated: 'If any man or woman be a witch (that is hath consulted with a familiar spirit) they shall be put to death'. Alse Young of Windsor, Connecticut, was the first witch to be executed in North America in 1647. Prior to the Salem witch-hunt, some 80 people had been accused of practising witchcraft: fifteen women and two men had been executed. Most of the cases were rooted in long-term suspicions against the accused – mainly women on the fringes of society. Most of the charges were for *maleficia*. JPs were often reluctant to hunt for witches or to credit popular mistrust of unpleasant neighbours. Influenced by judicial

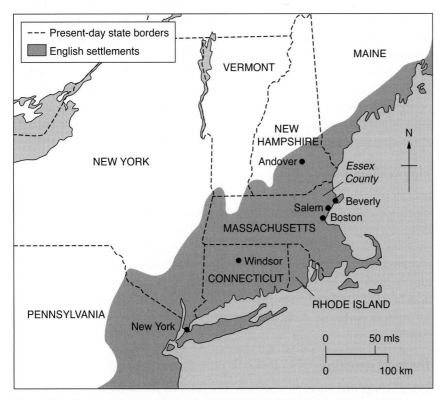

Figure 5.2 English colonies in the Massachusetts area of North America by the late seventeenth century.

scepticism in England (see page 173), they demanded proofs, not presumptions. Accordingly, accused witches were usually acquitted. Nevertheless, many people in Puritan Massachusetts believed that Satan and his agents were present and active on earth.

The 1688–9 Boston case

In 1688, four of John Goodwin's children began to behave strangely. They cried out as sudden pains seemed to pass through their bodies, flapping their arms like birds. Cotton Mather, a Boston minister, examined the children and concluded they had been bewitched. Mary Glover, an old washerwoman, was found guilty and executed. Cotton Mather described the Goodwin case in his book *Memorable Providences Relating to Witchcraft and Possessions* (1689).

The political situation in Massachusetts

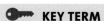

KEY TERM

Theocracy A state in which God is regarded as the sole sovereign and the laws of the realm are seen as divine commands. The clergy thus become the main officers of the state.

In 1684, the royal charter by which Massachusetts had been governed ran out. The old charter had allowed the colonists considerable freedom, enabling the Puritan Church to establish something of a **theocracy**. An unpopular Dominion of New England now replaced the charter government. In 1689, Sir Edward Andros, governor of the Dominion, was ousted following the Glorious Revolution in England when the Catholic king, James II, was replaced with the Protestant co-rulers William and Mary. Simon Bradstreet and Thomas Danforth resumed their posts as governor and deputy governor. However, they lacked constitutional authority to rule until a new charter was introduced. No one could predict exactly what this would say. But Puritans feared that the colony would lose its autonomy and that God's commonwealth in Massachusetts would be overthrown. Their fears came to pass. A new charter, approved in England in October 1691, stated that Massachusetts should conform to English law and allow religious toleration.

King William's War

In 1689, tensions erupted between English colonists in Maine and French-supported Wabanaki Native Americans in what became known as King William's War. News of hostilities awakened memories of King Philip's War (1675–6). While this war had ended in victory, many men had died in the fighting and hundreds of women and children had been slaughtered or taken captive. Over the winter of 1691–2, a stream of refugees fleeing Native American raids brought reports of massacres and predictions of savagery to come. Children, in particular, may have been worried by what they heard from their parents.

The local situation

Salem Village had some 600 residents. The place was known for its many internal disputes, mainly about property, grazing rights and Church privileges. There was also a bitter feud between the two most prosperous families, the

Putnams and Porters. The Putnams wanted to sever the Village from Salem Town, establishing institutions of local government and worship. The Porters, by contrast, favoured closer ties to the Town. The Putnams' supporters, who came mainly from the western side of the Village, are often depicted as mainly engaged in subsistence farming. The Porters' supporters, by contrast, are usually depicted as being more entrepreneurial and commercial in outlook. Recent research has suggested that the economic division between the two sides was by no means as clear-cut as was once thought. Nevertheless, families in Salem Village generally committed themselves to one side or the other. Disputes over lands often became tests of 'clan' loyalty.

The Church ministry in Salem inevitably became a focal point of tension. The Putnams, anxious for the Village to have its own congregation, appointed George Burroughs as minister in 1681: he lasted until 1682. Deodat Lawson replaced Burroughs but his appointment soon divided the community. In 1689, Samuel Parris became the Village minister. Parris, a quarrelsome man who had the support of the Putnam family, increased the divisions, preaching against those who opposed him. The anti-Parris faction retaliated in October 1691 when the Putnam-dominated rate committee was ousted and a Porter-dominated group took over. By January 1692, Parris was worried, particularly as the rate committee controlled his salary.

Initial events, February to May 1692

In Salem Village in February 1692, Betty Parris, aged nine, daughter of Reverend Parris, began to behave oddly, lashing out and diving under furniture. Her cousin, eleven-year-old Abigail Williams, followed suit. Both girls complained of being pinched and pricked with pins. Their behaviour was similar to that of the Goodwin children in Boston three years earlier. William Griggs, the local doctor, decided that the girls' illness was not natural but instead the work of the Devil. Reverend Parris was not immediately convinced. He continued to pray for their recovery. Other ministers prayed with him: John Hale from nearby Beverly and Deodat Lawson, Parris's predecessor. Prayer failed. The girls' fits grew worse. Ominously, other girls who visited Betty and Abigail soon appeared afflicted with their ailments. These girls included:

- eleven-year-old Ann Putnam Jr, whose father was Sergeant Thomas Putnam
- Mercy Lewis, aged nineteen, a servant in Thomas Putnam's household
- Mary Walcott, aged eighteen, a niece of the Putnams
- Elizabeth Hubbard, aged seventeen, Dr Griggs' niece.

The girls screamed, threw things around the room, and contorted themselves into peculiar positions. Their behaviour, John Hale declared, was 'beyond the power of epileptic fits or natural disease to effect'. He too was convinced that the fits were symptoms of possession.

The cause of the symptoms

There have been various medical and psychological explanations for the girls' symptoms. These include:

- Psychological hysteria in response to fear of Native American attack, Satan and a recent smallpox epidemic.
- Possession neuroses, resulting from a belief in the existence of demons and witches.
- Convulsive ergotism, caused by eating rye bread made from grain infected by ergot, a fungus from which the drug **LSD** is derived: this can cause delusions, muscle spasms and vomiting.
- Asthma attacks.

Modern historians are less inclined to believe in biological explanations. The case for hallucinations, caused by ergot poisoning, for example, has now been refuted by scientists who have pointed out that the girls invariably had their fits 'to order' at the same time – a most improbable occurrence if they were indeed suffering from ergotism. Moreover, no one died, which would have been likely if they had indeed been poisoned by the ergot fungus. Historians today prefer to explore motivations such as jealousy, spite and a need for attention to explain behaviour that they insist was simply acting, the other girls and young women copying Betty and Abigail's symptoms. It may be that Betty and Abigail were copying the behaviour of the Goodwin children (see page 138), of which they were aware.

Witch cake

At some point in February 1692, Mary Sibley, a neighbour of Parris, instructed John, one of the minister's Native American slaves, to make a witch cake, using traditional English magic to discover the identity of the witch who was afflicting the girls. The cake, made from rye meal and urine from the afflicted girls, was to be fed to a dog. According to folklore, when the dog ate the cake the witch herself would be hurt and identified by her cries of pain. Tituba, John's wife or partner, made the cake. Historians continue to debate whether Tituba was of African or Native American descent – or both. Like Sibley, Tituba assumed that the best remedy to *maleficium* was counter-magic. Parris later criticised Sibley for her actions, admonishing her for 'going to the Devil for help against the Devil'.

Accusations

Sometime between 25 February (when Tituba fed the witch cake to an unsuspecting dog) and 29 February (when the first arrest warrant was issued), Betty, Abigail, Ann Putnam and Mercy Lewis named their afflicters, claiming that they had seen the apparitions of three people responsible for causing their distress. They named Sarah Good, Sarah Osborne and Tituba. Each of the women satisfied many of the traits typical of the 'usual suspects' for witchcraft accusations:

KEY TERM

LSD Lysergic acid diethylamide: a drug that causes hallucinations and psychedelic episodes.

- Tituba, a slave, was visibly, socially and legally an outsider. The girls may have named her because she had already become the focus of suspicion.
- Good was a disreputable beggar who had long been suspected of practising witchcraft.
- Osborne was old and rarely attended church meetings.

The local eminence of Ann Putnam's family gave urgency to the proceedings:

- Sergeant Thomas Putnam, his brother Edward and his brother-in-law Joseph Hutchinson pressed local JPs for action.
- When the interrogations began, the Putnam family sat by the girls and threw their weight behind the prosecutions.
- Many of the other accusers were connected to the Putnams.

Some historians have seen the accusations as part of the Putnam–Porter quarrel. It may be that later accusations, principally those levelled against Rebecca Nurse and her sisters, would take this form. But the first denunciations, and most of the later ones, do not suggest that the witchcraft charges resulted from local feud.

Investigation

Once the Putnams brought their suspicions to Essex County JPs Jonathan Corwin and John Hathorne, the two men issued warrants for the three women named by the girls and arranged for an inquest. The JPs, both veteran politicians, were not Village men but they knew Salem and its people. The first hearings, which began on 1 March, were essentially gatherings of neighbours. The examinations of Tituba, Good and Osborne began in a tavern but so many came to see the hearings that they were moved to the meeting house. Here the two JPs confronted for the first time the girls' convulsions. Apparently bitten and pinched by invisible agents, they twisted their arms and backs and contorted their faces. Sometimes they could not speak: at other times they could not stop speaking. Most of those who watched were convinced that the girls were afflicted.

Sarah Good, in defending herself, chose to accuse Sarah Osborne of afflicting the girls. This immediately gave credibility to the charges of witchcraft. Tituba initially denied any complicity. But when the JPs refused to believe her denials, she gave the JPs what they wanted. She admitted that she had been approached by a tall man from Boston with white hair who told her he was God. Sometimes he wore dark coats. At other times he appeared as a dog or hog. The JPs assumed he was the Devil. Tituba confirmed that Good and Osborn were both witches. She also asserted that many other people in Massachusetts were engaged in the 'Devil's conspiracy'. Possibly Tituba was so frightened by the proceedings that she allowed the JPs to prompt her. But it is also possible that she was manipulating the situation in her own interest. By confessing, she had some power. Her confessions exacerbated the fear that more witches lurked in the community.

Over several days witnesses were brought forward to give evidence of *maleficium* against the three women. Satisfied that the charges were well founded, the JPs had Tituba, Good and Osborne imprisoned while they awaited trial.

New charges

Tituba had told the JPs there were other witches and sure enough new witches appeared. On 11 March, Ann Putnam was afflicted by the spectral forms of Martha Corey and Rebecca Nurse, a claim supported by Abigail Williams. By voicing scepticism about the girls' accusations, Martha had drawn attention to herself, while Rebecca's family was engaged in a long-standing quarrel with the Putnams. The charges against the two women deeply troubled people because both were upstanding members of the community. If they could be witches, then anybody could be a witch. Both women challenged the investigation – to no effect. Both were imprisoned.

Meanwhile Ann Putnam's mother (also called Ann) claimed she too had been afflicted by Corey and Nurse. She later claimed she was visited by the ghosts of two people who told her they had been murdered by John Willard, a neighbour. Willard, she believed, was a witch who had also caused the death of her own four-month-old baby, Sarah.

When Deodat Lawson preached in the meeting house at Salem Village on 20 March, Betty Parris sat near the front with Abigail and Ann. At the meeting Abigail cried out: 'Look where Goodwife Cloyse sits on the beam suckling her yellow bird [her familiar] between her fingers.' Sarah Cloyse, Rebecca Nurse's sister, was examined by JPs at the end of March. The girls, who again appeared to suffer fits, accused Cloyse of being a witch. She too was imprisoned.

The girls continued their accusations, charging Mary Easty (another of Nurse's sisters), John and Elizabeth Proctor and Elizabeth Cary, all upright citizens. A few days later, Giles Corey (Martha's husband), Bridget Bishop and Mary Warren were arrested and examined. In April, Abigail and Deliverance Hobbs, Sarah Wildes and Elizabeth Howe were accused.

Most of the suspects tried to talk their way out of the accusation but few were practised at public speaking. Moreover, by now the girls had polished their performance. The examiners, notably Hathorne, prompted them into fits by asking them to identify the suspects, cuing the girls to act out their afflictions. The suspects were often asked to touch one of the girls while they were having a fit. If the fit stopped, it was assumed that the accused was guilty. The JPs were men of strong Puritan conviction. The more charges they heard, the more convinced they became that the Devil was indeed at work in the colony.

So dramatic were the events that on 11 April deputy governor Thomas Danforth and several of the colony's councillors visited Salem to witness the spectacle. They were not disappointed. The meeting house was packed. The girls duly performed, along with the Native American John who had started to have fits of his own. Danforth, unsure whether to believe the girls, left the matter unresolved and returned to Boston.

On 30 April, Reverend George Burroughs, Lydia Dustin, Susannah Martin, Dorcas Hoar and Sarah Morey were arrested. In May, the girls turned their attention to the township of Andover, accusing Martha Carrier of witchcraft. A month later, Ann Putnam and Mary Walcott went to Andover where, blindfolded, they were touched by a parade of men and women suspected of witchcraft. They named four as witches. When the girls had finished their task, Andover's citizens started accusing one another (see below).

In May, as the accusations increased, John Alden, a Boston sea captain, and Philip English, a prosperous merchant, fled, preferring to lose their property than their lives. Meanwhile, Sarah Osborne, one of the first three accused, died in gaol on 10 May.

The girls' evidence

The girls had become witch-finders. By May they had only to name someone to secure an arrest. Fully aware that witches could be put to death, they knew that false accusation was also punishable by death. If the girls began as mischievous innocents, they were now involved in serious business. Historians have speculated who led them. Given that Betty, Abigail and Ann Putnam were probably too young to lead the older girls, Mercy Lewis would seem to be the most likely leader. Of all the girls, she was the most imaginative and compelling in her accusations.

The girls were good listeners and adults around them inadvertently provided clues of people long suspected of deviant ways or unpopular beliefs. Among these were the **Quakers** of Essex County, long persecuted and in 1692 uneasily tolerated. George Burroughs, reputed to be a **Baptist**, was also vulnerable to witchcraft accusations.

Confessions

Confined to gaols, some of the suspects began to confess to being in league with the Devil. The first had been Tituba. The next was Abigail Hobbs, who admitted to seeing the Devil and confessed to pinching Putnam and Lewis at his command. Hobbs now became an informer, accusing others of being witches. When the JPs wanted confirmation that George Burroughs was the leader of the witches' coven, Hobbs obliged. She more than Tituba gave the magistrates what they wanted: evidence of a conspiracy of witches that threatened the colony. Mary Warren and Deliverance Hobbs also confessed. They told the examining JPs that there were over 300 witches in Massachusetts, that they flew to mass meetings and that the Devil led services for them. They were brought periodically from prison to accuse new suspects. More arrests followed, including Sarah Wildes, William Hobbs, Nehemiah Abbott, Edward and Sarah Bishop, and Mary English.

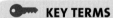 **KEY TERMS**

Quakers Members of the Religious Society of Friends, founded in England by George Fox in the 1640s. They rejected the ministry and sacraments of the established Church. Adopting a plain style of dress and way of life, they refused to take oaths and opposed the use of titles.

Baptists Protestant Christians who baptise, by immersion, only those old enough consciously to accept the Christian faith.

Interestingly, Tituba was cleared by a grand jury in May. The bill of indictment brought against her charged her with making a contract with the Devil (to which she confessed) but not with harming anyone. The rejection of the indictment suggests that the jury believed that Tituba herself had been afflicted by witches. It is not known when she was released or what happened to her thereafter.

The situation in May

By the end of May, 62 people were in custody. Most lived in Salem or nearby Andover but the witch-hunt was starting to spread to other townships, threatening to overwhelm the institutions of criminal justice.

On 14 May, a new governor of Massachusetts, William Phips, arrived from England with the power to do something about the crisis. Phips's main concern was defeating the Native Americans and French in Maine. On 27 May, he created a special Court of Oyer (to hear) and Terminer (to decide) deal with the Salem situation. William Stoughton, the chief judge of the court, was lieutenant governor of the colony. Phips feared that unless something was done quickly there would be more accusations and perhaps the spread of cases all over the colony. Having created the court, Phips went off to fight the Native Americans in the north.

Trials and executions

Between June and September 1692, many of the accused witches were tried by the Court of Oyer and Terminer which met five times, each time for a brief span of days. The judges called grand juries and submitted to them the evidence regarding all the people in custody. If indicted by the grand jury, the defendant went on trial. Trials were swift and were conducted in the English adversarial fashion (see pages 92–3). Stoughton and the other judges, including Hathorne and Samuel Sewall, were essentially partisans, adopting a semi-prosecutorial stance, questioning witnesses and pressuring jurors. The Crown, moreover, had prosecution lawyers while the defendants had to speak for themselves. Most did their best, cross-examining prosecution witnesses and bringing in witnesses who testified to their good character.

The source evidence

Although the pre-trial examinations and eyewitness accounts of the sessions of the court survive, along with bundles of depositions taken for use at trial, all records of the trials themselves have been lost. However, some records were made available to Cotton Mather, who wrote a defence of the trials: *Wonders of the Invisible World* (see below). Robert Calef wrote a counter-book, *More Wonders of the Invisible World*, five years later, with materials supplied him by opponents of the trials. Calef, like Mather, had not been present at the trials. Unlike Mather, he thought the proceeding a deadly farce, mixing superstition and the evil determination of the ministers to use the trials to cement their power over the colony.

Spectral and other evidence

Much, but by no means all, of the evidence used against the accused was spectral evidence: the testimony of the girls who claimed to see the apparition of the person who was allegedly afflicting them. (The girls and women sometimes claimed they could see the witch's familiar rather than the witch herself.) Opponents of the use of this evidence claimed that the Devil was able to impersonate innocent people. But others contended that the Devil could not use a person's shape without the person's permission. Therefore, when the afflicted claimed to see the apparition of a specific person, this should be accepted as evidence that the accused had been complicit with the Devil. Controversy over this issue ran through the proceedings. After accusations of spectral appearance had been made by the girls and others, other folk provided additional accusations of malefic acts against the suspects.

It was once thought that people were found guilty at Salem largely because of the charges of spectral appearance. However, historian Wendel Craker (1997) showed that it was the non-spectral charges which were crucial. The judges, advised by Cotton Mather (see below), seem to have followed the directions of the English Puritan William Perkins (see page 87) with regard to the rules governing evidence in witchcraft trials. By Perkins' formula, spectral evidence could be used to indict but not to convict. For this, either confession or evidence of non-spectral acts of witchcraft was required. The testimony concerning *maleficium* had to be by at least two people of good character. The court obeyed the ecclesiastical recommendations. Seventy-nine people were charged only with spectral appearance: half of the total accused. Not one of them was called by the court to answer charges. Without exception, the twenty persons put to death had been charged with *maleficium*.

The first trial

The court convened in Salem Town on 2 June with William Stoughton as chief magistrate. Bridget Bishop's case was the first brought to the grand jury which endorsed all the indictments against her. She went to trial the same day. Disliked and mistrusted in the community, she had faced charges of witchcraft ten years earlier and there were plenty of people prepared to give evidence against her. The girls, writhing as usual, also testified that her spectre afflicted them. Found guilty, Bishop was executed on 10 June.

On 3 June, the grand jury endorsed indictments against Rebecca Nurse and John Willard. But they did not immediately go to trial. Instead, the court adjourned until 30 June, allowing time to reflect on what had occurred. Not all were impressed by what they had witnessed. Appalled by the conduct of the trial, Major Nathaniel Saltonstall resigned from the bench. Some of the ministers present, including John Hale and Samuel Willard, a Boston minister, condemned the girls' writhing and the reappearance of medieval forms of 'proof' like the touching test. Given the unease, the court sought the advice of Massachusetts'

Cotton Mather

1666   Born in Massachusetts, the son of Maria and Increase Mather. Increase was a noted preacher and president of Harvard College

1678–81   Attended Harvard College

1688–9   Involved in the case of the Goodwin children in Boston (see page 138)

1689   Published *Memorable Providences Relating to Witchcraft and Possessions*

1692   Played an influential role in the Salem witch trials

1693   Published *Wonders of the Invisible World*, defending the Salem trials and the use of spectral evidence

1722   Published *The Christian Philosopher*, the first systematic book on science published in America

1728   Died

Cotton Mather was one of the most influential Puritan religious leaders in Massachusetts in the late seventeenth and early eighteenth centuries, writing more than 450 books and pamphlets. As well as greatly influencing the moral tone of America, he was also a force to be reckoned with in secular matters. In 1688–9, he was among the leaders who succeeded in overthrowing the unpopular Dominion of New England government in Massachusetts (see page 138).

Mather's role in the Salem witch trials remains controversial. In *More Wonders of the Invisible World* (see page 144), Robert Calef bitterly criticised Cotton Mather for his role in supporting the trials and for accepting the validity of spectral evidence. However, Mather has his defenders. They point out that in 1692 his advice about whether spectral evidence should be considered was cautious. While supporting the prosecution of the Salem witches, for example, he said 'do not lay more stress on pure spectral evidence than it will bear … It is very certain that the Devils have sometimes represented the shapes of persons not only innocent but also very virtuous. Though I believe that the just God then ordinarily provides a way for the speedy vindications of the persons thus abused.' After 1693, he never admitted publicly to any regret for in his part in the Salem trials and remained a vehement defender of the entire proceedings.

most influential ministers. The close ties between ministerial and magisterial roles in New England made the judges' recourse to the ministers a natural step. The Puritan clergy, who had been highly politicised since the founding of the colony, were an informal network of political advisers.

Cotton Mather's influence

Cotton Mather appeared to be the best source of knowledge on witches:

- He had written an account of the bewitching of the Goodwin children (see page 138).
- His father, Increase Mather, was hugely respected.

Cotton Mather wrote the ministerial response: *The Return of Several Ministers to the Governor and Council in Boston*. It was issued on 15 June. Cotton had long feared witches and the Devil. While cautioning the judges not to rely on spectral evidence alone (see Source D, page 147), he did not reject spectral evidence outright. Nor did he condemn the outcome of the first trial. His conclusion recommended 'the speedy and vigorous prosecution of such as had rendered themselves obnoxious, according to the direction given in the laws of God, and the wholesome statutes of the English nation, for the detection of witchcrafts'. Thus, Mather encouraged the judges to complete the work they had begun.

SOURCE D

From part of Cotton Mather's report: 15 June 1692 (available at: http://en.wikipedia.org/wiki/Salem_witch_trials).

Presumptions whereupon persons may be committed, and, much more, convictions whereupon persons may be condemned as guilty of witchcrafts, ought certainly to be more considerable than barely the accused person's being represented by a spectre unto the afflicted; inasmuch as it is an undoubted and notorious thing, that a demon may, by God's permission, appear, even to ill purposes, in the shape of an innocent, yea, and a virtuous man. Nor can we esteem alterations made in the sufferers, by a look or touch of the accused, to be an infallible evidence of guilt, but frequently liable to be abused by the Devil's legerdemains [tricks].

According to Source D, why was Mather cautious about using spectral evidence and touch-tests in court?

The second and third court sessions

From 30 June through to early July, grand juries endorsed indictments against Sarah Good, Elizabeth Howe, Susannah Martin, Elizabeth and John Proctor, Martha Carrier, Sarah Wilds and Dorcas Hoar. Sarah Good, Elizabeth Howe, Susannah Martin and Sarah Wildes, along with Rebecca Nurse, went on trial. All five women were found guilty and executed on 19 July.

On 2 August, the third session of the court convened. Grand juries indicted George Burroughs, Mary Easty, Martha Corey and George Jacobs. Trial juries convicted Martha Carrier, George Jacobs, George Burroughs, John Willard, Elizabeth and John Proctor. Elizabeth Proctor was given a temporary stay of execution because she was pregnant. On 19 August, Martha Carrier, George Jacobs, George Burroughs, John Willard and John Proctor were executed.

Confessions

In July, accusations began again. A constable invited the Salem girls to Andover to uncover the cause of his wife's illness. Ann Putnam and Mary Walcott went and duly found witches. The first persons named were Ann Foster, her daughter, Mary Lacey Sr, and her granddaughter, Mary Lacey Jr. All three immediately confessed to making a pact with the Devil and implicated the five victims about to be hanged in Salem as having been present at a sabbat they themselves had attended. Cotton Mather described this as a remarkable providence, vindicating the court's judgment.

After this, both accusations and confessions proliferated at a rapid rate. Roughly a third of those charged – 50 out of 156 – admitted complicity. Forty-three of the 50 confessions came during the Andover phase of the accusation. This upsurge in confessions is remarkable. Did the confessors hope they would escape execution by confessing?

It has often been stated that confession was the surest way of escaping execution. Robert Calef asserted as much. He observed: 'Though the confessing witches were many; yet not one of them that confessed their own guilt and abode by their confessions were put to death.' On the surface, this argument seems valid. Only six confessors were brought to trial and only one was executed: Samuel Wardwell, who had renounced his confession. Thus, it appears that most of those who were executed could have saved their lives by lying. However, as Wendel Craker (1997) has pointed out, those who were indicted early did not know that those who confessed would escape execution. Moreover, there is no evidence that the court targeted those intransigent prisoners who maintained their innocence or intended to free those who confessed.

The situation in September 1692

By early September, scores of people stood accused of witchcraft and JPs were rushing all over Essex County taking depositions, particularly in the Andover area. Cotton Mather was jubilant as the number of cases increased and as Andover defendants began to confess *en masse* to their supposed crimes. He now declared what he had long believed, that the entire colony was beset with witches and that the executions were warranted.

The fourth and fifth court sessions

In September, grand juries indicted eighteen more people. On 19 September, Giles Corey, a 71-year-old farmer, refused to plead guilty or innocent. Accordingly, he was pressed beneath an increasingly heavy load of stones in an attempt to make him enter a plea. It took him two days to die. His refusal to plead is usually explained as a way of preventing his property from being confiscated by the Crown but it may be that his death was a protest against the court's methods.

Four suspects pleaded guilty and eleven others were tried and found guilty. On 22 September, eight more witches were executed – Corey, Wardwell, Scot, Easty, Parker, Pudeator, Redd and Parker. Abigail Faulkner was given a temporary reprieve because she was pregnant. Another condemned witch, Mary Bradbury, managed to escape from prison.

Wonders of the Invisible World

In September 1692, Cotton Mather began writing *Wonders of the Invisible World: Being an Account of the Trials of Several Witches, Lately Executed in New England*, as a defence of the trials. Completed in mid-October, the book was published with a letter of endorsement by William Stoughton. Mather was able to use court records, supplied to him by his friend Stephen Sewall, clerk of the court. Cotton set out to prove that the convictions were justified. The impassioned language with which he defended the court's actions has led to his being perceived as one of the chief fomenters of the witchcraft episode.

The problem of confessions

Confessions were not formally considered by the court until the last set of trials in late September. This, the first time that anyone from Andover was tried, was also the first time that anyone who had confessed was tried. Before the court could meet again to pass judgment, Governor Phips delayed the October sitting and then disbanded the court (see below). Ironically, and probably more by luck than judgement, those who confessed thus escaped execution.

The end of the witch-hunt

The witch-hunt came to an end because of opposition from many Church leaders and action by Governor Phips.

Ministerial opposition

From the start of the Salem witch-hunt, Puritan ministers had been divided on the issue. Samuel Willard, a Boston minister, spoke openly against the trials. He also wrote – anonymously – a pamphlet *Some Miscellany Observations* in which he stated his objections to the trials, starting with his suspicions of the girls' veracity.

Increase Mather's intervention was more decisive. Cotton Mather's father was the acknowledged head of the Ministerial Association, a body comprising the Puritan Church leaders in Massachusetts. His opinion thus carried weight with the judges and with Governor Phips, who returned from the fighting in Maine (see page 144) in early October. Having initially stayed in the background, Increase Mather presented a pamphlet, *Cases of Conscience Concerning Evil Spirits,* to the association on 3 October. Critical of spectral evidence, he declared that evidence of witchcraft must be as clear as evidence of any other felony and stated 'it were better that ten suspected Witches should escape than one innocent person should be condemned'.

The actions of Phips

The extent of Increase Mather's influence on Phips is debatable. It may be that Phips was already determined to stop the witchcraft trials. It must have been clear to Phips that far from settling matters as he had hoped, the actions of the Court of Oyer and Terminer had inflamed the situation. It had become a standing witch tribunal and no one seemed safe against the wrath of the tormented girls. Phips therefore disbanded the court and also reprieved the five people who were in gaol awaiting execution.

The Superior Court of Judicature 1693

In January 1693, a new Superior Court of Judicature, Court of Assize and General Gaol Delivery convened in Salem, headed by Stoughton. Phips now specifically prevented Stoughton from admitting spectral evidence. The first cases tried in January were of the five people who had been indicted in

September. All were found not guilty. Grand juries were held for many of those remaining in gaol. Charges were dismissed against many. But 31 more people were indicted and tried, only three of whom were found guilty. The fact that most were acquitted was an indication of the change of mood. When Stoughton, still obsessive in pursuit of witches, wrote the warrants for the execution of the three convicted women and the others remaining from the previous court, Phips pardoned them. Stoughton now resigned from the court. The court continued its witchcraft work through February to May 1693. All those brought it before it were found not guilty. In May, Phips freed those still in prison: many had been unable to pay their fees for food and board in order to secure their release. While accusations of witchcraft continued to appear, the authorities, secular and religious, refused to take them seriously.

The aftermath

The witch trials had some effect on North America as a whole, if only that no one was executed as a convicted witch after 1692. The trials had a much greater impact on Salem itself. Moreover, the recriminations and fall-out from what had occurred continued for many years.

The impact of the witch-hunt on Salem

The witch-hunt seems to have had a serious economic impact on Salem and the surrounding area. The numbers of people involved in the trials meant that fields were left untended, farm work was neglected and the planting season was interrupted. Many of the families who had had their lands confiscated as a result of witchcraft accusations were left without homes or money. Consequently, economic conditions were probably much worse in 1693 than they had been in 1692, particularly as local taxation increased.

Just as important were the hatreds and resentments arising from the witch-hunt. It took many years before what had happened at Salem was forgiven and forgotten by those who had been falsely imprisoned or lost family members, friends or loved ones. Joseph Green, who replaced Parris as minister of Salem in 1696, attempted to heal the scars by seating the accused next to the accusers at his sermons – apparently with some success.

Criticisms and regret

The Salem trials were soon followed by intense criticism and expressions of regret from judges and jury members that innocent blood had been shed:

- From 1693 to 1697, Robert Calef, a Boston cloth merchant, collected correspondence, court records and petitions, and other accounts of the trials and placed them, for contrast, alongside portions of Mather's *Wonders of the Invisible World* under the title *More Wonders of the Invisible World*. The book, published in London in 1700, was a damning attack on Cotton Mather.

- John Hale, the minister in Beverly, who was present at many of the proceedings, completed his book *A Modest Enquiry into the Nature of Witchcraft* in 1697. (It was published in 1702.) Expressing regret over the actions taken, Hale admitted: 'Such was the darkness of that day, the tortures and lamentations of the afflicted, and the power of former presidents that we walked in the clouds and could not see our way.'

In Salem, Reverend Parris admitted in 1694, 'I may have been mistaken'. He lost his church post in Salem in 1696. In January 1697, Samuel Sewall publicly acknowledged his guilt as a judge in the witch trials. A number of jurors similarly repented. Cotton Mather, in 1697, in the privacy of his diary, recorded his fears that God would punish his family for 'not appearing with vigour enough to stop the proceedings of the judges'. In 1706, Ann Putnam publicly asked forgiveness. She claimed that she had not acted out of malice but was deluded by Satan into denouncing innocent people. She was accepted for full membership of the Salem Village church. Not one of the false accusers was punished for their actions. Abigail Williams appears to have died from her afflictions soon after 1692. Betty Parris went on to marry and have five children and died aged 78.

The process of pardon

Meanwhile, those who had been accused and imprisoned and the relatives of those who had been executed soon petitioned the General Court (the Massachusetts' Parliament), seeking:

- a declaration of the innocence of those individuals convicted
- compensation for the families of those who had been executed.

In 1697, the General Court declared a day of fasting and soul-searching for the tragedy that had occurred at Salem. In 1702, it finally declared the trials unlawful but gave little in the way of compensation to those families who had suffered. In 1703, another petition was put forward, requesting a more equitable settlement for those wrongly accused. Still not enough was done. Accordingly, in 1709, 22 people who had been convicted of witchcraft, or whose relatives had been convicted, presented the General Court with a petition in which they demanded both a reversal of attainder and compensation for financial losses. In October 1711, the General Court passed a bill reversing the judgment against the people listed in the 1709 petition and two months later the sum of £578 and 12 shillings (£578.60) was authorised to be divided among the survivors and relatives of those accused. But not all the condemned were exonerated. Not until 1957 was an act passed pronouncing the innocence of all those accused.

Summary diagram: The Salem witch trials

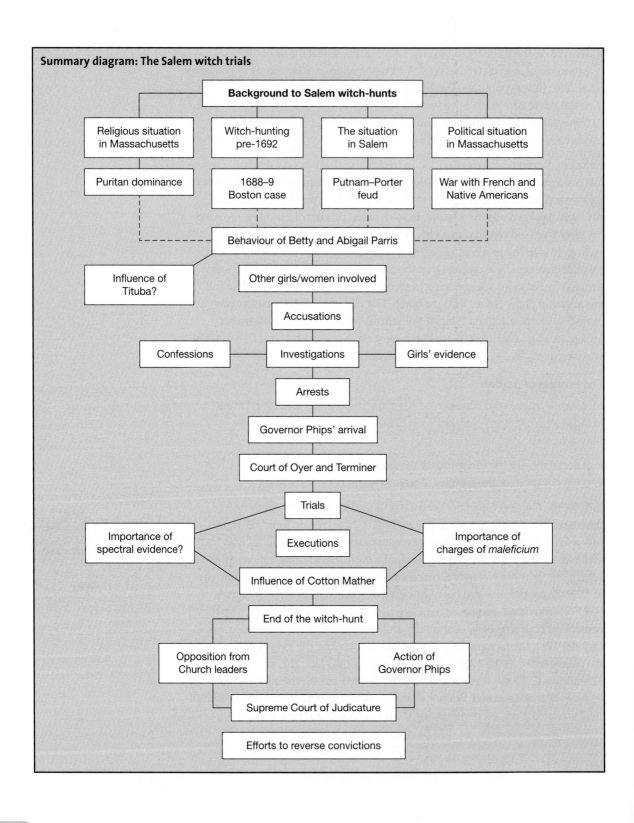

4 Key debate

▶ *Why did the Salem witch trials occur?*

There would have been no witch panic without a strong belief in the threat posed by witchcraft. However, belief in witchcraft had existed in New England for several decades and not resulted in a major witch-hunt. So why did the Salem trials occur?

EXTRACT 1

From B. Rosenthal, *Salem's Story: Reading the Witch Trials of 1692*, Cambridge University Press, 1995, p. 192.

The orgy of accusations cut across towns and villages and across gender, class and age. People fed all sorts of names to the accusers, either in sincere belief that a particular person was a witch or for motives rooted in malice, greed, or the need to justify the proceedings. Yet there was no grand conspirator behind it all; instead varieties of individuals, for varying motives, responded to the open invitation of the society in which they lived to provide names to those who had been defined as the witch-finders of their day.

EXTRACT 2

From J.P. Demos, *Entertaining Satan: Witchcraft and the Culture of Early New England*, Oxford University Press, 1982, pp. 384–5.

Why, in particular, did this one episode [of witchcraft trials in Salem] attain such massive proportions – i.e., in the sheer quantity of persons involved? The early 1690s seem, in the first place, to have been a time of extreme and pervasive anxiety in New England. The difficulties experienced during the preceding fifteen years had added up to an almost intolerable sum: the wars were more devastating, the epidemic illnesses more prevalent and 'mortal', the constitutional changes more unsettling, than in any earlier period of the region's history. It was not hard to see in all this a general movement of Divine Providence against New England. Meanwhile, too, there were powerful undercurrents of social change – old enough in their origins, but newly visible in some of their effects.

> Evaluate the interpretations in Extracts 1 and 2. Explain which you think is a more convincing explanation of what caused the Salem witch trials.
>
> **?**

Boyer and Nissenbaum (1974) stressed the importance of local quarrels, particularly the rivalry between the Putnams and the Porters. Certainly the Putnam family played an important role in proceedings. Many of the girls were connected to them in some way. However, the notion that the Putnam family was pulling the strings does not quite add up. The first three victims were not obvious opponents. More importantly, the Putnams did not know the vast majority of those accused of witchcraft.

Recent research suggests that broad social and economic interpretations do not really explain what occurred in Salem. There is little evidence that those who supported the witch-hunts were essentially subsistence farmers who feared change and who opposed increasing commercialism. Nor is there much to suggest that the prosecutors were impelled by selfish economic motives. While some people did benefit from the confiscation of the property of those who were executed as witches (not least George Corwin, Sheriff of Essex County and nephew of JP Jonathan Corwin), there is no evidence that motives of this sort prompted the initial charges.

It has recently been claimed that economic hardship, the result of decades of cold weather, had an impact on developments. People, unhappy with their lot, sought scapegoats – as, according to Behringer, did many Europeans in the 'mini ice age' (see page 26). However, dire economic conditions affected much of Massachusetts both before and after 1692. The cold weather explanation thus begs the question why the witch-hunts in the colony were limited to Salem and its surrounding area in the single year 1692.

What is clear is that the Salem victims suffered from malice. The question remains: whose malice and who was to blame?

- A few Puritan clergy – Parris, Hale, Lawson – played a crucial role in supporting the witch-hunt at the start. Cotton Mather also threw his not inconsiderable power behind the trials. Nevertheless, most Puritan clergy seem to have opposed the trials. Ultimately, it was opposition from the clergy which helped to bring the trials to a close.
- The civic authorities must also shoulder responsibility for what occurred. It is hard to blame Governor Phips. Although he set up the Court of Oyer and Terminer, most of the court's activities occurred in his absence. As soon as he returned from fighting Native Americans, he brought the court's proceedings to a halt. It is far easier to blame William Stoughton, Lieutenant Governor and Chief Judge. He, more than anyone else, influenced the judicial course of events and was still eager to execute witches in 1693. However, as Craker suggests, the Court of Oyer and Terminer moved cautiously and operated within established guidelines.

The Salem trials are probably best ascribed to mass hysteria, induced by the fevered imaginations of the girls, women and later some men who claimed to be afflicted. The girls were the initial villains. However, they would not have been listened to if there had not been a very real fear of witches among the ordinary people of Salem. The identification of demonic power with the Native Americans, with whom the colonists were at war, may have aggravated the fear of the Devil and made it more imperative to identify his confederates. But most citizens were simply anxious to punish the perpetrators of *maleficia*. It was the voice of neighbours which pushed the jurors: the witnesses who swore under oath that they were certain that the defendant had harmed them. Although the girls' visions led to the witch-hunts, not one person was hanged on the basis of spectral evidence alone. The factor that attracted the court's attention was the charge of non-spectral acts of malefic witchcraft.

Chapter summary

Scottish witch-hunting is associated with the Calvinist Kirk, which wanted to create a godly state. There was relatively little witchcraft under the 1563 Scottish Act before 1590. James VI was involved in the North Berwick witch trials of 1590–1, when it appeared that a large group of witches, in association with the Earl of Bothwell, were conspiring to kill him. James, who was personally involved in interrogating some of the suspects, later wrote a book on the dangers of witchcraft: *Daemonologie*. Witch-hunting continued after 1591, supported by the government and the Kirk. Although witch-hunting subsided somewhat after 1597, large witch-hunts occurred in Scotland in 1649–50 and 1661–2. Some 1500 Scottish people are thought to have been killed.

The Salem witch trials occurred in Massachusetts in New England in 1692–3. They are associated with the religious and political situation in Massachusetts as well as with King William's War with the French and Native Americans. The accusations resulting from the apparent possession of a group of girls and young women led to the arrests of over 150 people. Twenty people were convicted of witchcraft in the Court of Oyer and Terminer and executed. No one was executed for spectral evidence alone and (ironically) virtually none of the 50 people who confessed to being witches were executed. Governor Phips, with the support of some important Puritan ministers, ended the panic in 1693. Debates continue about who was to blame for the Salem trials.

Refresher questions

Use these questions to remind yourself of the key material covered in this chapter.

1. What caused the North Berwick witch-hunt?
2. What impact did James VI have on Scottish witch-hunting?
3. What was the role of Bothwell in the 1590–1 witch-hunt?
4. Why was witch-hunting so severe in Scotland in the 1590s?
5. How important was the Kirk in Scottish witch-hunts?
6. What caused the Salem witch-hunt?
7. How important was the Puritan church in the Salem witch-hunt?
8. What evidence was used to convict the Salem 'witches'?
9. Why did the Salem witch-hunt end?
10. Who was mainly responsible for the Salem witch trials?

Question practice

ESSAY QUESTIONS

1 How accurate is it to say that the Scottish government was responsible for initiating witch trials in the years from 1590 to 1597?

2 How accurate is to say that the failure of the central Scottish administration to control events in the localities was the primary reason for the persecution of witchcraft in the years 1590–7?

3 How far were Puritan ministers responsible for the Salem witch-hunt in the years 1692–3?

4 How far were the actions of Governor Phips of Massachusetts responsible for the ending of the Salem witch trials?

INTERPRETATION QUESTION

1 Read the two passages and then answer the question. Evaluate the interpretations in both of the passages and explain which you think is more convincing as an explanation for the causes of the Salem witch trials.

PASSAGE A

From W.D. Craker, *Witchcraft at Salem* in *New Perspectives on Witchcraft, Magic and Demonology: Volume 3*, edited by B.P. Levack, Routledge, 2001, pp. 350–1.

The arguments set forth here has been designed to demonstrate that the court [of Oyer and Terminer] performed a much more finely tuned balancing act than is generally recognized. It tried no one based solely on spectral evidence; it hanged no one who had not been charged with what in that day was considered empirical evidence; and its formal consideration of confession came last in the trials and became the issue upon which the court foundered. When the court, in its own day, answered criticism for violating protocols, it is evident that it literally spoke the truth – even though the truth did not succeed in its attempt to shield the colony from what Cotton Mather called a 'heartquake'.

But understanding that does not, of itself, move the scholar closer to a theoretical understanding of why the Salem episode broke with such force upon the colony, nor why it overflowed the elaborate protective barriers raised by the colony's officials until it overtook the innocent caught in its path. That the victims of the Salem trials suffered from malice is abundantly clear. But the question remains, 'Whose malice?' Over the years focus has shifted from the clergy, to the accusers, and to the courts. But none of the conclusions offered are either comprehensive or compelling. The same can be said for attempts to explain the episode by impersonal forces such as mercantile capitalism, misogyny, or classical understandings of deviance. …

All that has been done here has been to demonstrate that the court moved with caution and within established guidelines. If its actions are to be viewed as deliberate deception to cover its own malice, then the court moved more cannily than it is generally given credit for. If the court, itself, was self-deceived, then the source of that self-deception remains to be more adequately explained.

PASSAGE B

From P.C. Hoffer, *The Devil's Disciples: Makers of the Salem Witchcraft Trials*, Johns Hopkins University Press, 1996, pp. 199–200.

Salem's agony reminds us of the contingency of historical events. Chance brought Tituba and Samuel Parris together, compounded by Betty's illness and Cotton Mather's need to be needed, a hard winter and a harder war, without which there would have been no trials and no executions …

As the gathering of these particular players was accidental, the stage on which they performed was set by another, larger contingency. In 1692, Salem was contested ground, not just by the Putnam and Porter clans, but by whole cultures. Forest and glade reached to the northwestern edge of the village, almost touching the busy coastal lands that joined the village on the east. The village was the 'edge' of the two worlds, where a vast Atlantic commercial system, throughout whose reaches people and consumer durables were in constant motion, met a wilderness, whose natives, long put upon by foreign force, still struggled to protect their ways and their land. There witchcraft beliefs and warfare fed each other, creating the stresses and shaping the images of the crisis.

To Salem had also come the burden of war. In its physical manifestation, King William's War brought devastation, panic and death. In moments when the guns were still, the war was fought with words. Salvos of Puritan sermons condemning Roman Catholic France cratered the ground on which accusers and accused trod. In eastern New England the last battles of the Reformation raged. Cotton Mather and Samuel Parris agreed with Richard Baxter, whose works the New Englanders eagerly read, that Satan and his minions had joined forces with the French and their Indian [Native American] allies. The advance scouts of the enemy columns were the witches of Salem.

SOURCE ANALYSIS QUESTIONS

1 Assess the value of Source 1 as evidence for revealing first the causes and then the course of the North Berwick witch trials. Explain your answer, using the source, the information given about its origin and your own knowledge about the historical context.

2 Assess the value of the Source 2 for revealing popular attitudes to witchcraft and as evidence for what occurred in the interrogation of suspected witches at Salem in the years 1692–3. Explain your answer, using the source, the information given about its origin and your own knowledge about the historical context.

SOURCE 1

From an excerpt from *Newes from Scotland*, published in late 1591. This was the first work printed about the North Berwick witches. Although its author or authors remain unknown, it was essentially Scottish government propaganda, an attempt to explain and justify what had occurred. Quoted in L. Normand and G. Roberts, *Witchcraft in Early Modern Scotland*, University of Exeter Press, 2000, pp. 311–12.

Within … Tranent … David Seton, who, being deputy bailiff in the said town, had a maidservant called Geillis Duncan, who used secretly to be absent and to lie forth of [to stay overnight away from] her master's house every other night. This Geillis Duncan took in hand to help all such as were troubled or grieved with any kind of sickness or infirmity, and … did perform many matters most miraculous. Which things, … she began to do them upon a sudden, having never done the like before, made her master and others to be in great admiration [astonishment], and wondered thereat. By means whereof [in consequence of this] the said David Seton had his maid in some great suspicion that she did not those things by natural and lawful ways, but rather supposed it to be done by some extraordinary and unlawful means. Whereupon her master began to grow very inquisitive, and examined her …; whereat she gave him no answer. Nevertheless, her master to the intent that he might the better try and find out the truth … with the torture of the pilliwinks [a type of thumbscrew] upon her fingers, which is a grievous torture, and binding or writhing her head with a cord or rope, which is a most cruel torment also, yet would she not confess anything. Whereupon they, suspecting that she had been marked by the devil (as commonly witches are), made diligent search about her, and found the enemy's mark to be in … the forepart of her throat: which being found, she confessed that all her doings was done by the wicked allurements and enticements of the devil, and that she did them by witchcraft. After this her confession, she was committed to prison where she continued for a season; where immediately she accused these persons following to be notorious witches, and caused them forthwith to be apprehended one after another: viz. Agnes Sampson, the eldest witch of them all, dwelling in Haddington, Agnes Tompson of Edinburgh, Doctor Fian, alias John Cunningham, master of the school at Saltpans [Prestonpans] in Lothian … These were by the said Geillis Duncan accused, as also George Mott's wife dwelling in Saltpans, Robert Grierson, skipper, and James Bandilands, with the porter's wife of Seton, the smith at the Brig halls [covered markets in Edinburgh], with innumerable others in those parts … of whom some are already executed.

SOURCE 2

From the examination of Bridget Bishop at Salem Village on 19 April 1692 before JPs John Hathorne and Jonathan Corwin. Several of the girls and young women who had accused her of afflicting them were present at the inquest. Bishop was indicted by the JPs and later tried and executed. Transcribed from the 'Salem Witchcraft Papers' (available at: http://salem.lib.virginia.edu/).

Bridget Bishop being now coming in to be examined relating to her accusation of suspicion of sundry acts of witchcrafts the afflicted persons are now dreadfully afflicted by her as they do say.

[Hathorne] Bishop what do you say you here stand charged with sundry acts of witchcraft by you done or committed upon the bodies of Mercy Lewes and Ann Putnum and others?

[Bishop] I am innocent I know nothing of it I have done no witchcraft.

[Hathorne] Look upon this woman and see if this be the woman that you have seen hurting you Mercy Lewes and Ann Putnum and others do now charge her to her face with hurting of them?

[Hathorne] What do you say now you see they charge you to your face?

[Bishop] I never did hurt them in my life I did never see these persons before I am as innocent as the child unborn.

The afflicted persons charge her, with having hurt them many ways and by tempting them to sign to the devil's book at which charge she seemed to be very angry and shaking her head at them saying it was false they are all greatly tormented (as I conceive) by the shaking of her head.

[Hathorne] Good Bishop what contract have you made with the devil?

[Bishop] I have made no contract with the devil I never saw him in my life. Ann Putnam sayeth that she calls the devil her God.

[Hathorne] What say you to all this that you are charged with can you not find in your heart to tell the truth?

[Bishop] I do tell the truth I never hurt these persons in my life I never saw them before.

[Mercy Lewes] Oh good Bishop did you not come to our house the Last night and did you not tell me that your master made you tell more then you were willing to tell?

[Hathorne] Tell us the truth in this matter how comes these persons to be thus tormented and to charge you with doing?

[Bishop] I am not come here to say I am a witch to take away my life.

[Hathorne] Who is it that doth it if you do not they say it is your likeness that comes and torments them and tempts them to write in the book. What Booke is that you tempt them with?

[Bishop] I know nothing of it I am innocent.

[Hathorne] Do you not see how they are tormented you are acting witchcraft before us what do you say to this why have you not an heart to confess the truth?

[Bishop] I am innocent I know nothing of it. I am no witch. I know not what a witch is.

[Hathorne] Have you not given consent that some evil spirit should do this in your likeness?

[Bishop] No I am innocent of being a witch I know no man woman or child here.

[Hathorne] What do you say to these murders you are charged with?

[Bishop] I am innocent. I know nothing of it.

Now she lifts up her eyes and they are greatly tormented again.

CHAPTER 6

The end of witch-hunting

During the seventeenth and eighteenth centuries, prosecutions and executions for witchcraft declined and eventually came to an end. The decline occurred in all European countries where witch-hunts had taken place. Eventually the laws that had authorised the prosecutions were repealed. This chapter will examine how and why witch persecution ended by focusing on the following:

★ Reasons for the decline of European witch-hunting

★ The end of witch-hunting in England

Key dates

1597	Foundation of Gresham College	**1690**	Publication of John Locke's *Essay Concerning Human Understanding*
1656	Publication of Ady's *A Candle in the Dark*		
1660	Foundation of the Royal Society	**1691–3**	Publication of Bekker's *The Bewitched World*
1662	The case of the Demon Drummer of Tedworth	**1712**	The case of Jane Wenham
		1718	Publication of Francis Hutchinson's *An Historical Essay Concerning Witchcraft*
1677	Publication of Webster's *The Displaying of Supposed Witchcraft*	**1736**	British Witchcraft Act

1 Reasons for the decline of European witch-hunting

▶ *Why did European witch-hunting come to an end?*

Given that witch-hunting was a localised phenomenon, it is not surprising that the decline and eventual end of witch-hunting occurred at different times across Europe and for different reasons. In some countries, such as the Dutch Republic, the reduction in prosecutions was evident by 1600. (The last Dutch burning was in 1603.) In others, like Poland, it did not begin until the mid-eighteenth century. In some places, the decline in prosecutions was gradual. In others, it came to an end remarkably quickly. Nevertheless, some common features in the decline of witch-hunting are discernible. Ironically, as historian Brian Levack points out, some of the forces that encouraged the growth of witch-hunting – legal practices, religious beliefs, publications and socio-economic forces – were also instrumental in its decline.

New legal procedures

According to Levack, the main cause for the decline of witch-hunting was the establishment of new rules for conducting witchcraft trials. This occurred because many judges and legal writers across Europe doubted that many of those persons who were prosecuted were actually guilty.

The regulation of local justice

The decline in witchcraft prosecutions in most countries began when judicial authorities who staffed the central institutions of various states took measures to control the actions of local judges or inferior courts. These efforts often began in response to large witch-hunts that had spun out of control. The classic example of the way in which higher judicial authorities contained the witch-hunting zeal of local officials comes from northern France, where most people were subject to the jurisdiction of the *parlement* of Paris, the royal court to which people found guilty of capital offences could appeal. A witch panic in Champagne-Ardennes region in 1587–8, which claimed hundreds of lives and the abandonment of due legal process, resulted in the Paris *parlement's* intervention. It demanded that henceforward all sentences of death in witchcraft cases within its jurisdiction be reviewed. This policy, formally adopted in 1604, was published as an edict in 1624.The *parlement's* reversal of many death sentences led to a sharp decline in the number of indictments.

In the Holy Roman Empire, the law faculties of the universities helped to apply the brakes to local witch-hunting. The imperial code of 1532, the *Constitutio Criminalis Carolina*, required that when local courts confronted difficult cases they would consult with the jurists in the law faculty of a nearby university. During the sixteenth and early seventeenth centuries, witchcraft consultations, by spreading learned witch beliefs, probably did more to facilitate than to restrain prosecution (see page 5). But, by the late seventeenth century, the consultations began to have the opposite effect as jurists started to advise extreme caution in the prosecution of witchcraft.

The restriction and prohibition of torture

In the seventeenth and eighteenth centuries, the use of torture in all criminal cases, but particularly in witchcraft cases, came increasingly under attack. Those, like Friedrich Spee von Langenfeld (see page 75), who were critical of the use of torture, argued:

- The evidence obtained from torture was unreliable since innocent persons made false admissions in order to stop the pain.

- Witchcraft trials should conform to more exacting legal requirements. Torture should not be allowed on the basis of circumstantial evidence or because suspects had been named by confessing witches as accomplices.

Torture was eventually abolished in many areas: Prussia (1754), Saxony (1770), Sweden (1782) and France (1788). Its actual abolition usually came after the effective end of witchcraft prosecutions and was in large part inspired by humanitarian concerns that had not been prominent in earlier critiques. The decline in witch prosecutions probably had more to do with the regulation and limitation of torture than with its formal elimination.

New standards of evidence

As the seventeenth century progressed, European judges became reluctant to accept the evidence that was presented to them in witchcraft cases:

- There was a growing reluctance to accept confessions as sufficient proof of guilt, whether those confessions were extracted by torture or made 'freely'. Confessions of pacts with the Devil or sabbat attendance were increasingly attributed to mental illness.
- There was a growing acceptance that events attributed to supernatural agency may have had natural causes. The burden of proof was on the prosecution to rule out the possibility of natural causation: if natural causation was possible then the 'witch' was not guilty.
- Even if harm was apparently caused by supernatural means, lawyers could demand concrete evidence that the witch had been responsible for its infliction. This was hard to obtain – unless it could first be proved that the witch had made a pact with the Devil – which was even harder to prove.
- The revelation that some of those who claimed to be possessed had faked their symptoms contributed to the greater caution in the handling of all witchcraft accusations.
- There was doubt about the validity of spectral evidence. The most effective challenge to its judicial use came from those who claimed that the Devil might have used his powers of illusion to misrepresent innocent persons.
- Judges were increasingly unwilling to accept the testimony of children, criminals, servants and alleged accomplices. Given that such people were not allowed to testify against the accused in ordinary crimes, it seemed unfair that they should be allowed to do so in witchcraft cases.

As a result of the legal changes, witchcraft eventually became so hard to prove that judges stopped trying by the early seventeenth century. The difficulty in securing convictions had the effect of reducing the number of charges brought in the first place.

The experience of witch-hunting

Experience of the effects of witch-hunts during the sixteenth and seventeenth centuries led many authorities to view them as counterproductive. Rather than having a stabilising and purifying effect on local communities, it became apparent that they could often have the reverse effect, bringing only fear and destruction. There was an awareness that many innocent people were killed in witch-hunts. False accusations, particularly by children, added to the disquiet. Moreover, many people became convinced that possessions were fraudulent and exorcisms shams.

Change in the religious climate

Just as religious beliefs had played a significant part in the rise of witch persecutions, so, too, developments in theology played an important part in their decline:

- One outcome of the Reformation was a closer study of the Bible. Apart from Exodus (see page 23), the Bible contained few references to witchcraft and none to Devil-worship.
- By the seventeenth century, Protestant theologians increasingly saw God operating benignly in the contemporary world through natural forces and laws, rather than through miracles.
- There was a growing tendency to stress the sovereignty of God. If God was supreme, *maleficia* could only occur with His permission. Thus, the punishment of witches should end.

After the end of the Thirty Years' War in 1648, there was an era of relative calm in the history of Western Christianity. The quarrels about religious dogma which had characterised the previous 100 years were less important. A new spirit of tolerance began to characterise many Protestant communities in the late seventeenth century. This tolerance, manifested mainly towards members of other religious denominations, spread to those suspected of witchcraft. It is probably no coincidence that witch-hunting first began to decline in the Dutch Republic, a country known for its early religious tolerance. By the last decades of the seventeenth century, a more secular, rational age was dawning. Protestant and Catholic authorities abandoned their determination to use their secular power to create an ideal Christian community. One crucial effect of the new outlook was a decline in the commitment of God-fearing Christians to purify the world by burning witches.

By the mid-seventeenth century, a coherent body of theological thought existed which cast doubt on the whole business of diabolical activity and witchcraft. Just as publications had played a part in legitimising and aiding the most frenetic era of witch-hunting, so books and pamphlets were to prove part of its demise.

> ### Balthasar Bekker
>
> Between 1691 and 1693, Balthasar Bekker, a Dutch Calvinist pastor and biblical scholar, published a massive four-volume treatise, *The Bewitched World* – a sustained attack on witch beliefs (see Source A). The book, translated into English, German and French, was widely circulated. Bekker denied the pact with the Devil, the sabbat, conception by a demon, demonic possession and the practice of harmful magic. For Bekker, the Devil was nothing more than a symbol of evil with no power to intervene in the operations of the material world. Once the Devil was reduced to this status, the possibility that a human being could commit the crime of witchcraft vanished. Indeed, Bekker suggested that when accusations of witchcraft were made, the state should prosecute the accusers.

SOURCE A

> *In what ways is Source A a major attack on the notion of witchcraft?*

From Balthasar Bekker, *The Bewitched World*, volume 1, published 1695.

An Abridgement of the Third Book

… In the 12th [chapter] I run over again the whole Scripture from the beginning to the end, from the Covenant of God with Abraham to our Saviour and examining whether from whatever has been said upon that subject, there is any occasion to infer that the Devil may likewise on his part make his detestable compacts. I demonstrate that the opinion which supposes such contracts between the Devil and men by virtue of which they are said to have performed all their witchcrafts, can by no means consist with what is contained in the doctrine of the Holy Scripture, nor with the dispensation of God's covenant as well before the Law as under the Law, and much less under the Gospel.

Social and economic developments

Changes in the fabric of European social life during the period 1550–1650 may have contributed to witch-hunting (see pages 25–7). Arguably, there was an improvement in economic and social conditions after 1650:

- Inflation levelled off.
- There was some improvement in real wages.
- The effects of warfare on civilian populations were greatly reduced.
- There is some evidence that plague pandemics worked themselves out.

The relative economic upturn perhaps meant the soil for witch-hunting was less fertile than it had been previously.

Change in the intellectual climate

The decline of witch-hunting received its direction from men who were unwilling to abandon completely their belief in the reality of witchcraft.

However, a number of changes occurred in the intellectual world of the early modern period that fostered disbelief in the power of witches. By the seventeenth century, there was a growing tendency in all fields of thought to:

- reject dogma and inherited authority
- question everything.

Scientists (often called natural philosophers in the early modern period), in particular, endeavoured to arrive at new certainties in the understanding of the natural environment. There was a growing conviction that the physical world functioned like a machine, in an orderly, regular fashion and in accordance with immutable laws. This had the potential for undermining the belief that the Devil (or even God) could intervene in the natural world's operation. Several thinkers had particular influence in bringing about what has been called the Scientific Revolution.

Nicolas Copernicus (1473–1543)

Copernicus, a Polish mathematician, challenged the assumption that the earth was the centre of the universe in a treatise published in 1543. For many years, most scientists preferred to regard Copernicus's theory that the earth went round the sun as nothing more than a convenient mathematical theory. But by the end of the sixteenth century, Copernicus's theory had moved into the centre of intellectual and religious controversy.

Johannes Kepler (1571–1630)

Kepler, court astronomer to Holy Roman Emperor Rudolf II, built on Copernican cosmology. On the basis of the observations of Danish astronomer Tycho Brahe, Kepler proved that the planets in the earth's solar system moved in elliptical rather than circular orbits around the sun. His laws defined the revolution of planets by means of mathematical formulae. In his *Harmonices Mundi* (1619) there was no place for divine or demonic intervention.

Kepler had a personal experience with witch-hunting. His mother Katherina lived in Württemberg in southern Germany. Around 1615, she fell out with her neighbours who subsequently accused her of bewitching their children. In 1620, Katherina was imprisoned. Eventually, she was released but her imprisonment had taken its toll and she died soon afterwards.

Galileo Galilei (1564–1642)

Born in Pisa in Italy, Galileo was a physician, mathematician, engineer, philosopher and astronomer. Often described as the 'father of modern science', his many achievements included improvements to the telescope and consequent astronomical observations. Like Kepler, Galileo stated that the laws of nature are mathematical.

Galileo's discoveries revolutionised the European concept of the universe more effectively than either Copernicus or Kepler. Convinced that the earth went round the sun, Galileo was at odds with the papacy, which continued to insist that the earth was the centre of the universe. In 1633, he was convicted by the Roman Inquisition of suspicion of heresy and spent the remainder of his life under house arrest.

Francis Bacon (1561–1626)

Bacon was an English philosopher, statesman, jurist, essayist and author who served as attorney general and lord chancellor. His writings stressed the need for observation and experiment and the mutual benefit which practical skills and scientific theory could derive from each other – the so-called **empirical** scientific approach. Bacon's ideas, particularly his support for a planned procedure of investigation into all things natural, proved influential both in his lifetime and for decades after his death.

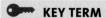

René Descartes (1596–1650)

Descartes was the outstanding French thinker of his day. Fearing Catholic persecution, he spent most of his adult life in the Netherlands. Like Galileo, Descartes thought of himself as a faithful Catholic, yet not only did he accept the ideas of Copernicus but he constructed a whole philosophical system without reference to the Church or to Christianity. In his *Discourse on Method* (1637), he declared his resolution 'to seek no other knowledge than that which I might find within myself, or perhaps in the great book of nature'. He deduced his view of human knowledge and of the laws governing the physical universe from first principles, mainly by mathematical reasoning. He argued that the world was a pure mechanism, governed by its own physical laws and without the further intervention of God who had created it or of any spirits.

The spread of scientific thinking

Scientific learning and investigation became more widespread:

- New chairs of science and medicine were founded in the major universities.
- Scientific academies appeared in Italy and France in the sixteenth century.
- England played an important role in spreading scientific knowledge in the seventeenth century.

Gresham College

Gresham College was founded in London in 1597 under the will of Sir Thomas Gresham. By the 1640s and 1650s, the Gresham College group was a loose collection of natural philosophers whose members were committed to scientific method and experimental science. They included many of England's great thinkers such as the astronomer Christopher Wren, who went on to display his architectural skills after the Fire of London in 1666.

The Royal Society

Founded in 1660, the Royal Society of London for the Improvement of Natural Science was granted a Royal Charter by Charles II in 1662. Its members, many of whom were initially linked to Gresham College, were influenced by the 'new science'. The Royal Society conducted meetings where various scientific experiments took place. Along with the French *Académie des Sciences*, established in 1666, and other learned societies, the Royal Society published details of the experiments, ensuring that new ideas reached a wider audience.

English influence

In the late seventeenth century, a number of English intellectuals influenced both British and European thought. Some were scientists. Others were social scientists, seeking laws that would apply to society and government.

Isaac Newton (1642–1727)

Newton, often regarded as England's greatest thinker, was a professor of mathematics at Cambridge University. His fame rests on his fundamental work on light and on his invention of calculus, a mathematical procedure used especially to calculate rates of change. Above all, he is known for his theory of universal gravitation, published in his book *Mathematical Principles of Natural Philosophy* in 1687. The theory finally achieved what Galileo had begun, the discovery of the mathematical laws of mechanics that were equally valid on earth and throughout the universe. Newton's ideas dominated scientists' view of the physical universe for the next three centuries. It was largely through the Royal Society that Newton's work became nationally and internationally known.

Thomas Hobbes (1588–1679)

English philosopher and mathematician Thomas Hobbes stressed the importance of deductive reasoning and scientific **materialism**. He subscribed to a mechanistic view of nature and denied the existence of witches and demons. His interests lay in mathematics, geography and the classics, until the breakdown of the English political and social order in the 1640s (see pages 106–7). Inspired to devise his own political theory, Hobbes sought to assimilate political thinking with that of natural science. His most famous work was *Leviathan*, published in 1651. In Hobbes's view, the state of nature was 'solitary, poor, nasty, brutish and short'. Accordingly, citizens should submit to the state, no matter whether the state was a monarchy or a republic, which would legislate on their behalf and maintain order. Hobbes's theory of government was secular in the sense that government was instituted by men, not by God.

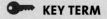 **KEY TERM**

Materialism The view that denies the independent existence of spirit and maintains that there is but one substance, matter. Everything both on earth and in the universe can thus be explained by studying natural forces.

John Locke (1632–1704)

Locke was a philosopher. His greatest work, the *Essay Concerning Human Understanding* (1690), was very much in the empirical tradition. It claimed, contrary to what was believed at the time, that:

- at birth, the human mind is a *tabula rasa* (blank tablet)
- people's ideas come from sense impressions.

Locke's *Two Treatises of Government* (1690) were enormously influential in moulding modern concepts of liberal democracy. He dismissed the idea of a divine right of kingship and asserted that any king who claimed absolute power could be legitimately removed. Locke, in keeping with his political philosophy, attacked the universal tool of absolute government, the censorship of the printed word. He drafted the arguments which were used in Parliament to achieve the repeal of the Act for the Regulation of Printing in 1695. This gave England a degree of freedom of the press which was not enjoyed in most of Europe.

The impact of the new ideas on witchcraft

There was no place for demons, spells and covens in the orderly universe governed by laws and mathematical proofs as put forward by the likes of Newton, Kepler and Galileo. However, the trickling down of new scientific ideas was a very gradual process. For most of the seventeenth century, the Scientific Revolution meant very little to the educated elite, never mind the great mass of illiterate Europeans. As Sharpe says, 'There was no decisive argument, debate or great work which ended the possibility that the educated man or woman might believe in witchcraft.' Historian James Sharpe (1997) adds: 'In natural philosophy, as with theology and with concepts of legal proof, such intellectual shifts as did occur are best interpreted as a gradual chipping away at witchcraft beliefs, a gradual process of marginalization, rather than a dramatic overturning of existing belief systems'. It was still possible for educated men to accept the new science/natural philosophy and support the reality of witchcraft until the end of the seventeenth century.

However, in the course of the eighteenth century, the movement known as the Enlightenment, with its stress on rationalism, eventually spread the scientific advances to a much wider public. As Sharpe says, 'it is undeniable that in the long run, however uncertainly and tangentially, that swirling mass of intellectual endeavour which historians refer to as the "Scientific Revolution of the Seventeenth Century" contributed to the process of the gradual invalidation of witchcraft beliefs'.

Decriminalisation

Once philosophical scepticism had become a hallmark of enlightened thought, legislators fell into step. In the eighteenth century, seven kingdoms – France (1682), Prussia (1714), England and Scotland (1736), the Habsburg Empire (1766), Russia (1770), Poland (1776) and Sweden (1779) – decriminalised witchcraft. In all other European countries, decriminalisation did not take place until after 1800. However, formal decriminalisation of witchcraft had little bearing on the broader processes of decline. Repeal of witchcraft legislation often occurred decades after the last witchcraft trials. Moreover, a late repeal of witchcraft did not necessarily mean a great deal. Ireland, a country with the fewest witchcraft executions, did not rescind its Witchcraft Act of 1587 until 1821.

Table 6.1 Last executions and last trials for witchcraft

Country or region	Last execution	Last trial
Parlement of Paris	1625	1693
Alsace	1683	1683
Franche-Comté	1661	1667
Cambresis	1679	1783
Dutch Republic	1609	1659
Luxembourg	1685	1685
Switzerland	1782	1782
Geneva	1652	1681
England	1685	1717
County of Essex	1645	1675
Scotland	1706	1727
Ireland	1711	1711
New England	1692	1697
Denmark	1693	1762
Sweden	1710	1779
Finland	1691	1699
Württemberg	1749	1805
Würzburg	1749	1749
Westphalia	1728	1732
Kempten	1775	1775
Augsburg	1728	1738
Bavaria	1756	1792
Nuremberg	1660	1725
Prussia	1714	1728
Austria	1750	1775
Hungary	1756	1777
Slovenia	1720	1746
Poland	1775	1776
Spain	1781	1820
Portugal	1626	1802
Palermo	1724	1788

From Brian Levack, *The Witch-hunt in Early Modern Europe*, Routledge, 2006, p. 280.

Conclusion

Just as the rise of European witch-hunting had no single cause and had many local characteristics, the same is true for its decline. Economics, personalities, publications, developments in legal practice and theology all played their part. So did the views of the intellectual elite, which rationally explained phenomena that had once seemed supernatural. A new generation of rulers and politicians, raised in the spirit of rationalism, began to suppress witch-hunting. Witch-hunts were increasingly seen to be irrational by those who no longer felt endangered by magic. By the eighteenth century, witch trials had been driven to the European peripheries – Poland, Slovenia and Hungary – where academic institutions and strong state administrations were absent or weak.

Nevertheless, the evidence suggests that traditional views of witchcraft among ordinary Europeans remained strong in the eighteenth century – and well beyond. In some areas, assaults on suspected witches continued into the twentieth century. The end of European witchcraft was in large part a product of modernity and progress, but one forced on ordinary people by governments and the intelligentsia.

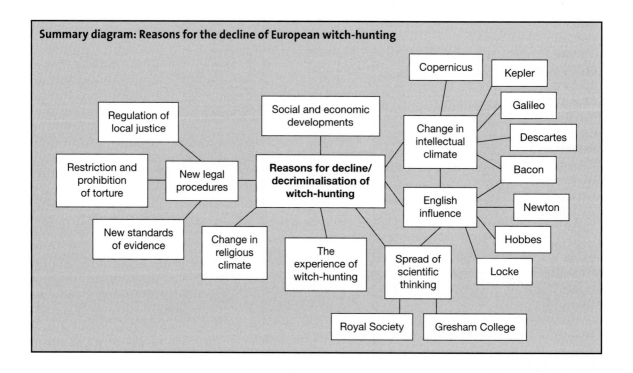

Summary diagram: Reasons for the decline of European witch-hunting

The end of witch-hunting in England

▶ *How did English witch-hunting come to an end?*

There had always been a strong streak of caution in English attitudes to witchcraft:

- The low conviction rates in English witch-trials suggest that assize judges were aware that accusations might come from malice or superstition.
- Some English writers, like Reginald Scot, had long argued that misfortunes attributed to witches should be ascribed to divine providence.

After the restoration of Charles II in 1660, the administrative and ruling elite, as well as leaders of the Anglican Church, were increasingly sceptical of witchcraft beliefs. Witch-hunting seemed symptomatic of the Civil War and **Interregnum** – an unhappy period of Puritan domination when religious fanatics like Hopkins had come to prominence. Witch trials declined sharply after 1660. Nevertheless, people, at all levels of society, continued to believe in witchcraft. Anglicans as well as Puritans feared that if people ceased to believe in witches, they would eventually cease to believe in the Devil and then in God.

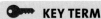 **KEY TERM**

Interrregnum The years from 1649 to 1660 when England had no king.

English writing on witchcraft in the late seventeenth and early eighteenth centuries

There were a number of important texts for and against witchcraft in the late seventeenth and early eighteenth centuries.

Thomas Ady

Ady, a physician, was the author of three sceptical books on witch-hunting. In *A Candle in the Dark, or a Treatise Concerning the Nature of Witches and Witchcraft* (1656), he attacked the delusion of witchcraft, mainly using the Bible as the base of his argument. His other works were *A Perfect Discovery of Witches* (1661) and *The Doctrine of Devils* (1676).

SOURCE B

From Thomas Ady, *A Candle in the Dark*, published in 1656. Quoted in R.H. Robbins, *The Encyclopedia of Witchcraft and Demonology*, Spring Books, 1959, p. 19.

Where is it written in all the Old and New Testaments that a witch is a murderer, or hath power to kill by witchcraft, or to afflict with any disease or infirmity? Where is it written that witches have imps sucking of their bodies? Where is it written that witches have biggs [nipples] for imps to suck on ... that the devil setteth privy marks upon witches ... that witches can hurt corn or cattle ... or can fly in the air? ... Where do we read of a he-devil or a she-devil called incubus or succubus, that useth generation or copulation?

What arguments does the author of Source B use to attack the notion of witchcraft?

John Webster

In 1677, John Webster published *The Displaying of Supposed Witchcraft*. Webster, after a career as a clergyman, schoolmaster and chaplain to parliamentary forces in the Civil War, became a medical practitioner. His book on witchcraft, while drawing on the medical and scientific knowledge of the day, was essentially written within a theological framework. 'Trust the scriptures' was his essential message and the scriptures said little about witchcraft. He ridiculed 'pitiful lying witchmongers' and the notion of demonic pacts, the feeding of imps and the use of demonic power to raise storms. Given the many gaps in human knowledge, he claimed it was better to wait for a natural explanation than to attribute the inexplicable to demons.

Webster's book was the first salvo in a heated debate with Joseph Glanvill (see textbox), a Somerset clergyman. Webster claimed that the misfortunes attributed to witches had natural causes while Granvill defended the belief in witchcraft on the grounds that the Devil worked through the forces of nature.

The Demon Drummer of Tedworth

In 1661, John Mompesson, from Tedworth (now Tidworth) in Wiltshire, brought a lawsuit against a man called Drury, an ex-drummer in Cromwell's army, for extorting money by false pretences. Drury was found guilty and forced to give up his drum to Mompesson. Soon afterwards, Mompesson's house was plagued by drumming at night. The situation grew worse: objects in the house began to move and tricks were played on the servants. Drury, questioned about the matter, admitted to bewitching Mompesson's house and boasted that Mompesson would have no peace until he returned the drum. Charged by Mompesson for the crime of employing an evil spirit, Drury was found guilty and imprisoned but later released on appeal.

The Tedworth case was investigated by Joseph Glanvill, a clergyman and member of the Royal Society. He visited Mompesson's house, collected eyewitness accounts and recorded hearing noises himself. Convinced that evil spirits were at work, he published his conclusions in 1668. Other investigators, sent by Charles II, found no evidence of spectral activity but as soon as they left, the drumming recommenced. It only came to an end after Drury left the country. It remains a mystery whether the drumming was the result of poltergeist activity or – more likely – a hoax.

Richard Boulton

The last major work in defence of the belief in witchcraft, *The Compleat History of Magick, Sorcery and Witchcraft,* was written by a medical doctor, Richard Boulton, in 1697. Boulton argued that the weight of evidence in favour of witchcraft was so great that it had to be accepted.

Francis Hutchinson

Boulton's *Compleat History* spurred Francis Hutchinson, a young clergyman, to write *An Historical Essay Concerning Witchcraft* (1718). Hutchinson's work, based solidly on developments in natural philosophy, rejected witch beliefs. Most of what was attributed to witchcraft, Hutchinson claimed, was explicable in terms of natural causes. He attributed witches purely to the imaginations of men.

The English legal process

By the 1660s, it was clear that the government and the legal profession were sceptical about witchcraft. But in England juries continued to determine judicial proof. Accordingly, accused witches were sometimes found guilty. Three women, for example, were executed for witchcraft in Exeter in 1682. All came from Bideford in Devon and all confessed and told tales of meeting the Devil. The last person in England sentenced to death and in all probability hanged for witchcraft was Alice Molland, condemned at Exeter in 1685.

However, by the late seventeenth century, a number of judges refused to countenance witchcraft prosecutions brought into their courts. Sir **John Holt** played a crucial role. In the 1690s, he dismissed at least eleven witch trials and in a final case even had a plaintiff examined for deceit. His opinions as chief justice persuaded lower courts to discontinue the practice of charging witches. By the eighteenth century, those who confessed to being witches were usually discharged as lunatics.

In Scotland, the number of trials began to decline around the same time, though Scottish courts remained more willing to accept evidence against witches. Thus, a serious outbreak of accusations occurred in 1697, resulting in the execution of seven supposed witches. The last witch to be burned was in 1727.

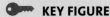 **KEY FIGURE**

John Holt (1642–1710)
An English lawyer who served as lord chief justice of England from 1689 to his death. He is usually credited with playing a major role in ending the prosecution of witches in English law.

> ## Jane Wenham
>
> On the home circuit, the last witchcraft trial came in 1712 in Hertfordshire when Jane Wenham was charged with witchcraft. The judge, Sir John Powell, showed scepticism throughout the proceedings, bullied prosecution witnesses, responded to the charge that she flew on a broomstick by joking that there was no law against flying, and secured a pardon for Wenham after the jury had returned a verdict of guilty. However, the fact that Wenham was initially convicted is evidence that witchcraft beliefs were still strong among local JPs, parish clergy and the population.

The 1736 Witchcraft Act

The Witchcraft Act of 1736 repealed the 1563 and 1604 English statutes against witchcraft and the Scottish statute of 1563. Henceforward, the law dictated that 'no prosecution, suit or proceeding shall be commenced or carried on against any person or persons for witchcraft, sorcery, enchantment … or for charging another with any such offence, in any court whatsoever in Great Britain'. The Act further made it an offence to 'pretend' to exercise or use any kind of witchcraft or sorcery. Thus, while it was now impossible to prosecute witches in an English or Scottish court, cunning folk could still be prosecuted, albeit as frauds rather than as agents of the Devil.

Local action

Local 'justice' continued. In 1737, for example, a woman was 'swum' in the River Ouse at Oakley in Bedfordshire. A large crowd gathered, including the local vicar. In 1751, Ruth Osborne was swum in a pond near Tring in Hertfordshire and died from her repeated immersions (see Source C). A large crowd was present, threatening the mayor who tried to halt the swimming. The government stepped in, executing a man who was accused of leading the affair. Nevertheless, cases of swim-tests continued to be reported in the late eighteenth and early nineteenth centuries.

The withdrawal of the elite

The seventeenth-century educated elite did not entirely abandon belief in witchcraft and magic:

- Famous scientist Sir **Robert Boyle** firmly believed in demons and witches.
- Isaac Newton (see page 167) maintained an active interest in alchemy.

As in the rest of Europe, the direct contribution of the Scientific Revolution to the decline of belief in witchcraft was minimal. However, by the eighteenth century, the mental world of the elite was changing:

KEY FIGURE

Robert Boyle (1627–91)

An Irish-born important British scientist. His work on air and gases was of considerable importance.

? Study Source C. How good a source is this illustration for what actually happened at Tring?

SOURCE C

The swimming of Ruth Osborne by a mob at Tring, Hertfordshire, 1751.

- Most educated people, while still overwhelmingly Christian, no longer accepted that they could see God's work in all daily happenings.
- The world of the educated Englishman or woman of 1700 was a far more secure and understood world than it had appeared a century before. There was a declining sense of the miraculous and less fear of Satan and his agents.

While ordinary folk retained their witchcraft beliefs, among the elite witchcraft was no longer fashionable. There was thus a divide between elite and popular culture. According to Sharpe, it may be that 'cultural distancing, on occasions amounting to downright snobbery, was a greater force in persuading polite society to reject witch-hunting than was the impact of rationalism.'

It should be said that educated men and women did not altogether dismiss belief in witches, apparitions and spirits. Eminent people like dictionary-compiler Dr Samuel Johnson, William Blackstone, one of the eighteenth century's foremost legal minds, and Methodist John Wesley continued to believe that there was such a thing as witchcraft. 'Giving up witchcraft is, in effect, giving up the Bible', wrote Wesley in 1768. While belief in witches among the elite undoubtedly declined terminally, lively interest in astrology reveals a continuing acceptance of the occult.

Continuation of witchcraft beliefs

Historians now realise that the history of witchcraft did not end with the legal denial of its existence. Witchcraft remained a reality for a large portion of the population. No words from on high could make people less scared of witches. Until the mid-nineteenth century, most British people were still part of an agrarian economy. Other than the very meagre relief provided by the Poor Law there was no safety net to fall back on when serious misfortune struck. The illness of a family member or of a pig or cow, for example, could cause considerable hardship and lead to suspicions of witchcraft.

In the absence of a legal means of dealing with witches, cunning folk were often consulted to identify the witch responsible and to instruct on the best course of action. A counter-spell such as a witch-bottle might be employed. Numerous examples of these have been found, some dating from the early twentieth century. In its simplest form it consisted of a bottle filled with the bewitched person's urine. Into this were put some sharp objects – thorns, pins or nails. The bottle was then sealed and either buried in the ground or heated in a fire. The bottle represented the witch's bladder and the thorns and pins were meant to cause him or her such excruciating pain that he or she would remove the spell.

Another popular method of breaking witches' power was to scratch them in order to draw blood. Since this constituted a physical assault, some who employed it found themselves in court for their action. There were scores of such trials, effectively witch-trials in reverse, in the nineteenth century.

Witchcraft beliefs were finally largely eradicated in the twentieth century by the spread of educated values and as a result of the erosion of the small-scale societies where fear of witches had flourished. People today are able to explain natural phenomena and personal misfortune in ways which do not (usually) involve witchcraft. We are more confident than our early modern forebears of being able to understand and control our cosmos. There is also a lack of any real notion of cosmic evil. Thus, whereas most people in 1600 believed in witchcraft, most people today do not. Nevertheless, belief in the occult and supernatural still remains strong. And the risk of modern 'witch-hunts' – a term now used when any minority is unfairly persecuted – remains a constant threat. As Sharpe says, knowledge of the early modern witch-hunts 'should encourage us to be critical of any intolerances and persecutory urges which still flourish, and to be vigilant in protecting that fragile and imperfect, yet still precious, rationality and tolerance which we have achieved'.

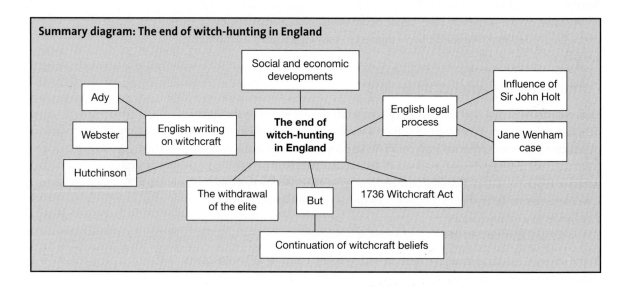

Summary diagram: The end of witch-hunting in England

- Social and economic developments
- Ady
- Webster
- Hutchinson
- English writing on witchcraft
- The end of witch-hunting in England
- English legal process
- Influence of Sir John Holt
- Jane Wenham case
- The withdrawal of the elite
- But
- 1736 Witchcraft Act
- Continuation of witchcraft beliefs

Chapter summary

Witch-hunting came to an end in Europe in the course of the seventeenth and eighteenth centuries. New legal processes – regulation of local justice, restriction and prohibition of torture, and new standards of evidence – played a crucial role. But other factors – the experience of witch-hunts, a change in the religious climate, social and economic factors – also played a part in ending the persecution. So did a change in the intellectual climate (usually called the Scientific Revolution). The work of men like Copernicus, Kepler and Galileo stressed the importance of observation and experiment. By the seventeenth century, natural philosophers and scientists like Bacon, Newton, Hobbes and Locke, and institutions such as Gresham College and the Royal Society, helped to spread new ideas about the natural world. As new laws were put forward to explain natural phenomena there was less room for belief in magic and the supernatural.

English witch-hunting came to an end thanks to the scepticism of the government and the Anglican Church after 1660. Judges were reluctant to convict witches. A number of books critical of witch beliefs, especially those by Ady, Webster and Hutchinson, were also influential. The 1736 Witchcraft Act officially brought witch persecutions to an end. However, people at local level continued to believe in witchcraft and continued to use old methods to deal with witches well into the nineteenth century.

Refresher questions

Use these questions to remind yourself of the key material covered in this chapter.

1 Why did European witch-hunting come to an end?

2 Why did new legal procedures help to bring about the decline of witch-hunting?

3 How far did changes in the religious climate affect witch-hunting?

4 How did changes in the intellectual climate help to bring about the decline of witch-hunting?

5 Who were the great natural philosophers and scientists of the seventeenth century?

6 Why did English witch-hunting come to an end?

7 Which early modern English authors were particularly important in attacking the belief in witchcraft?

8 Why did English courts stop finding witches guilty?

9 Why did ordinary folk continue to believe in witchcraft after 1736?

10 What evidence is there to suggest that witchcraft beliefs remained strong after 1736?

Question practice

ESSAY QUESTIONS

1 To what extent were the rise and decline of witch-hunting in Europe and Britain during the period from 1560 to 1660 the result of changes in legal practice?

2 How far do you agree with the view that the growth and decline of witch-hunting in the period from 1560 to 1660 were the result of pronounced changes in the religious climate in most European countries?

3 How accurate is it to say that the scientific revolution brought witch-hunting in Britain to a steady decline in the period 1650–1750?

CHAPTER 7

Conclusion

Although widespread belief in the existence of witchcraft pre-dated the early modern period, a notable intensification in prosecutions for it occurred in Europe after 1500. Between 1560 and 1660, some 50,000 people are thought to have been executed as witches. Debates over many aspects of the so-called 'witchcraze' continue. This chapter will attempt to reach some conclusions to some of the key issues by examining the following themes:

★ Reasons for the witchcraze

★ The nature of the persecutions

★ Reasons for the decline of witch-hunting

1 Reasons for the witchcraze

▶ *What were the main reasons for the witchcraze?*

Few historians now believe that there was one overarching cause for the escalation of early modern witch-hunting. Instead, it is generally accepted that there were a number of major causes and that these varied from area to area and from time to time. Most scholars today tend to focus on the following explanations: the mental world of the early modern period, political developments, the impact of the Reformation, changes in legal systems, the impact of catastrophes, socio-economic developments, a war on women and the impact of certain individuals.

The mental world of the early modern period

Debate over the nature of popular cultures and elite cultures looks set to rumble on (see pages 33–40). Most scholars now believe that there were evolving and diverse popular (and elite) cultures: Peter Burke's stark bipolar popular and elite model is usually regarded as too simplistic. However, most historians do accept that in the field of religion and magic, early modern Europeans – rich and poor, educated and illiterate, peasants and townsmen – held a number of common attitudes.

Religious attitudes

In 1500, people in western and central Europe accepted the practices and beliefs of the Catholic Church. Its calendar, festivals and rituals dominated people's lives. Moreover, most, elites and masses alike:

- saw God's presence in the world everywhere
- believed that the world around them was full of 'signs' which could be interpreted as portents: sunshine on St Vincent's day, for example, meant a good wine harvest
- believed they could ward off ill fortune by various means including prayer and the wearing of amulets which had been blessed by a priest.

Magic

Magical beliefs and practices permeated early modern European society:

- Elite intellectuals dabbled in prophecy, astrology and alchemy because they seemed to present paths to knowledge and understanding of the world.
- Most peasants seem to have had no sense of any meaningful division between religion and magic in their strategies for coping with life's problems.

If misfortune occurred, peasants sought aid from any or all of the local purveyors of magic: saints' shrines, parish priests or local people who had a reputation for harnessing the power of supernatural forces. Such folk existed across Europe. Contemporary English writers thought they probably equalled or even exceeded the parish clergy in numbers. Most people had recourse to 'white' magic at some time in their lives in an attempt to ensure the welfare of loved ones, livestock or crops. Most also feared the power of 'black' magic which could be directed to do harm.

Belief in witchcraft

Belief in witchcraft was general among ordinary Europeans. But the educated elites also embraced the reality of witchcraft. For Christian theologians the essence of witchcraft was the pact which the witch made with the Devil, agreeing to do his bidding (see page 2). By the sixteenth century, demonologists claimed that witches met together in sabbats (to which they had flown) to indulge in unspeakable acts, including eating babies and copulating with Satan. They were depicted as the ultimate heretics: enemies of God who sought to overthrow Christianity.

Most Europeans, rather than viewing witches as Devil-worshippers, focused on *maleficia*: with the effects of a witch's power rather than with its origins. They were concerned not with how misfortune occurred but with who had made it happen. The answer was often a particular woman who had long had a reputation for being able to cause harm by magical means. Nevertheless, learned ideas of Devil-worship gradually began to infiltrate popular understanding:

- Illustrated pamphlets portrayed witches riding on goats or broomsticks to sabbats and participating in orgies.
- Executions of witches attracted large crowds. The list of charges read out for all to hear usually included the fact that the condemned witches had been found to be in league with the Devil.

By the late sixteenth century, popular denunciations for witchcraft in many parts of Europe involved at least some parts of the demonic conception of witchcraft. Thus, there was a great deal of overlap between popular and elite attitudes, particularly because most judges lent great weight to the harmful acts of which the witches were accused in making their judgments.

Attacks on magic and superstition

The world-view of magic and superstition came under attack during the Reformation and to a lesser extent from the Counter-Reformation. Protestant reformers taught that misfortune was a punishment from God for sin and that the only theologically valid response was repentance and prayer. But many peasants continued to prefer the old ways and attempts to abolish the magical from popular religion proved to be an uphill task for reformers.

In the sixteenth and early seventeenth centuries, neither Protestant nor Catholic reformers denied the existence of the witch. Indeed, at the same time as they were trying to stamp out popular superstition, many religious authorities blamed society's misfortune on witchcraft.

Political developments

Some historians have related the persecution of witches to early modern political developments, especially the centralisation processes (state-building) and the authorities' quest for greater social discipline.

State-building

It was once claimed that centralised states used their increasing power to pursue and prosecute witches. However, historical research has shown that the mass persecutions usually occurred in smaller states or regions which were outside the control of the central government or where central authority had largely broken down (for example, in East Anglia in the English Civil War). In such areas, local courts, egged on by the people, could take charge of the process. In an age of state-building, a concerted witch-hunt was something of an aberration: it was likely to exacerbate social divisions to the detriment of order. Generally, strong governments sought to resist the considerable pressure from below for witch-burnings. Surrender to popular passions ran counter to what rulers were trying to achieve: the imposition of government on community. Authorities in strong, centralised states were more likely to end than to promote witch-hunts.

The quest for social discipline

A more convincing explanation for witch-hunting is the fact that some states sought greater social discipline. Uniting with religious authorities, some rulers (such as King James VI of Scotland) sought to create a more godly state. Witches were perceived as a huge threat to that state. The logical conclusion thus seemed to be to eradicate witches.

The impact of the Reformation

Many historians have noted the coincidence of the rise in witch prosecutions with the Protestant Reformation and the Catholic Counter-Reformation. This was not so much because Catholics accused Protestants and Protestants accused Catholics in an outburst of religious hostility. It was more to do with the fact that both movements encouraged the condemnation of witchcraft as a sin against God and Christian society. Catholic prince-bishops who launched large-scale witch-hunts did so, in part, because they were attempting to create a godly state in their small domains. Similarly, many Calvinist leaders, for example, in Scotland, pressed the government to take action against witchcraft. Catholic and Protestant leaders alike believed they must resist the forces of Satan.

Changes in legal systems

Historian Brian Levack regards the reinvigoration of Roman law across much of Europe as central to the process of witchcraft investigation (see pages 15–19). The new inquisitorial procedures involved intense questioning, the aim of which was to persuade the suspect to confess. Judges were allowed to torture suspects because the papacy had judged witchcraft to be an exceptional crime (see page 3). The use of torture generally ensured that people confessed to witchcraft crimes. It also usually ensured that they implicated others. Countries in Europe which did not allow the use of torture, for example England, saw relatively few witchcraft trials and almost no large-scale witch-hunts.

However, the use of inquisitorial procedures did not always lead to witch-hunts. The most famous Inquisitions in early modern Europe, those in Spain, Portugal and Italy, were in fact very lenient in their treatment of those accused of witchcraft. The Inquisition in Spain executed only a handful of witches, the Portuguese Inquisition only one and the Roman Inquisition none, although in each of these areas there were hundreds of witchcraft cases. Inquisitors firmly believed in the power of the Devil but they doubted very much whether the people accused of *maleficia* had actually made a pact with Satan that gave them special powers.

The impact of catastrophes

It is often claimed that a rise in witch prosecutions responded to particular catastrophes such as disease epidemics, crop failures or wars:

- Epidemics could result in an increase in witchcraft prosecutions. However, this did not usually happen. Moreover, in cities like Geneva, suspected plague-spreaders (many of whom were executed) were not necessarily regarded as witches.
- Historian Wolfgang Behringer claims that the 'mini ice age' in central Europe had a major impact on witch-hunting in south-west Germany (see pages 65–7) where witches became a useful scapegoat for people's misery.
- The greatest witch-hunts occurred in Germany during the Thirty Years' War (see page 67)

However, a rise in witch prosecution did not necessarily – or even usually – follow a particular catastrophe. Indeed, it has been claimed that a lack of crisis was more conducive to witch-hunting: authorities were not then distracted by war, famine or disease. Certainly the areas most affected by catastrophe were not necessarily those which experienced the highest rate of witchcraft trials.

Socio-economic developments

Historians Alan Macfarlane and Keith Thomas claimed that the worsening socio-economic developments in the late sixteenth century, resulting from a rising population, inflation and increasing poverty for those on the margins of society, had a major impact on witchcraft persecution (see pages 25–6). They claim that the economic situation exacerbated social tensions within villages. Macfarlane and Thomas showed that most of those accused of witchcraft in Essex were unpopular, antisocial and frequently aggressive women who were known for begging from their neighbours and verbally cursing those who turned them away.

Macfarlane and Thomas argued that worsening economic circumstances made people more reluctant to give to the poor, who were increasingly perceived as a threat and a problem. They claimed that the refusal of charity led to resentment and ill-feeling and in turn to the guilt of those who turned the needy away. Any subsequent misfortune could then be attributed to the malice of the offended party, leading to an accusation of witchcraft (and the assuaging of guilt).

All this is perhaps going too far. The socio-economic situation, even in Essex, never mind in England or Europe as a whole, was not quite as clear-cut as Macfarlane and Thomas argued. Nor is the 'charity refused' model very convincing. There is not much evidence, for example, that those who did not give alms felt particularly guilty.

However, Macfarlane and Thomas's emphasis on the fact that it was personal interaction within local communities which led to accusations, not actions from the evil elite above, is crucially important in the historiographical debates on witchcraft. There is no doubt whatsoever that fears, suspicions, grievances, jealousies and gossip at village level often led to the victimisation of individuals and eventually to their prosecution.

A war on women?

Given that an estimated 80 per cent of those accused of witchcraft were women, it is possible to equate the witch-hunts to a hate campaign by an increasingly misogynistic and patriarchal society (see page 28). However, the feminist view that witch persecutions were a war on women is far from convincing:

- The fact that twenty per cent of victims were men indicates that witch-hunting was a gender-related rather than gender-specific campaign. In some areas, for example, Iceland, Russia and Estonia, the majority of those convicted as witches were men.
- Many of the witnesses who testified against female witches were women.
- The sporadic nature of the prosecutions makes it unlikely that there was a co-ordinated campaign to target women.

Ultimately, witches were persecuted because they were regarded as witches, not because they were women.

Nevertheless, the imbalance remains and needs to be explained. Arguably:

- Women were disproportionately associated with witchcraft because of traditional perceptions of their susceptibility to sexual temptation, inconstancy, gullibility and deceitfulness.
- The predominantly female domestic roles of childrearing, treating the sick and food preparation also made them suspect when people, especially children, fell ill or died.
- Most women who were accused of witchcraft did not conform to the stereotype of the 'good' wife and mother: they were usually argumentative, wilful and aggressive.
- There was a widespread assumption that the crime of witchcraft was a female crime, just as the crime of highway robbery was a male crime.

The impact of individuals

The role of certain individuals in particular regions often proved crucial:

- A number of German prince-bishops, who were both religious and secular authorities in their bishoprics, were among the most active witch-hunters. A few, like Johann Georg Fuchs von Dornheim in Bamberg, took a leading role in prosecutions (see page 76).
- King James VI's role in supporting witchcraft persecution was crucial in Scotland. In *Daemonologie* (1597), he advocated the harshest punishment for witches.
- Certain judges played a key role. Nicolas Remy, for example, at the end of the sixteenth century, happily claimed responsibility for hundreds of deaths in lands that became eastern France.
- Witch-finders, like Matthew Hopkins in Essex, sometimes played a vital role.

Conclusion

The witchcraze therefore resulted from a complex interplay of various factors. There was no single, universal explanation. It needs to be added that the witch-hunts were not motivated by stupidity. Witchcraft provided both an explanation and a remedy (through counter-magic or trial) for the misfortunes people experienced. Accusations thus constituted both a rational and a reasonable response in their own terms. Most people, the elite and ordinary people alike, believed that the punishment of witches was an appropriate course of action. It is worth noting that in the normal run of witch-hunts, far more rage was directed at witches than at their persecutors. It should be also be said that most of the judges in witch cases seem to have acted from a spirit of duty and a concern for the public welfare.

Moreover, it does seem that some of those accused of witchcraft were in fact guilty. It is remarkable how often the accused came to believe in their own guilt and produced elaborate confessions, even when no torture was used or threatened. Suspected witches often seemed to have believed in their own powers, which could serve as a way to earn a living or gain influence over their neighbours and within their community. Geoffrey Scarre and John Callow (2001) thought it 'without doubt' that some of those accused of witchcraft were guilty of employing magic in an attempt to harm their enemies or settle scores. 'Surely some early modern people must have tried to kill with magic', writes Gaskill: 'it would be incredible if they hadn't.'

 # The nature of the persecutions

▶ *Was there actually a witchcraze?*

Estimates of 9 million executions for witchcraft have long since been abandoned. Exact figures of those prosecuted and executed as witches are difficult to obtain because of the patchy survival of sources. Recent research suggests that some 100,000 people were prosecuted and between 40,000 and 60,000 executed. In some respects, this is a shockingly high figure: indeed, ten times as many people may have been executed for witchcraft as for heresy in the early modern period. However, in other respects, the figure is relatively small, especially given the very real fear that witches roused. The fact that half of those who were accused were found not guilty is also surprising.

The process

In the sixteenth century, most secular rulers north of the Alps passed witchcraft statutes authorising the death penalty for witches who harmed people through the use of magic or sorcery. These civil laws, such as the English and Scottish witchcraft statutes of 1563, tended to focus more on *maleficia* and less on pacts with the Devil.

The charge of witchcraft

Most witch trials began with an accusation of *maleficia* in a village or town. Individuals accused someone they knew of using magic to spoil food, make children ill, raise hailstorms or do other types of harm. Local communities often preferred to wait until other avenues had been explored before recourse to the law. Peasants might deal with the suspected witch at local level by:

- scratching her and drawing blood to nullify her spell
- trying to counter the spell with white magic.

Prosecutions were not lightly brought, partly because of the costs of litigation and the local rifts which a prosecution could cause. Possible retribution from the accused's relatives (or the accused themselves) if the prosecution failed was a further deterrent, a fear firmly wedded to the belief in the supernatural powers of the supposed witch. Judges or magistrates usually required a number of witnesses to support the accuser and a substantial case history of supposed crimes. This explains why many of the accused were relatively old, having built up a reputation over a lifetime.

Large-scale hunts

Large-scale hunts were the outgrowth of smaller investigations, in which the circle of suspects brought in for questioning simply continued to grow unchecked. This was a relatively rare phenomenon. The worst hunts occurred in places where a popular fear of witchcraft was taken seriously by local judicial authorities which had enough autonomy to bend legal procedures explicitly to the extirpation of witches. Torture was used, not just to extract confessions, but to obtain the names of additional suspects. In areas of Europe in which the demonic concept of witchcraft never took hold, such as Iceland, Finland and Estonia, there were no large-scale hunts.

Mass panics tended to end when it became clear to legal authorities or to the local community that the people being executed were not what they understood witches to be, or that the scope of accusations defied credulity.

The involvement of children

Children were sometimes involved in witch-hunts. Some were victims, especially in Germany. (A quarter of the 160 witches executed in Würzburg between 1627 and 1629 were juveniles.) Some children were malicious dreamers – as in Salem (see pages 139–44). A few children seem to have believed themselves to be witches. In some areas, witchcraft was thought to be an inheritable condition and children grew up dreading the day of accusation.

Variations

The rise in prosecutions varied according to time and place and was dependent on a number of regional variables. Some areas were prone to mass trials, principally parts of the Holy Roman Empire. In other countries, notably France and England, large-scale hunts were much less common. In France, remarkable restraint was exercised by the judges and the leading sovereign court, the *parlement* of Paris, which had jurisdiction over much of France. It was in the French borderlands – Lorraine, Franche-Comté, Normandy and the Pyrenees, that most witches were executed. These areas were unstable and further away from central control.

Spain, Portugal, Ireland and Russia experienced very little by way of persecutions. In Spain and Portugal, prosecutions were undertaken by the Inquisition (see above). This was more concerned with enforcing orthodoxy than locating diabolism.

Persecution in southern Germany

Persecution of witches in the Holy Roman Empire was patchy. In many parts of what is today Germany, the restraint of judicial processes often prevented large-scale persecution. This was true in small states like Rothenburg (which had only three witch executions in its entire history) and the Palatinate. It was also true in larger states like Austria and Bavaria. But elsewhere, especially in south-western Catholic German states, for example, Trier, Mainz, Würzburg, Ellwangen, Bamberg and Cologne, there were mass witch panics.

There are a number of explanations for the mass panics:

- Much of south-west Germany consisted of very small government units, whose rulers were largely unhindered in their legal or judicial moves by any higher authority.
- The ruling Catholic prince-bishops saw persecuting witches as a way to demonstrate their piety and concern for order. Some of the worst panics followed the aggressive restoration of Catholicism by Counter-Reformation prince-bishops.
- Climatic problems, usually cold and wet summers and late hailstorms, led to pressure from below for some action to be taken against witches who were blamed for the bad weather.
- It may be that some rulers promoted witch trials to deflect criticism and to appease popular pressure.
- The Thirty Years' War led to increased turmoil and fear, destabilising local communities.

Suspicion grew into accusations, accusations into trials, which in turn generated more accusations and trials. No one was above suspicion. Between 1626 and 1631, Philipp Adolf von Ehrenberg, prince-bishop of Würzburg, executed 900 people for witchcraft including large numbers of atypical victims – wealthier people, children and men. In total, there were over 20,000 German executions – almost half the European total.

Interestingly, witch-hunting declined during the 1630s, at a time when many communities in south-west Germany were facing increasing problems arising from famine, plague, economic collapse and the threat of marauding armies.

Persecution in Britain and North America

There were considerable regional variations with regard to witch persecution in Britain. (England and Scotland were separate countries until the Act of Union in 1707.) Scotland saw more witch-hunts than England. In England, witch-hunts occurred mainly in Essex and the south-eastern counties. There were relatively few prosecutions and even fewer executions in Wales and Ireland, which were both controlled by England.

England

Some 500 witches were probably executed in England. Nearly half of these died in East Anglia – especially Essex. England's apparent leniency has been explained by its different legal system, based on common law rather than continental-style Roman law. English law treated witchcraft as a felony rather than a heresy (so that witches were hanged rather than burned). More importantly, England banned the use of torture, which reduced the likelihood of confession and the incrimination of others which often lay behind mass convictions on the Continent. The use of the jury system may also have led to many witches being found innocent. (However, jury trials of witches in Denmark did not lead to lighter sentences.) In England, the emphasis of the charges was invariably on the practice of malevolent magic rather than contact with the Devil.

The most serious witch-hunting occurred when the traditional legal system broke down in the 1640s during the Civil War. Matthew Hopkins and his partner John Stearne were able to exploit wartime disruption to style themselves instruments of justice. They extracted confessions in pre-trial investigations by using methods, especially sleep deprivation, which were akin to torture. The result was about 100 executions – one-fifth of England's total for the early modern period. Hopkins and Stearne's persecution took place in East Anglia, a Puritan-controlled area (Hopkins and Stearne were themselves strongly Puritan). Many English Puritans, keen to establish a godly state, wished to eradicate witchcraft.

Scotland

Scotland had a legal system not dissimilar to that of England. However, King James VI, who believed strongly in the threat of witchcraft, allowed the use of torture to extract confessions. The so-called North Berwick persecutions that occurred in the 1590s had a political as well as a religious side. James

believed that his political enemies, notably the Earl of Bothwell, had sought
to use witchcraft against him. James was also anxious to have the support of
the Scottish Kirk. He thus approved royal commissions to hunt down witches.
James's political concerns did not mean that he was insincere about witchcraft.
As Gaskill says, 'Demonology and state ideology merged: James the absolutist
monarch and James the witch-hunter were the same man on the same royal
business.' Many leading Scottish Calvinist ministers believed that witchcraft
was a threat to their efforts to create a godly society. The result was that
Scotland, a country with only a quarter of the population of England, probably
executed three times as many witches. The Scottish pattern of prosecution had
more similarities with some continental countries, especially German states,
than with England.

Salem

The colonists who settled in New England took the English notions of witchcraft
with them. But relatively few people were executed as witches. Salem was the
only 'big' case. For all its notoriety both at the time and since, it resulted in about
150 arrests but only nineteen executions and one person crushed to death for
refusing to plead. (Several people died in prison while awaiting trial.) What
happened at Salem was extraordinary, particularly because the persecution
came at a time when witchcraft as a crime was abating in England. Leading
Puritan ministers might have done more to prevent the panic; the extent to
which they supported it remains debatable. The greatest irony of the Salem trials
was that only people who refused to confess were executed: those who, in effect,
perjured themselves were spared. This was probably as much through luck as
judgement (see pages 147–8).

Many Americans – historians, novelists, playwrights and scientists – have tried
to explain Salem. Among the various interpretations are divine retribution (a
contemporary rationale), class conflict, village factionalism, a scam to grab the
victims' property, the coming of capitalism, political repression, mental illness
and 'acid-trip' – the idea that victims ate rye bread infected with ergot.

In truth, it was the belief in witchcraft which led to the 1692 hysteria. That
hysteria was made possible by Salem's remoteness from central government:
London was 3000 miles away. 'Like most crazes', says Gaskill, 'Salem was not
about the growth of the state but its weakness and failure.' But there would have
been no witch trials in Salem had it not been for local fears, rage and belief in
the power of witches. Thus, for a few months witchcraft became a terrifying
reality. The fear of witches was greater than the fear of injustice. But order was
eventually restored by Governor Phips, who was advised by Increase Mather
and other Puritan ministers, many of whom had initially supported the trials.

The witnesses at Salem may well have been hysterical. But the judges were
essentially sober and learned men. They tried to do right in what they saw as the
most difficult and urgent crisis to affect their colony.

Was there a witchcraze?

The differences in the intensity of prosecution between countries have led historians to downplay the notion of a European-wide witchcraze in the early modern period.

Across Europe, the estimate that only 40–50 per cent of those who came to trial for witchcraft were actually executed does not suggest that the judgements were driven by panic. Indeed, the leniency or caution of the judges in witchcraft cases is quite impressive. Given the perceived threat supposedly posed by witches, far more might have been expected to have been condemned. The conviction rate for similar 'moral' crimes which were prosecuted in this period was far higher. Infanticide (an almost exclusively 'female' crime) resulted in the execution of most of those accused. The relatively low conviction rate for witches was despite the fact that every effort was made to load the case against accused witches by allowing the usually inadmissible testimony of women, children, felons, servants and those with a vested interest in the outcome.

Most witchcraft historians now point out that isolated trials and executions, although more frequent than before, continued to be the norm in most countries. The mass panics in Germany were exceptions to the rule. Indeed, it has been suggested by Rowlands (2003) that 'areas which did not experience witch-hunts may well have been the early modern norm rather than the exception'.

3 Reasons for the decline of witch-hunting

▶ *Why did witch-hunting in Europe come to an end?*

A number of sixteenth-century authors, for example Johann Weyer and Reginald Scot, were sceptical of the danger posed by witches (see page 7). Weyer concluded that the Devil was more than capable of undertaking acts of *maleficia* without human assistance. By the late seventeenth century, it was clear that many of Europe's intellectual, legal, political and religious elite had no time for witches or witchcraft. Their scepticism was decisive in bringing legal prosecution to an end.

Intellectual scepticism

Changes in the intellectual world, usually called the Scientific Revolution, fostered disbelief in the power of witchcraft. The ideas of Copernicus, Kepler, Galileo, Bacon, Descartes, Newton, Hobbes and Locke (see pages 165–8) challenged traditional thinking of the way the universe operated. Their ideas also challenged the notion of witchcraft. However, as Geoffrey Scarre and John Callow point out, the responsibility of the Scientific Revolution for ending the witch trials can be exaggerated because 'the theories of the scientific revolutionaries did not obtain a firm basis in educated consciousness until the age of witch trials was past'.

Political scepticism

The experience of witch-hunts convinced many secular authorities that witch-hunts were counterproductive. Far from having a stabilising and purifying effect, witch panics brought fear and disorder. By the eighteenth century, the ruling elites were sceptical of witchcraft accusations and were determined to control popular passions. Stronger centralised governments also had greater control over regions within their states – the areas where witch-hunts had been common.

Religious scepticism

By the late seventeenth and early eighteenth centuries, many leading theologians, both Catholic and Protestant, were sceptical of witchcraft. Balthasar Bekker (see page 164) argued that God's love was supreme. The Devil, by contrast with God, was a miserable, impotent figure. In 1718, English Bishop Francis Hutchinson (see page 172) attributed witches to 'the imaginations of men': witch-ordeals were 'the meanest of paganist and popish superstitions' and spectral evidence was 'far from being legal proof'. Protestant theologians, in particular, saw God operating benignly through natural forces and laws rather than through malice. Moreover, most leading churchmen were less concerned with establishing godly states on earth. Sin was increasingly envisaged more as the result of specifically human and social weaknesses rather than the work of the Devil.

Legal scepticism

By the mid-seventeenth century, many judges and magistrates felt uneasy with the concept of witchcraft. Most accepted that justice had often been perverted by popular action and believed that a large number of innocent people had been executed. While many judges still accepted that there might be witches, most had come to think that attempts to punish them were futile and dangerous and might do no more than play the Devil's game. Other judges and magistrates were convinced that witchcraft was an impossibility. In *De Crimine Magiae* (1701), for example, Christian Thomasius, an influential German law professor, maintained that witchcraft was a clerical invention. Most judges were also sceptical of:

- the use of torture in witchcraft cases
- the validity of spectral evidence.

The contribution of sceptical judges and magistrates was crucial in bringing witch-hunts to an end. The *parlement* of Paris, for example, introduced the automatic appeal of all witchcraft cases from the French provinces as early as 1624 and in 1640 forbade the prosecution of witchcraft cases altogether – a position not officially decreed by the French Crown until 1682.

By 1700, across Europe, forced confessions for witchcraft were frequently dismissed in law courts and voluntary ones were taken to signify mental illness. Witchcraft trials and convictions thus diminished.

Conclusion

Witch-hunts in the sixteenth and early seventeenth centuries provide an example of the overlap of popular and elite attitudes. For many decades, the elites and ordinary people worked together in a common cause in many parts of Europe. Traditional witch beliefs continued to remain part of mass culture in most parts of Europe well into the nineteenth century – and sometimes beyond. But by the early eighteenth century, the elites in western and central Europe had abandoned their belief in witchcraft. This process of 'withdrawal' from traditional culture did not take place in a single generation but occurred at different times in different areas. Witch-hunts continued in Poland and other parts of eastern Europe well into the late eighteenth century.

But by 1700 most of the European elites had a more rational, less fearful view of the world – and the potential of evil forces within it. Belief that Satan interfered directly in human affairs had begun to wane. This provided a coherent intellectual context for increased scepticism of witchcraft.

Elite opinion was only indirectly influenced by the ideas of Kepler, Galileo, Descartes, Bacon and Newton. For many, rejection of witchcraft was as much a matter of culture as intellect: witchcraft was perceived to be a superstition of the masses from which the European elites wished to distance themselves. The elites proceeded to impose their beliefs – albeit slowly – on the rest of society and witchcraft persecutions came to an end. By the late eighteenth century, witchcraft seemed so self-evidently nonsensical to Europe's intellectual elite that it was not worth refuting. Scepticism of witchcraft and the occult generally has been regarded as a badge of reason ever since.

Question practice

ESSAY QUESTIONS

1 'The European witch-hunts were primarily a war against women.' How far do you agree with this view in the period from 1560 to 1660?

2 'Regional variations make it impossible to generalise about reasons for the rise and fall in European witchcraft prosecutions.' How far do you agree with this view in the period from 1550 to 1650?

3 'Witch persecutions in the period from 1560 to 1660 depended on the support of the elites.' How far do you agree with this view?

4 'Areas which did not experience large-scale witch-hunts may well have been the early modern norm rather than the exception.' How far do you agree with this view in the period from 1550 to 1660?

Edexcel A level History

Sources guidance

Edexcel's Paper 3, Option 33: The witch craze in Britain, Europe and North America, c.1580–c.1750 is assessed by an exam comprising three sections:

- Section A is a source analysis assessment. It tests your knowledge of one of the key topics in depth.
- Section B requires you to write one essay from a choice of two, again testing your knowledge of key topics in depth (see page 198 for guidance on this).
- Section C requires you to write one essay from a choice of two. Questions relate to themes in breadth and test your knowledge of change over a period of at least 100 years (see page 202 for guidance on this).

The sections of the exam relate to the sections of the paper in the following way:

Section A and Section B	Test your knowledge of the key topics in depth	Persecuting witches: <ul><li>The North Berwick witches in Scotland, 1590–1 and the aftermath to 1597</li><li>The Lancashire witches of 1604–13</li><li>The great witch-hunt in Bamberg, Germany, 1623–32</li><li>Matthew Hopkins and the East Anglian witch craze, 1645–7</li><li>Cotton Mather and the Salem witch-hunt, 1692–3</li></ul>
Section C	Tests your knowledge of the themes in breadth	Challenges to the witch craze, c.1580–c.1750: <ul><li>Changing attitudes to witchcraft in Britain</li><li>The wider intellectual context: the coming of the age of science and reason</li></ul>

The following advice relates to Paper 3, Section A. Paper 3 is only available at A level, therefore there is no AS level version of this paper.

Paper 3 Section A

Section A of Paper 3 comprises a single compulsory question which refers to one source.

The question

The Section A question will begin with the following stem: 'Assess the value of the source for revealing …'. For example:

> Assess the value of the source for revealing Matthew Hopkins' motives for persecuting witches in East Anglia in the years 1645–7 and how he approached the interrogation of suspected witches.

> Explain your answer, using the source, the information given about its origin and your own knowledge about the historical context.

The source

The source will be a primary or contemporary source: it will have been written contemporary to c.1580–c.1750, the period that you are studying. The source will be around 350 words long. It will be accompanied by a brief passage which will set out the essential provenance of the source. Here is an example:

SOURCE I

From Matthew Hopkins' pamphlet, *The Discovery of Witches*, published in 1647.

The Discoverer never travelled far for it, but in March 1644 he had some seven or eight of that horrible sect of Witches living in the Towne where he lived, a Towne in Essex called Maningtree, with divers other adjacent Witches of other towns, who every six weeks in the night (being always on the Friday night) had their meeting close by his house and had their severall solemne sacrifices there offered to the Devill. One of which this discoverer heard speaking to her Imps one night, and bid them goe to another Witch, who was thereupon apprehended and searched, by women who had for many yeeres knowne the Devill's marks, and found to have three teats about her, which honest women have not: so upon command from the Justice they were to keep her from sleep two or three nights, expecting in that time to see her familiars, which the fourth night she called in by their severall names, and told them what shapes, a quarter of an houre before they came in, there being ten of us in the roome, the first she called was

1. Holt, *who came in like a white kitling.*
2. Jarmara, *who came in like a far Spaniel without any legs at all, she said she kept him fat, for she* slapt her hand on her belly and said he suckt good blood from her body.
3. Vinegar Tom, *who was like a long-legg'd Greyhound, with an head like an Oxe, with a long taile and broad eyes, who when this discoverer spoke to, and bade him goe to the place provided for him and his Angels, immediately transformed himselfe into the shape of a child of foure yeeres old without a head, and gave halfe a dozen turns about the house, and vanished at the doore.*
4. Sack and Sugar, *like a black Rabbet.*
5. Newes, *like a Polecat.*

All these vanished away in a little time. Immediately after this Witch confessed severall other Witches, from whom she had her Imps, and named to divers women where their marks were, and Imps, and Imps names, as Elemanzer, Pyewacke, Peckin the Crown, Grizzel, Greedigut, &c. which no mortall could invent, and upon their searches the same Markes were found, the same number, and in the same place, and the like confessions from them of the same Imps, (though they knew not that we were told before).

Understanding the question

To answer the question successfully you must understand how the question works. The question is written precisely in order to make sure that you understand the task. Each part of the question has a specific meaning.

Assess the value of the source[1] for revealing Matthew Hopkins' motives for persecuting witches in East Anglia in the years 1645–7[2] and how he approached the interrogation of suspected witches[3].

Explain your answer, using the source, the information given about its origin and your own knowledge about the historical context.

1 You must evaluate how useful the source could be to a historian. Evaluating the extent of usefulness involves considering its value and limitations in the light of your own knowledge about the source's historical context. Important information about the context of the source is included in the information given about the source.
2 The question focuses on two specific enquiries that the source might be useful for. The first is Matthew Hopkins' motives for persecuting witches.
3 The second enquiry is how he set about interrogating suspected witches.

You should use the source, the information about the source and your own knowledge of the historical context to make a judgement about how far the source is useful to a historian engaged in two specific enquiries. Crucially, you must consider both enquiries; an answer which only focuses on one of the enquiries is unlikely to do well.

Source skills

Section A of Paper 3 tests your ability to evaluate source material. Your job is to analyse the source by reading it in the context of the values and assumptions of the society and the period from which it came.

Examiners will mark your work by focusing on the extent to which you are able to do the following:

- Interpret and analyse source material:
  - At a basic level, this means you can understand the source and select, copy, paraphrase and summarise the source to help answer the question.
  - At a higher level, your interpretation of the source includes the ability to explain, analyse and make inferences based on the source.
  - At the highest levels, you will be expected to analyse the source in a sophisticated way. This includes the ability to distinguish between information, opinions and arguments contained in the source.
- Deploy knowledge of historical context in relation to the source:
  - At a basic level, this means the ability to link the source to your knowledge of the context in which the source was written, using this knowledge to expand or support the information contained in the source.
  - At a higher level, you will be able to use your contextual knowledge to make inferences, and to expand, support or challenge the details mentioned in the source.
  - At the highest levels, you will examine the value and limits of the material contained in the source by interpreting the source in the context of the values and assumptions of the society from which it is taken.
- Evaluate the usefulness and weight of the source material:

  - At a basic level, evaluation of the source will be based on simplistic criteria about reliability and bias.
  - At a higher level, evaluation of the source will be based on the nature and purpose of the source.
  - At the highest levels, evaluation of the source will be based on a valid criterion that is justified in the course of the essay. You will also be able to distinguish between the value of different aspects of the source.

Make sure your source evaluation is sophisticated. Avoid crude statements about bias, and avoid simplistic assumptions such as that a source written immediately after an event is reliable, whereas a source written years later is unreliable.

Try to see things through the eyes of the writer:

- How does the writer understand the world?
- What assumptions does the writer have?
- Who is the writer trying to influence?
- What views is the writer trying to challenge?

Basic skill: comprehension

The most basic source skill is comprehension: understanding what the source means. There are a variety of techniques that you can use to aid comprehension. For example, you could read the sources included in this book and in past papers. In this context you could:

- Read the sources out loud.
- Look up any words that you don't understand and make a glossary.
- Make flash cards containing brief biographies of the writers of the sources.

You can demonstrate comprehension by copying, paraphrasing and summarising the sources. However, keep this to the minimum as comprehension is a low-level skill and you need to leave room for higher-level skills.

Advanced skill: contextualising the sources

First, to analyse the sources correctly you need to understand them in the context in which they were written. Source 1 reflects Matthew Hopkins' view. Your job is to understand the values and assumptions behind the source.

- One way of contextualising the source is to consider the nature, origins and purpose of the source. However, this can lead to a formulaic essay.
- An alternative is to consider two levels of context. First, you should establish the general context. In this case, Source 1 was written towards the end of Matthew Hopkins' life. Second, you can look for specific references to contemporary events, people or debates in the sources. For example, when considering his motives for persecuting witches, the details in the source can be put in context in the following way:
  - 'The Discoverer' (Hopkins is speaking about himself) says he first became aware of witches in March 1644 (did he really mean 1645?) in Maningtree (today usually spelt Manningtree) in Essex.
  - Hopkins says there were 'seven or eight' witches in Manningtree and 'divers' (many) others in nearby towns.
  - Hopkins states that the Manningtree witches met 'close by his house' every six weeks at night and offered sacrifices to the Devil.
  - Hopkins infers that he heard one of the witches speaking to her imps. (You will need to stress the importance of imps in the context of English witchcraft.) This led to the apprehension of another suspect who was questioned. This presumably was Elizabeth Clarke.
  - Hopkins describes the process of interrogation, asserting that he had been given authority by the local justice of the peace to deprive the suspect of sleep for several days.

- On the fourth night, Clarke's imps 'appeared in force' and were apparently observed by ten people present in the room.
- Hopkins asserts that other women who were implicated by Clarke were found to have witches' marks and imps with the exact names that Clarke had provided.
- Hopkins implies that this is proof that witchcraft existed in the area of Essex where he lived.

Using context to make judgements

- Start by establishing the general context of the source:
  - Ask yourself, what was going on at the time when the source was written, or the time of the events described in the source?
  - What are the key debates that the source might be contributing to?
- Next, look for key words and phrases that establish the specific context. Does the source refer to specific people, events or books that might be important?
- Make sure your contextualisation focuses on the question.
- Use the context when evaluating the usefulness and limitations of the source.

For example:

Source 1 is valuable to a historian investigating Hopkins' motives for persecuting witches because he provides what he sees as convincing evidence that witchcraft existed in the area around Manningtree in Essex. Hopkins believed that the suspected witches met every six weeks on Friday nights. He states that the women who searched the suspects found evidence of 'the Devil's marks', for example three teats. And, improbable though it may appear to us, he testifies to seeing – along with ten other witnesses – a variety of familiars (or imps) who were eventually summoned by Elizabeth Clarke, his first victim. Clarke then implicated a number of other women. Her testimony with regard to their Devil's marks and the name of their familiars was supported when these women, in turn, were interrogated. Hopkins regarded this as proof that witchcraft existed and posed a real threat to his local area. Hopkins seems to have accepted that familiars did appear. It is reasonable to infer that he believed that those who read his tract would also accept the evidence. He was surely aware that magistrates, juries and judges in seventeenth-century England were influenced in witchcraft cases by confessions from suspected witches, and also by evidence of familiars and witches' marks.

The source also provides evidence of Hopkins' methods of interrogation. He used experienced women – probably midwives – to search the suspects' bodies to find 'the Devill's marks'. With the backing of the local magistrate, he then deprived Clarke of sleep for three nights. Sleep deprivation remains an effective form of torture. Most victims will usually confess to what their interrogators ask. Eventually, Clarke confessed to being a witch. She was also persuaded to accuse other women of being witches. The appearance of various animals was seen as proof of the suspect having familiars. In England, uniquely, most people thought that communion with Satan was achieved through familiar spirits, disguised as animals. Elsewhere in Europe, imps were rarely mentioned in witchcraft cases. Instead, witches were thought to communicate with the Devil at sabbats where they met to worship and devise malevolent plots. Perhaps the senses of Hopkins and the other witnesses who claimed to see the familiars were similarly affected by lack of sleep. Hopkins seems to have genuinely believed that his methods were just and proper and were essential in the battle to root out witches. Finally, it is clear from the source that Hopkins was not acting alone. He had the support of a magistrate, a team of female body searchers and a large number of witnesses. Many people in East Anglia in the 1640s, like Hopkins, regarded witchcraft as a major threat to their communities.

The two paragraphs above thus make inferences from details in the source to suggest that it is of considerable use for both lines of enquiry: Hopkins' motives and his methods.

Essay guidance (1)

Paper 3

To get a high grade in Section B of Paper 3 your essay must contain four essential qualities:

- focused analysis
- relevant detail
- supported judgement
- organisation, coherence and clarity.

This section focuses on the following aspects of exam technique:

- The nature of the question.
- Planning your answer, including writing a focused introduction.
- Deploying relevant detail.
- Writing analytically.
- Reaching a supported judgement.

The nature of the question

Section B questions are designed to test the depth of your historical knowledge. Therefore, they can focus on relatively short periods, or single events. Moreover, they can focus on different historical processes or 'concepts'. These include:

- cause
- consequence
- change/continuity
- similarity/difference
- significance.

These different question focuses require slightly different approaches:

Cause	1 To what extent were the Lancashire witch trials of 1612 the result of the socio-economic situation in the Pendle area?
Consequence	2 How far were the actions of Governor Phips of Massachusetts responsible for the ending of the Salem witch trials?
Continuity and change	3 To what extent did the nature of the East Anglian witch-hunt change over the course of the years 1645–7?
Similarities and differences	4 'The Scottish witch-hunts of 1591–7 had the same key features as the North Berwick witch-hunts of 1590–1.' How far do you agree with this statement?
Significance	5 How significant was the Bamberg witch-hunt within Germany in terms of the overall persecution of witches in the period 1623–32?

Some questions include a 'stated factor'. A common type of stated factor question would ask how far one factor caused something. For example, for question 1 in the table, 'To what extent were the Lancashire witch trials of 1612 the result of the socio-economic situation in the Pendle area?', you would be expected to evaluate the importance of 'the socio-economic situation in the Pendle area' – the 'stated factor' – compared to other factors.

Planning your answer

It is crucial that you understand the focus of the question. Therefore read the question carefully before you start planning. Check the following:

- The chronological focus: which years should your essay deal with?
- The topic focus: what aspect of your course does the question deal with?
- The conceptual focus: is this a causes, consequences, change/continuity, similarity/ difference or significance question?

For example, for question 5 in the table on page 198 you could point these out as follows:

How significant[1] was the Bamberg witch-hunt[2] within Germany[3] in terms of the overall persecution of witches in the period 1623–32[4]?

1 Conceptual focus: significance, specifically to the situation within Germany.
2 Topic focus: the Bamberg witch-hunt.
3 Topic focus: witch-hunting in Germany.
4 Chronological focus: 1623–32.

Your plan should reflect the task that you have been set. Section B asks you to write an analytical, coherent and well-structured essay from your own knowledge, which reaches a supported conclusion in around 40 minutes:

- To ensure that your essay is coherent and well structured, it should comprise a series of paragraphs, each focusing on a different point.
- Your paragraphs should come in a logical order. For example, you could write your paragraphs in order of importance, so you begin with the most important issues and end with the least important.
- In essays where there is a 'stated factor', it is a good idea to start with the stated factor before moving on to the other points.
- To make sure you keep to time, you should aim to write three or four paragraphs plus an introduction and a conclusion.

The opening paragraph

The opening paragraph should do four main things:

- answer the question directly
- set out your essential argument
- outline the factors or issues that you will discuss
- define key terms used in the question – where necessary.

Different questions require you to define different terms, for example:

'The East Anglian witch-hunt was the result of the breakdown of traditional authority.' How far do you agree with this explanation?

You will need to define – and describe – 'traditional authority'.

How accurate is it to say that there would have been no witch persecutions in Bamberg had it not been for the Counter-Reformation?

In this example, it is vital that you define and discuss the nature of the Counter-Reformation.

Here's an example introduction in answer to question 2 in the table on page 198:

How far were the actions of Governor Phips of Massachusetts responsible for the ending of the Salem witch trials?

Sir William Phips, who became governor of the colony of Massachusetts in May 1692 as the witch craze in the Salem area was gaining momentum, helped to bring the Salem witch-hunt to an end later in 1692[1]. Phips is not usually seen as the man mainly responsible for the witch trials. Nor should he be seen as single-handedly bringing the witch persecutions to an end[2]. There were other factors at work, not least the pressure of leading Puritan ministers, which helped to bring an end to witch-hunting in Salem[3].

1 The essay starts with a clear focus on the question.
2 This provides some indication of your essential argument and says something about Phips' power as governor.
3 The final sentence provides more indication of the way that the essay intends to go, particularly with regard to the importance of Puritan ministers within Massachusetts.

The opening paragraph: advice

- Don't write more than a couple of sentences on general background knowledge. This is unlikely to focus explicitly on the question.
- After defining key terms, refer back to these definitions when justifying your conclusion.
- The introduction should reflect the rest of the essay. Don't make one argument in your introduction and then make a different argument in the essay.

Deploying relevant detail

Paper 3 tests the depth of your historical knowledge. Therefore, you will need to deploy historical detail. In the main body of your essay your paragraphs should begin with a clear point, be full of relevant detail and end with explanation or evaluation. A detailed answer might include statistics, proper names, dates and technical terms. For example, if you were writing a paragraph about Phips' actions in the autumn of 1692, you might include Cotton Mather's *Wonders of the Invisible World* as well as Increase Mather's intervention in October 1692, which influenced Phips' decision to set up a new court.

Writing analytically

The quality of your analysis is one of the key factors that determines the mark you achieve. Writing analytically means clearly showing the relationships between the ideas in your essay. Analysis includes two key skills: explanation and evaluation.

Explanation

Explanation means giving reasons. An explanatory sentence has three parts:

- a claim: a statement that something is true or false
- a reason: a statement that justifies the claim
- a relationship: a word or phrase that shows the relationship between the claim and the reason.

Imagine you are answering question 1 in the table on page 198:

> To what extent were the Lancashire witch trials of 1612 the result of the socio-economic situation in the Pendle area?

Your paragraph on the socio-economic situation should start with a clear point, which would be supported by a series of examples. You would round off the paragraph with some explanation:

Therefore, the socio-economic situation in the Pendle area was only a minor factor in causing the Lancashire witch trials[1] because[2] similar conditions before 1612 and worse conditions after 1612 did not spark further witch-hunts[3].

1 Claim.
2 Relationship.
3 Reason.

Make sure of the following:

- The reason you give genuinely justifies the claim you have made.
- Your explanation is focused on the question.

Reaching a supported judgement

Your essay should reach a supported judgement. The obvious place to do this is in the conclusion of your essay. Even so, the judgement should reflect the findings of your essay. The conclusion should present:

- a clear judgement that answers the question
- an evaluation of the evidence that supports the judgement.

Finally, the evaluation should reflect valid criteria.

Evaluation and criteria

Evaluation means weighing up to reach a judgement. Therefore, evaluation requires you to:

- summarise both sides of the issue
- reach a conclusion that reflects the proper weight of both sides.

So, for question 4 in the table on page 198:

> 'The Scottish witch-hunts of 1591–7 had the same key features as the North Berwick witch-hunts of 1590–1.' How far do you agree with this statement?

the conclusion might look like this:

In conclusion, while the Scottish witch-hunts of 1591–7 did undoubtedly follow the North Berwick persecutions, they were in many ways different[1]. The factors which brought about the 1590–1 witch-hunts were not the same as those which brought about the later witch persecutions[2]. The North Berwick persecutions very much concerned politics as well as witchcraft. King James VI feared that there was a plot, probably involving Bothwell and certainly involving witches, to kill him. Once this danger had passed, the witch-hunts might have ended. Instead, they continued for several more years. James's fear of witchcraft was certainly a common factor in 1590–1 and thereafter. However, after 1591, James had far less control of events than in 1590–1. The later Scottish hunts were more the result of local factors than government-organised pogroms. It was James's determination to re-establish control of events that helped to reduce witch-hunting in Scotland after 1597[3]. In short, while the witch-hunts of the years 1591–7 were sparked by the 1590–1 persecutions, they had several different features[4].

1 The conclusion starts with a clear judgement that answers the question.
2 This sentence begins the process of weighing up the different factors involved in the two witch-hunts.
3 The conclusion summarises James VI's role in events.
4 The essay ends with a final judgement that is supported by the evidence of the essay.

The judgement is supported in part by evaluating the evidence, and in part by linking it to valid criteria. In this case, one such criterion is the distinction between the causes of the 1590–1 witch-hunt and the causes of the witch-hunts post-1591.

Essay guidance (2)

Paper 3, Section C

Section C is similar in many ways to Section B. Therefore, you need the same essential skills in order to get a high grade:

- focused analysis
- relevant detail
- supported judgement
- organisation, coherence and clarity.

Nonetheless, there are some differences in terms of the style of the question and the approach to the question in Sections B and C. Therefore, this section focuses on the following aspects of exam technique:

- The nature of the question.
- Planning your answer.
- Advice for Section C.

The nature of the question

Section C questions focus on the two themes in breadth:

- Changing attitudes to witchcraft in Britain.
- The wider intellectual context: the coming of the age of science and reason.

Questions can address either theme or both themes. There are two questions in Section C, of which you must answer one. However, you are not guaranteed a question on both themes, therefore you have to prepare for questions on both of the themes.

Section C questions are designed to test the breadth of your historical knowledge and your ability to analyse change over time. Therefore, questions will focus on long periods, of no less than 100 years.

Section C questions have a variety of forms but they have one of two essential foci. They will focus on either:

- the causes of change: for example, the factors, forces or individuals that led to change

or

- the nature of change: the ways in which things changed.

Significantly, the exam paper may contain two causes of change questions or two nature of change questions: you are not guaranteed one of each. Finally, questions can focus on different aspects of change over time:

- Comparative questions: ask you to assess the extent of change and continuity of an aspect of the period.
- Patterns of change questions: ask you to assess differences in terms of the rate, extent or significance of change at different points in the chronology.
- Turning point questions: ask you to assess which changes were more significant.

Comparative question	How far do you agree that legal developments played a decisive role initially in helping the spread of witchcraft persecution and then in bringing witch-hunting in England and Scotland to an end in the period 1580–1750?
Patterns of change question	How accurate is it to say that the scientific revolution brought witch-hunting in Britain to a steady decline in the period 1650–1750?
Turning point question	'The publication of Reginald Scot's *The Discoverie of Witchcraft* in 1584 was a turning point in the growth of witchcraft scepticism in Britain in the period 1580–1750.' How far do you agree with this statement?

Planning your answer

It is crucial that you understand the focus of the question in order to make an effective plan. Therefore, read the question carefully before you start planning. Different questions require a different approach. Here are suggestions about how to tackle some of the common types of question:

How far do you agree that legal developments played a decisive role initially in helping the spread of witchcraft persecution and then in bringing witch-hunting in England and Scotland to an end in the period 1580–1750?

This is a comparative question which focuses on the causes of change. In this case, you should examine the significance of 'legal developments', the stated factor, and compare it to other possible causes of change.

> How accurate is it to say that the scientific revolution brought witch-hunting in Britain to a steady decline in the period 1650–1750?

This is a patterns of change question which focuses on the nature of change. Here, you should examine the pattern of the so-called scientific revolution which helped to change the approach to human understanding and knowledge. You should consider how far this development took place at an even rate and to what extent it affected the elite classes, never mind the mass of people in Britain.

> 'The publication of Reginald Scot's *The Discoverie of Witchcraft* in 1584 was a turning point in the growth of witchcraft scepticism in Britain in the period 1580–1750.' How far do you agree with this statement?

This is a turning point question which focuses on the nature of change. Therefore, you should examine the significance of the stated turning point, and compare it to two or three other turning points from the period 1580–1750. Significantly, you should not just focus on Scot or the 1580s: you must consider other possible turning points. Additionally, when considering how far an event was a turning point you must consider both the changes it caused and the ways in which things stayed the same.

Advice for Section C

In many ways a Section C essay should display the same skills as a Section B essay (see page 198). However, Section C essays focus on a much longer period than Section B essays and this has an impact on how you approach them.

The most important difference concerns the chronology. In order to answer a Section C question properly you must address the whole chronology, in this case the period 1580–1750. In practice, this means choosing examples from across the whole range of the period. Specifically, it is a good idea to have examples from the early part of the period, the middle of the period and the end of the period. For example, if you were answering the question:

> 'The publication of Reginald Scot's *The Discoverie of Witchcraft* in 1584 was a turning point in the growth of witchcraft scepticism in Britain in the period 1580–1750.' How far do you agree with this statement?

The question states a possible turning point from 1584 – the early part of the period. Therefore, if you are considering other possible turning points you should choose one from the middle part of the chronology and one from the later part to make sure you cover the whole period.

Equally, if you are dealing with the question:

> How accurate is it to say that the scientific revolution brought witch-hunting in Britain to a steady decline in the period 1650–1750?

you should analyse examples of the development of changing approaches to human understanding and knowledge throughout the whole period. This could include developments such as:

- early: the impact of Kepler, Galileo and Bacon
- middle: the foundation of Gresham College and the Royal Society
- late: the impact of Hobbes, Newton and Locke.

In so doing, you would be addressing the full chronological range of the question.

OCR A level History

Essay guidance

In the OCR A Unit Y312: Popular culture and the witchcraze of the 16th and 17th centuries there are two elements:

- The thematic essay, which will require you to consider developments over approximately 100 years. You will answer two essays from a choice of three.
- The in-depth interpretation element, where you will comprehend, analyse and evaluate the ways in which the past has been interpreted by historians.

There are a number of skills that you need to develop if you are to reach the higher levels in the marking bands:

- understand the wording of the question
- plan a thematic answer to the question set
- write a focused opening paragraph
- avoid irrelevance and description
- write analytically and thematically
- make comparisons within the themes, showing similarity and difference across the whole period
- write a conclusion which reaches a supported judgement based on the argument in the main body of the essay.

The skills are made very clear by both mark schemes, which emphasise that the answer must:

- focus on the demands of the question
- be supported by accurate and relevant factual knowledge
- be analytical and well structured
- reach a supported and developed judgement about the issue in the question
- demonstrate evidence of well-developed synthesis across the whole period.

These skills are the same as those you have developed for essay writing in Units 1 and 2. However, in this unit there is a significant emphasis on *synthesis* across the whole period.

Understanding the wording of the question

To stay focused on the question set, it is important to read the question carefully and focus on the key words and phrases. Unless you directly address the demands of the question you will not score highly. Remember that in questions where there is a named factor you must write a good analytical paragraph about the given factor, even if you argue that it was not the most important.

Types of questions you might find in the exam	The themes you might consider in answering them
1 How important was the impact of religious change and confessional strife on witch-hunting in the period from *c.*1500 to *c.*1650?	You should weigh up the impact of religious changes, associated with the Reformation and Counter-Reformation, against other factors in the development of witch persecution: • Legal developments • Social and economic factors • The impact of disasters and the search for scapegoats.
2 'The invention of the printing press in the fifteenth century was of vital importance with regard to the growth of the persecution of witches.' How far do you agree with this view of the period from 1500 to 1700?	You might consider the relative importance of the printing press in spreading ideas on witchcraft by comparing it with other developments: • The impact of legal procedures • Religious developments • Social and economic factors • Popular and elite cultures.

Types of questions you might find in the exam	The themes you might consider in answering them
3 How far did the reasons for witchcraft persecutions in the period from 1500 to 1650 remain the same?	You should consider a range of factors that led to the growth of witch-hunting, including: • The legal system, especially the inquisitorial system and the use of torture • Religious changes and confessional strife • Social and economic developments • The search for scapegoats following natural disasters.
4 'Popular and elite cultures drew increasingly apart in the years from 1550 to 1700.' How far do you agree with this view?	You might consider the notion of popular culture(s) and elite culture(s). You might also consider some of these themes: • The impact of religious change • Political change • Intellectual developments • The impact of economic and social change • The withdrawal of the elite.

Planning an answer

Many plans simply list dates and events – this should be avoided as it encourages a descriptive or narrative answer, rather than an analytical answer. The plan should be an outline of your argument; this means you need to think carefully about the issues you intend to discuss and their relative importance before you start writing your answer. It should, therefore, be a list of the themes or issues you are going to discuss and a comment on their relative importance in relation to the question.

For question 1 in the table, your plan might look something like this:

- Religious change in Europe: the Reformation and Counter-Reformation coincided (roughly) with the witchcraze.
- The impact of the Reformation on witchcraft.

- Other factors were important: the intellectual foundations for witch-hunting had been established before the Reformation.
- Legal developments in Europe, including the inquisitorial system and the use of torture, were crucially important.
- The economic and social context played a vital role.
- The role of wars and natural disasters, including plague and the 'mini ice age', led to the demand for scapegoats.
- Demand for persecution of witches came from below rather than being imposed from above.

The opening paragraph

Many students spend time 'setting the scene'; the opening paragraph becomes little more than an introduction to the topic – this should be avoided. Instead, make it clear what your argument is going to be. Offer your view about the issue in the question – how important was the impact of religious change and congressional strife on witch-hunting – and then introduce the other issues you intend to discuss. In the plan, for example, it is suggested that legal changes may have been more important than religious developments. This should be made clear in the opening paragraph, with a brief comment as to why you think legal developments were more important than religious changes. This will give the examiner a clear overview of your essay, rather than it being a mystery tour where the argument becomes clear only at the end. You should also refer to any important issues that the question raises. For example:

The Reformation and Counter-Reformation roughly coincided with the European witchcraze of the sixteenth and seventeenth centuries. It can be argued that the profound religious developments which took place in early modern Europe encouraged the growth of witch-hunting[1]. However, exactly how the Protestant Reformation and the Catholic Counter-Reformation contributed to the growth of witch persecution remains a subject of huge debate; as does the contribution of

Protestants and Catholics to witch-hunting. The fact that the Reformation had a negative as well as a positive effect on European witch-hunting means that it would be a mistake to blame the entire European witch-hunt on the Reformation, the Counter-Reformation or both[2]. Other factors, especially legal changes, social and economic development, and the impact of natural disasters, especially the 'mini ice age', had a major impact on European witch-hunting – an impact that was more important than religious change and congressional strife[3].

1 The opening two sentences are very much geared to the set question.
2 The following two sentences cast some doubt on the impact of religious change on witch-hunting.
3 This sentence indicates the way that the essay will progress, suggesting that the impact of religious change was less important than other factors.

The answer should then go on to discuss the issues raised in the opening paragraph.

Avoid irrelevance and description

It is hoped that the plan will stop you simply writing all you know about the reasons for the growth in the persecution of witches and force you to weigh up the role of a range of factors. Similarly, it should also help prevent you from simply writing about the religious changes and confessional strife. You will not lose marks if you do that, but neither will you gain any credit, and you will waste valuable time.

Write analytically

This is perhaps the hardest, but most important skill you need to develop. An analytical approach can be helped by ensuring that the opening sentence of each paragraph introduces an idea, which directly answers the question and is not just a piece of factual information. In a very strong answer it should be possible to simply read the opening sentences of all the paragraphs and know what argument is being put forward.

If we look at question 3, 'How far did the reasons for witchcraft persecution in the period from 1500

to 1650 remain the same', the following are possible sentences with which to start paragraphs:

- Legal developments, especially the introduction of the inquisitorial system of criminal procedure, had a vital impact on witch-hunting throughout the period, especially in continental Europe.
- The use of torture on witchcraft suspects was of crucial importance in forcing witches to confess and implicate others, ensuring that witch-hunts grew in intensity throughout most of the period.
- The Protestant Reformation, the Catholic Counter-Reformation and the bitter conflict between Protestants and Catholics during the early modern period had an effect on the growth of the European witch-hunt throughout the period.
- Social and economic developments, particularly those affecting the popular masses, played a role in generating witch persecution.
- Natural disasters, including wars, epidemics and problems arising from climatic change, affected witch persecution, especially the desire to find scapegoats to blame for people's suffering in particular countries and at particular times.

Such a plan would enable you to discuss the role of legal developments in the growth of witch-hunting as well as other factors which led to persecution. The final sentence of each paragraph should reach a judgement on the role played by the factor you are discussing in the growth of witch-hunting. This approach would ensure that the final sentence of each paragraph links back to the actual question you are answering. If you can do this for each paragraph you will have a series of mini-essays, which discuss a factor and reach a conclusion or judgement about the importance of that factor or issue. For example:

The use of torture during the course of witchcraft trials played a major role in witch persecution across much of Europe, especially in Germany, throughout the period[1]. Torture resolved the problem of insufficient evidence and made possible the conviction of almost anyone who incurred the suspicion of witchcraft. When torture was used on a regular basis, the rate of convictions in witchcraft persecutions was often as high as 95 per cent. When it was not used, for example in England, the conviction rate was well below 50 per cent. Torture also enabled the authorities to acquire the names of witches' alleged accomplices. This encouraged the type of large chain-reaction witch-hunts, common in several south German states like Bamberg[2]. Without the widespread use of torture, it is unlikely that there would have been mass persecution of witches[3].

1 A clear view about the impact of torture is offered.
2 This view is explained and supported by evidence.
3 The final sentence establishes the importance of torture with regard to European witch-hunting.

The conclusion

The conclusion provides the opportunity to bring together all the interim judgements to reach an overall judgement about the question. Using the interim judgements will ensure that your conclusion is based on the argument in the main body of the essay and does not offer a different view. For the essay that answers question 3 (see page 205), you can assess the importance of legal developments in witchcraft persecution in Europe in the early modern period. You will also need to comment on other factors, particularly if you have argued that a different factor (or factors) was more important than legal changes. If you think that legal developments were the most important factor, you will need to explain why they were more important than the other factors or issues you have discussed.

In reaching a judgement for question 3 (on page 205) you might conclude:

Legal developments in Europe in the early modern period were therefore crucial in the witch-hunting process[1]. This is not to say that legal changes determined the entire process of witch persecution. Other factors also played a vital role. These include religious change and confessional strife, social and economic developments, the impact of natural disasters and the desire to find scapegoats, and intellectual support for witch-hunting from leading theologians. It is also worth stressing that without grass-roots pressure from local people who feared the power of witchcraft, there would have been very few persecutions[2]. Nevertheless, legal developments help to explain why the great witch-hunt took place when it did. Intensive witch-hunting did not begin until many European courts had adopted inquisitorial procedures and had begun to use torture. Thus, as historian Brian Levack says, 'The great European witch-hunt was essentially a judicial operation'[3].

1 Reiterates the importance of the named factor.
2 Explains why other factors were also important in developments.
3 Reaches an overall judgement that emphasises the importance of one factor while not denying the importance of others.

Interpretations guidance

For each of the in-depth interpretation elements, four key topics are listed in the specification and a question will be set on one of the topics. The four topics for Popular culture and the witchcraze of the 16th and 17th centuries are as follows:

- Popular culture.
- The main reasons for the growth and decline in the persecution of witches.
- The persecuted.
- Response of the authorities to witchcraft.

Although this is an A level paper it is not a historiography paper. The aim of this element of the unit is to develop an awareness that the past has been interpreted in different ways. The question will require you to assess the strengths and limitations of the two interpretations of an issue related to one of the specified in-depth topics. The interpretations will always be from historians and will not be primary sources.

You should be able to place the interpretation within the context of the wider historical debate on the key topic. However, you will not be required to know the names of individual historians associated with the debate or to have studied the specific books of any historians.

There are a number of skills you will need to develop if you are to reach the higher levels in the mark bands:

- Remain focused on the question throughout the answer.
- Assess and evaluate the two interpretations in the wider context of the historical debate about the issue.
- Apply your knowledge of the topic to the interpretations in order to evaluate their strengths and weaknesses.

- Ensure that you consider both interpretations.
- Reach a supported judgement as to which interpretation you think is more convincing.

Approaching the question

It might be helpful to think of a four-paragraph structure:

- In the first paragraph, explain the interpretations in the two passages and place them in the wider debate.
- In the second paragraph, apply your own knowledge to interpretation A to evaluate the validity of its view about the issue in the question. In doing this, your own knowledge should be used to analyse the strengths and weaknesses of the view in the interpretation.
- Repeat the second point, but for interpretation B.
- In the final paragraph, reach a supported and balanced judgement as to which view you think is more convincing.

You do not need to evaluate the provenance of the interpretation and therefore comments on the author and their background will not gain marks.

Here is an example of a question you will face in the exam:

Evaluate the interpretations in both of the passages and explain which you think is a more convincing explanation for the decline in the persecution of witches.

PASSAGE A

The main cause of the decline in witchcraft prosecutions in the seventeenth and eighteenth centuries was the establishment of new rules for conducting witchcraft trials and the application of new, more demanding standards of evidence for the conviction of witches. The pressure to make these changes originated in the objections that judges and legal writers had to the ways in which the trials were being conducted. As a consequence of these changes in judicial procedure, witchcraft trials resulted in a larger number of acquittals, the mass panics in which scores of witches perished no longer recurred and the courts became increasingly reluctant to initiate prosecutions in the first place.

The judges, inquisitors, magistrates and writers who responded to the trials in this critical way can best be defined as judicial sceptics. In the context of witchcraft the word 'scepticism' usually denotes the attitudes of those who doubt or deny the existence of witches or the possibility of their crime. Judicial sceptics did not necessarily adopt such a stance.

The essence of their intellectual position was a genuine doubt whether those persons who were being prosecuted were actually guilty as charged, and this concern led in turn to a more general uncertainty as to whether the crime could ever be proved at law. Some judicial sceptics may have also harbored a more fundamental philosophical doubt whether witchcraft even existed. But judicial scepticism could, and in most cases did, coexist with a firm belief in the reality and possibility of the crime.

The three most significant changes in the conduct of witchcraft trials that led to a decline in prosecutions were the regulation of local witchcraft trials by higher authorities, the restriction or prohibition of torture, and the demand for more persuasive evidence to support the conviction of witches.

B.P. Levack, The Witch-hunt in Early Modern Europe, 2006.

PASSAGE B

As the seventeenth century progressed, advances in medical science began to solve some of the mysteries of death and disease that had formerly been blamed upon maleficent magic. Leading scientists were eager to challenge old opinions and traditions, of which magic was one of the foremost. Belief in witchcraft thus rapidly became unfashionable among the educated elite, who scorned the credulous and naïve attitude of those who sought the services of their local cunning man or astrologer, or accused a member of their community of practicing maleficent magic.

There was also an emerging belief in an orderly universe, governed by God and nature, rather than the caprices of the Devil. According to this world view, the confessions of suspected witches who claimed to have made pacts with Satan or killed people by maleficent magic were completely unfeasible. 'It is simply impossible for either the

Devil or witches to change or alter the course that God hath set in nature', claimed the English clergyman John Webster.

With advances in science came greater knowledge of the human body and thus the treatment of disease. By the end of the seventeenth century, flourishing trade had brought a wealth of new drugs into England, including quinine which was used to treat malaria. There was also a new emphasis upon self-help in preventing the spread of disease, such as increased hygiene and quarantine during bouts of the plague. Other advances gradually made people feel more in control of their environments, notably industrialization and the growth of urban centres.

T. Borman, Witches: James I and the English Witch-Hunts, 2013.

In answering the question, the opening paragraph could consider the views of the two interpretations and place them in the context of the debate:

Historians continue to debate the main causes for the decline in the persecution of witches in the late seventeenth century. Some, for example, stress the importance of the scientific revolution and the growth of rationalism and enlightened thinking. Others put more emphasis on judicial developments[1]. Passage A is firmly in the judicial development camp. It stresses the importance of judicial scepticism across Europe. It claims that many judges may well have continued to believe in witchcraft. However, the vast majority doubted whether the crime could ever be proved in law. The passage then emphasises the importance of three other judicial developments: the regulation of local witchcraft trials by higher authorities; the restriction or prohibition of the use of torture; and the demands of judges and courts for more persuasive evidence to support the conviction of witches[2].

1 The opening places the passages in the wider context of the debate about the decline of witchcraft persecution in the late seventeenth century.
2 The next part explains Passage A in relation to the issue raised in the question and supports its view by summarising part of the interpretation.

A strong answer would go on to examine some of the points raised in Passage A in greater detail, especially with regard to judicial scepticism, the regulation of local witchcraft trials, the decline of the use of torture, and the demands of courts for more conclusive evidence. It would then reach an overall judgement about the validity of the views in Passage A.

The answer for the question could then go on to evaluate Passage B:

While Passage A focuses on judicial developments, Passage B stresses the growth of rationalism and enlightened thinking, especially the greater understanding of medicine and remedies for serious illnesses. The result was that among the educated elite classes belief in witchcraft 'rapidly' became unfashionable[1]. Passage B makes no mention of judicial scepticism, although judges would clearly be among the educated elite who 'scorned the credulous and naïve attitude' of the masses[2].

1 The opening sentences summarise Passage B's general approach to the issue.
2 The next sentence links the two passages. There may be some common ground between them, although the emphasis in the two passages is very different.

In evaluating Passage B, the response might go on to consider other intellectual developments including the impact of Johannes Kepler, Galileo Galilei and Isaac Newton, as well as the development of the empirical scientific approach to human understanding and knowledge. The foundation of Gresham College (1644) and the Royal Society (1662) and the works of Thomas Hobbes and John Locke might also be mentioned.

The student should then consider the strengths and weaknesses of Passage B before writing a concluding paragraph that brings together the two interim judgements to reach an overall judgement as to which view is more convincing.

In the conclusion, the following might be argued:

Both passages focus on important factors in the decline of witchcraft persecution. In one sense Passage A is more focused: it concentrates solely on judicial developments. However, it implies that those developments occurred across Europe and had similar effects across the Continent. Passage B – which focuses more on developments in England – stresses the importance of the so-called scientific revolution and the importance of the elite's withdrawal from belief in witchcraft. While the emphases of the two passages are thus very different, both provide convincing explanations for witch-hunting's gradual demise. It is hard to decide which provides the better explanation, particularly as there is some common ground between the two passages. Passage A obviously implies that those involved in judicial proceedings – the judicial elite – withdrew their support from persecuting witches**[1]**. On balance, however, Passage A's stance is more convincing than that of Passage B. Legal changes can certainly be seen to have a direct impact on witchcraft persecution. Changes in intellectual thinking, by contrast, are more nebulous. The impact of rationalism and enlightened thinking was often slow to filter down. Much of the educated elite was largely unaware of the ideas of Newton and other great thinkers until the eighteenth century. Witchcraft persecution, however, slowed down considerably across most of western and central Europe in the late seventeenth century. This being the case, Passage A's explanation wins – just!**[2]**

1 The answer sums up the evidence before making a final judgement and is not afraid to suggest that the judgement is a difficult one.
2 The judgement is developed and the answer explains why, despite the strengths of Passage B, Passage A is more convincing.

Timeline

1420s	Large-scale witch-hunts in the Alpine region
1440s	Johannes Gutenberg began printing in Germany
1476	William Caxton began printing in England
1484	Pope Innocence VIII's papal bull *Summis desiderantes affectibus*
1486	Kramer published *Malleus Maleficarum*
1488	Publication of Lichtenberger's *Prognostications*
1517	Martin Luther's *Ninety-Five Theses*: the start of the Reformation
1545–63	Meeting of the Council of Trent
1560–1660	Large-scale witch persecutions across Europe
1563	English and Scottish Witchcraft Acts
1581–93	Trier witch-hunt
1584	Publication of Reginald Scot's *The Discoverie of Witchcraft*
1590–1	North Berwick witch-hunt
1590–7	National Scottish witch-hunt
1597	Publication of *Daemonologie*
1597	Foundation of Gresham College
1597	The case of the Boy of Burton

1604	English Witchcraft Act
1612	Pendle witches
1626–31	Wurzburg and Bamberg witch-hunts
1626–34	Cologne witch-hunt
1634	The Pendle fraud
1645–7	East Anglian witch-hunt
1649–50	Scottish witch-hunt
1656	Publication of Thomas Ady's *A Candle in the Dark*
1660	Foundation of the Royal Society
1661–2	The last major Scottish witch-hunt
1662	The case of the Demon Drummer of Tedworth
1677	Publication of Webster's *The Displaying of Supposed Witchcraft*
1690	Publication of John Locke's *Essay Concerning Human Understanding*
1691–3	Publication of Balthasar Bekker's *The Bewitched World*
1692–3	Salem witch trials
1712	The case of Jane Wenham
1718	Publication of Francis Hutchinson's *An Historical Essay Concerning Witchcraft*
1736	British Witchcraft Act

Glossary of terms

Anthropological approaches Examinations of present-day societies (which are often seen as being 'pre-modern') which try to explain the actions of past societies.

Auto-da-fé A ritualised public penance.

Baptists Protestant Christians who baptise, by immersion, only those old enough consciously to accept the Christian faith.

Calendar A list of events.

Capital crime A crime punishable by a death sentence.

Cathars Twelfth-century French dissidents from Catholicism. The sect, sometimes known as the Albigensians, was wiped out in the fourteenth century by the Inquisition.

Commonwealth A term used in the early modern period to describe the public or the nation.

Diabolism Devil worship.

Diet A meeting of the states that made up the Holy Roman Empire.

Ducking-stool A stool or chair in which people who had committed a not very serious offence were tied and ducked in a pond or river.

Early modern Europe The period from c.1450 to c.1700; the years that are regarded as bridging the medieval and modern worlds.

Empirical/empiricism The belief that all knowledge is based on observation and direct experience.

Enlightenment The name given to a school of European thought of the eighteenth century. Those influenced by the Enlightenment believed in reason and human progress.

Franconia A region of south-western Germany.

General Assembly The ruling body of the Scottish Calvinist Church.

Guilds Associations of workers, formed in medieval Europe, to further their members' common purposes and interests. Most guilds represented specific crafts or trades. They became very powerful, exercising a monopoly over both production and trade and controlling recruitment by the apprenticeship system.

Heresy A belief contrary to the authorised teaching of the Catholic Church.

Holy Roman Empire This territory comprised most of present-day Germany. From the thirteenth century, the emperors (in theory elected) were almost always members of the Habsburg family which ruled Austria. The Empire consisted of hundreds of small states.

Huguenots French Protestants.

Humanists Supporters of humanism – an intellectual movement that was strong in the late fifteenth and early sixteenth centuries. Humanists, while by no means rejecting Christianity, turned away from the theological bias of the medieval period and concentrated instead on human achievements.

Indictments The formal charges on which suspects stand trial.

Inquisition A tribunal, established in the thirteenth century, to preserve the supremacy of Catholicism by suppressing heresy by means of formally organised persecution.

Interrregnum The years from 1649 to 1660 when England had no king.

Jesuit A member of the Catholic religious order the Society of Jesus, founded in 1534 by Ignatius Loyola. Jesuits were known for their aggressive religiosity as 'the soldiers of Christ'.

Justice of the peace A person commissioned to perform certain judicial and other functions within a specified locality in England and Wales.

Lollards Followers of English reformer John Wycliffe (c.1329–84) who advocated the primacy of the scriptures over the teaching of the Church.

Lowland Scotland Southern Scotland.

LSD   Lysergic acid diethylamide: a drug that causes hallucinations and psychedelic episodes.

Maleficium   A harm committed by magic (plural *maleficia*).

Marxist historians   Historians who believe that history has been deeply shaped by economic circumstances. They are influenced by the ideology of the philosopher Karl Marx.

Masques   A form of dramatic entertainment, consisting of a combination of verse, dance and music, usually with a plot based on a mythological theme. Masques were elaborately staged with expensive costumes and scenery.

Materialism   The view that denies the independent existence of spirit and maintains that there is but one substance, matter. Everything both on earth and in the universe can thus be explained by studying natural forces.

Papal bull   An edict issued by the pope.

Parlement   A provincial high court in pre-revolutionary France for hearing appeals of local legal cases.

Patriarchal society   A social system which is dominated by men.

Popery   A derogatory term for Catholicism. It suggested that Catholics were part of an international conspiracy led by the pope against Protestantism.

Presbyteries   A presbytery was a Church council consisting of the ministers, presbyters and elders of the Kirk.

Privy Council   The central governing body convened by royal summons.

Quakers   Members of the Religious Society of Friends, founded in England by George Fox in the 1640s. They rejected the ministry and sacraments of the established Church. Adopting a plain style of dress and way of life, they refused to take oaths and opposed the use of titles.

Renaissance   An intellectual and cultural movement that began in Italy in the fourteenth century, spread to northern Europe and flourished until the mid-sixteenth century. Fundamental to the Renaissance (which means rebirth in French) were the revival of classical learning, art and architecture, and the concept of the dignity of man, which characterised humanism.

Ruling elite   The governing class, mainly comprising royalty, the aristocracy and the rich and powerful. The elite are the leading members of any social group.

Sabbat   A witches' midnight meeting.

Serf   An agricultural labourer who was tied to working on his lord's estate.

Skimmingtons   Public humiliations. The word is possibly derived from a ladle used in cheese-making, which women may have used to beat their husbands.

Subsistence farming   Farming in which land will yield just enough to support the farmer and his family, leaving little or nothing to be sold.

Suffragan   An assistant.

Theocracy   A state in which God is regarded as the sole sovereign and the laws of the realm are seen as divine commands. The clergy thus become the main officers of the state.

Thirty Years' War   This conflict from 1618 to 1648, mainly fought in Germany, involved most of the countries of western and central Europe and was one of the most destructive wars in European history. Initially a religious war between Protestants and Catholics, it eventually became a power struggle between France and Spain.

Tribute   Payment as an acknowledgement of submission.

Waldensians   Members of a dissident Christian group which began in the French Alps in the twelfth century. Religious persecution scattered them to other areas including Bohemia and Germany.

Yeomen   Farmers who owned a relatively small amount of land, on which they themselves usually worked.

Further reading

General texts

J. Barry *et al.*, editors, *Witchcraft in Early Modern Europe* (Cambridge University Press, 1996)
A major collection of essays

M. Gaskill, *Witchcraft: A Very Short Introduction* (Oxford University Press, 2010)
A very useful – and short – introduction to witchcraft

R. Golden, *Encyclopedia of Witchcraft*, four volumes (ABC-CLIO, 2006)
Too detailed for most readers but a splendid book

B.P. Levack, *The Oxford Handbook of Witchcraft in Early Modern Europe and Colonial America* (Oxford University Press, 2015)
The latest work by one of the best authorities on early modern witchcraft

B.P. Levack, editor, *The Witchcraft Sourcebook* (Routledge, 2004)
An excellent collection of documents with very useful commentaries on the sources

D. Oldridge, editor, *The Witchcraft Reader* (Routledge, 2002)
Provides a selection of the best historical writing on witchcraft

R.H. Robbins, *Encyclopedia of Witchcraft and Demonology* (Spring Books, 1959)
Hard to acquire but a very useful text if you are able to find it

R. Thurston, *The Witch Hunts: A History of the Witch Persecutions in Europe and North America* (Routledge, 2006)
Another useful work on all aspects of witch-hunting

Witch-hunting in Europe

W. Behringer, *Witchcraft Persecutions in Bavaria* (Cambridge University Press, 1997)
Worth dipping into but perhaps a bit too focused for most readers

W. Behringer, *Witches and Witch Hunts* (Cambridge University Press, 2004)
An essential read by an expert on German witch-hunting

R. Briggs, *Witches and Neighbours* (Penguin, 1998)
A regional study of witchcraft in the Lorraine and Franco-German borderlands

S. Clark, *Thinking with Demons: The Idea of Witchcraft in Early Modern Europe* (Oxford University Press, 1997)
An important contribution to the intellectual history of witchcraft

B.P. Levack, *The Witch-hunt in Early Modern Europe* (Pearson, 2006)
Probably the best single work on witch-hunting in Europe

L. Roper, *Witch Craze: Terror and Fantasy in Baroque Germany* (Yale University Press, 2006)
Well worth reading

G. Scarre and J. Callow, *Witchcraft and Magic in Sixteenth- and Seventeenth-century Europe* (Palgrave, 2001)
A useful short introduction

Witchcraft in England

Tracy Borman, *Witches: James I and the English Witch-hunts* (Vintage, 2014)
A very readable book on a particular witch-hunt in James's reign but it has much to say about witch-hunting in England generally

Malcolm Gaskill, *Witchfinders: A Seventeenth-century English Tragedy* (John Murray, 2005)
An excellent example of history as gripping literature

C. Goodier, *1612: The Lancashire Witch Trials: A New Guide* (Palatine Books, 2011)
A short, lively book on the witch trials of 1612

B.P. Levack, editor, *New Perspectives on Witchcraft, Magic and Demonology, Volume 3: Witchcraft in the British Isles and New England* (Routledge, 2001)
A splendid collection of essays which are not otherwise easily accessible

A. Macfarlane, *Witchcraft in Tudor and Stuart England: A Regional and Comparative Study* (Routledge, 1999)
An enormously influential work which brought an anthropological approach to the study of English witchcraft, particularly in Essex

R. Poole, editor, *The Lancashire Witches: Histories and Stories* (Manchester University Press, 2002)
A splendid collection of essays on the Pendle witch-hunt

J.A. Sharpe, *Instruments of Darkness: Witchcraft in Early Modern England* (University of Pennsylvania Press, 1997)
A brilliant book – essential reading for everyone

J.A. Sharpe, *Witchcraft in Early Modern England* (Pearson Education, 2001)
An excellent short book on witchcraft in England

K. Thomas, *Religion and the Decline of Magic* (Penguin, 2003)
A bit dated now but remains an encyclopaedic study of religion, magic and witchcraft in early modern England

Witchcraft in Scotland

J. Goodare, editor, *The Scottish Witch-hunt in Context* (Manchester University Press, 2002)
A useful collection of essays

C. Larner, *Enemies of God: The Witch Hunt in Scotland* (Chatto & Windus, 1981)
Still the definitive study of Scottish witchcraft

B.P. Levack, *Witch-hunting in Scotland: Law, Politics and Religion* (Routledge, 2007)
An excellent study which challenges some of Larner's views

P.G. Maxwell-Stuart, *Satan's Conspiracy: Magic and Witchcraft in Sixteenth-century Scotland* (Tuckwell Press, 2001)
A useful collection of material

Lawrence Normand and Gareth Roberts, *Witchcraft in Early Modern Scotland: James VI's Demonology and the North Berwick Witches* (University of Exeter Press, 2000)
A useful book on the situation in Scotland. It contains excellent sources and commentary on the documents

The Salem witch trials

P. Boyer and S. Nissenbaum, editors, *Salem-Village Witchcraft: A Documentary Record of Local Conflict in Colonial New England* (Northeastern University Press, 1972)
An excellent collection of material

P. Boyer and S. Nissenbaum, editors, *Salem Possessed: The Social Origins of Witchcraft* (Harvard University Press, 1974)
This social explanation of the Salem witch trials is no longer generally accepted but this book remains as an important contribution to the debate

J. Demos, *Entertaining Satan: Witchcraft and the Culture of Early New England* (Oxford University Press, 1982)
A bit dated now but still merits attention

D.K. Goss, *The Salem Witch Trials: A Reference Guide* (Greenwood Publishing, 2007)
This is a useful reference guide

P.C. Hoffer, *The Devil's Disciples: Makers of the Salem Witchcraft Trials* (Johns Hopkins University Press, 1996)
A very readable and balanced book which helps to explain why the Salem witch-hunt spun out control

C.F. Karlsen, *The Devil in the Shape of a Woman: Witchcraft in Colonial New England* (Vintage, 1987)
This provides useful social background on other witchcraft accusations in seventeenth-century New England

M.B. Norton, *In the Devil's Snare: The Salem Witchcraft Crisis of 1692* (Random House, 2002)
An essential read

B. Rosenthal, *Salem Story: Reading the Witch Trials of 1692* (Cambridge University Press, 1993)
A useful book which goes back to the main sources

B. Rosenthal, *Records of the Salem Witch-hunt* (Cambridge University Press, 2009)
This book assembles all the documentary evidence in one massive volume

Popular culture

P. Burke, *Popular Culture in Early Modern Europe* (Ashgate, 2009)
A pioneering work which examines the broad sweep of pre-industrial Europe's popular culture

B. Kumin, editor, *The European World 1500–1800: An Introduction to Early Modern History* (Routledge, 2009)
A concise and authoritative introduction to the period, containing useful essays by a variety of specialists

R. Muchembled, Lydia Cochrane and L. Cochrane, *Popular Culture and Elite Culture in France 1400–1750* (Louisiana State University Press, 1985)
This book examines popular and elite cultures in France in the early modern period

B. Reay, *Popular Cultures in England 1550–1750* (Routledge, 1998)
An impressive examination of popular cultures in England in the early modern period

J.A. Sharpe, *Early Modern England: A Social History 1550–1760* (Hodder Arnold, 1997)
An excellent survey of all aspects of life and culture in early modern England

Index